HOMIES AND HERMANOS

HOMIES AND HERMANOS

God and Gangs in Central America

by

ROBERT BRENNEMAN

OXFORD
UNIVERSITY PRESS

Oxford University Press, Inc., publishes works that further
Oxford University's objective of excellence
in research, scholarship, and education.

Oxford New York
Auckland Cape Town Dar es Salaam Hong Kong Karachi
Kuala Lumpur Madrid Melbourne Mexico City Nairobi
New Delhi Shanghai Taipei Toronto

With offices in
Argentina Austria Brazil Chile Czech Republic France Greece
Guatemala Hungary Italy Japan Poland Portugal Singapore
South Korea Switzerland Thailand Turkey Ukraine Vietnam

Published by Oxford University Press, Inc.
198 Madison Avenue, New York, New York 10016

www.oup.com

Library of Congress Cataloging-in-Publication Data
Brenneman, Robert E.
Homies and hermanos : God and gangs in Central America / Robert Brenneman.
p. cm.
Includes bibliographical references (p.) and index.
ISBN 978-0-19-975384-0 (hardcover : alk. paper) — ISBN 978-0-19-975390-1 (pbk. : alk. paper)
1. Church work with juvenile delinquents—Central America. 2. Ex-gang members—Religious life—Central America. 3. Christian converts—Central America. 4. Evangelicalism—Central America. I. Title.
BV4464.5.B74 2012
259′.5—dc22 2011010636

1 3 5 7 9 8 6 4 2

Printed in the United States of America
on acid-free paper

For Rachel Sue
and for América Gabriela

Table of Contents

Acknowledgments

Where to begin? A work of this nature passes through many, *many* stages and I am grateful to everyone who read and commented on a chapter or a paper that became a chapter. Among them are Chris Smith, Andy Weigert, Jessica Collett, David Smilde, Chris Hausmann, Steve Offut, Georgi Derlugian, Randall Collins, Ed Flores, Andrew Johnson, Gaby Ochoa, Meredith Whitnah, Mark Baker, Claudia Dary, Lily Keyes, Natalie Elvidge, and the members of the Research on Religion and Society seminar at Notre Dame. In addition, many scholars provided comments on presentations of my work at the University of Illinois at Chicago, the University of Vermont, Calvin College, Boston University, and Notre Dame, as well as at multiple meetings for the Association for the Sociology of Religion and the Society for the Scientific Study of Religion. John Hagedorn, Randall Collins, Nelson Portillo, Robert Fishman, and Luis Vivanco stand out among those who offered thoughtful comments. Two anonymous reviewers at Oxford University Press provided excellent, detailed critiques of a first draft of this manuscript that helped me to focus my efforts and improve the book. Cynthia Read's expert advice and strong encouragement throughout the process was also crucial.

Much earlier in the process, a number of Central Americans helped orient a sociologist of religion who was obviously wading into new territory. Emilio Goubaud, Maricruz Barillas, Fr. Julio Coyoy, Marco Castillo, Rodolfo Kepfer, Harold Sibaja, and Willy Hugo Perez in Guatemala as well as Ernesto Bardales, René Correa, Ricardo Torres, and Ondina Murillo in Honduras all gave me valuable insight and crucial leads that helped get the project off the ground. Dennis Smith, whose insight on Central American evangelicalism and Guatemalan politics has aided the careers of many a gringo scholar, took the time to sit down and talk religion and politics with me on more than one occasion over the years. I owe my curiosity about the sociology of Central American Pentecostalisms to having interpreted dozens of his *pláticas*. In graduate school and beyond, Carlos Mendoza has been an important conversation partner and an extremely knowledgeable connection to the world of Central American scholarship.

Thomas Scheff once compared academia to an urban street gang complete with its own set of rituals of belonging and status hierarchies. He was certainly on to something, and so I have many *compadres* and *ranfleros* to thank for walking with me through *chequeo* and (nonviolently) jumping me in. At Eastern Mennonite University, Omar Eby, Loren McKinney, Barb Graber, and Jay Landis instilled in me a love of human stories and a deep respect for the power of storytelling in facilitating human connection and transformation. I hope you will tolerate the fact that my first book is a work of social science and not a piece of literature. Ray Horst taught me to love Spanish and encouraged a preacher's kid from rural Michigan to think about graduate school for the first time. More important, in the classroom and abroad he introduced me to the violently beautiful Central America that he himself had fallen in love with decades earlier. *¡Gracias Ramoncito!* Around the same time, Doug Frank encouraged me to pay attention to the role of shame in social relations, though I ignored the advice for many years. At Notre Dame, Christian Smith proved an invaluable supervisor and mentor who never tired of hearing me doubt myself and my work—or never told me so if he did. That this book exists is at least as much to his credit as to mine. Other faculty whose encouragement must be mentioned include Maureen Hallinan, Rory McVeigh, Erika Sommers-Effler, Robert Fishman, Lyn Spillman, and David Sikkink. The Center for the Study of Religion and Society provided an excellent place to air some of the ideas contained here both in seminar format and in informal contexts. I greatly value the input of fellow graduate students Jonathan Hill, Brian Miller, and Chris Morrissey. Although we have no tattoos bearing witness to our solidarity, the encouragement and collegiality of this little band of lunchtime sociologists and cultural critics helped me survive a lonely patch of dissertation writing and self-doubt. At Saint Michael's College, Vince Bolduc has made me feel at home by being a good friend and capable mentor.

Several institutions provided me with crucial financial support for researching and writing the dissertation. The Kellogg Center at Notre Dame provided me with funding for travel, and the Institute for Study in the Liberal Arts at Notre Dame as well as the Society for the Scientific Study of Religion provided grants that subsidized the writing process. Mennonite Central Committee also awarded me a small (Mennonite-sized) alumni grant for research. More important, the MCC office in Honduras provided me with free lodging and a nighttime office in San Pedro Sula, and gave me a blessing that opened doors for me in a variety of neighborhoods and institutions. Thanks to Darrin, Julie, and Jeff for going out of your way to help me. Perhaps most important of all, MCC taught me how to get around Central America on a very tight budget. After years of living on a $62-per-month volunteer's stipend, my first grant of five grand seemed like a bottomless war chest.

In Guatemala, the staff at *¡Adios Tatuajes!* opened wide its doors for me due to the remarkable trust and passion of Edgar Franco. The current and former staff of SEMILLA must also be thanked both for the many years of friendship offered me prior to graduate school and for providing me with a place to work during the early stages of the dissertation. Rafael Escobar, Mario Higueros, Willy Hugo Pérez, and Hector Argueta have all contributed greatly to whatever knowledge and passion I possess regarding the intersections of religion and violence in Central America.

Ondina Murillo and the staff at Proyecto Paz y Justicia in La Ceiba, Honduras practically dropped everything whenever I was in town in order to help me. In particular, Dennis Mata, PPyJ's local peace and justice promoter and gang interventionist, introduced me to many former gang members of La López Arellano barrio and spent multiple afternoons discussing religion and life on the streets over fried chicken or plaintain chips. The respect that the *jovenes* of that neighborhood have for Hermano Dennis was obvious wherever we went, and allowed me to hit the ground running rather than spend weeks or months trying to develop leads and generate interviews. *¡Mil gracias vos!*

In San Salvador, the staff at JovenES and Proyecto San Andrés allowed me to tag along and went out of their way to help my project on short notice. Idalia Argueta at CRISPAZ and Fr. José Morataya at El Polígono also gave me generous, extensive interviews and contacts.

A veritable support group of family and friends kept me going on the project when I wondered if any of it would amount to anything. Norma and Jeremías Ochoa provided me free room and board (and grandkid-sitting) whenever I was in Guatemala, and Jeremías especially offered the unique advice and support that only a sociologist and father-in-law could provide. Mark Baker deserves to be singled out for timely support and encouragement that helped me name and escape my own "shame spiral" during multiple moments of writer's block. My three brothers gave patient support to their "black sheep" academic brother and tolerated my occasional sociological rant at family gatherings. I have my father to thank for passing on to me a sociability that disarmed skeptical gatekeepers and won over many an interviewee. But it was my mother who inspired me to the intellectual life and to social and cultural critique. More of a "kitchen sink intellectual" than an "armchair intellectual," for she could never sit still for a moment, Mom taught me to be curious about the world around me and to relish honest debate. That I have been the beneficiary of so many academic and travel opportunities not available to her is a knowledge that makes me all the more determined to make the most of them.

Of course, Mom and Dad also taught me the wonder and privilege of being part of a family—a privilege that can easily end up at loggerheads with the demands of publishing a book while teaching a load of courses. Thus I cannot escape acknowledging the fact that I have not always excelled at navigating the book-versus-family demands effortlessly. Many thanks to Gaby, Nico, and Gabito for tolerating my four-year obsession and for making real sacrifices that allowed this book to become a reality. In fact, Gaby did more than just pick up the slack for a dissertating husband. Her native ear was an invaluable resource whenever I needed to test a translation, which proved frequent since the book is filled with translated street slang. Even more important were the countless volunteer hours she put into transcribing interviews in order to speed up the transcription process and hustle up a stalled researcher. A measly *agradecimiento* here hardly begins to express the depth of my gratitude. Still, *¡De veras, te agradezco!*

I owe my greatest debt of gratitude to the sixty-three men and women who made this project possible by detailing their own experience of leaving the gang. It is my firm belief that the forthrightness of their sharing and the streetwise articulacy that characterizes so many of the interviews represent the key contribution of this book. I have tried to be true to their desire to tell their stories by beginning each chapter with extended pieces of a single ex-gang member's biography in his own words while incorporating the pithy phrases of multiple ex-gang members throughout the book. I sincerely hope that some element of the human resilience of these interviews has managed to survive translation and confronts the reader as it confronted me when I first conducted them. It is my prayer that sharing these stories may help to diminish the odds that any more of these youth will meet the fate of *el Panadero* and the many other ex- (and active) gang members whose lives have been extinguished by social cleansing and the boomerang of gang violence.

HOMIES AND HERMANOS

Introduction: JJ's Second Marriage

To get out of the gang alive is hard, HARD. Our leader, a ranflero [gang lord] once told me, "Here, there is only one way to get out, and that's in your pine-box suit."[1]
—Neftalí, former member of Guatemalan White Fence

Tattooed in bold cursive script across the shoulders of Juan José Tobar[2] are the words, "Why should I fall in love with life when I'm already married to death?"[3] Juan José, or "JJ" as his friends today call him, spent sixteen years as a member and then leader of a violent Guatemala City cell of the transnational gang called the "White Fence." The twenty-eight-year-old Guatemalan has spent years of his life in Guatemala City's juvenile detention centers, prisons, and hospitals and has survived three gunshots, nine stabbings, and the complete failure of one lung due to substance abuse. He candidly admits, though without any pride or pleasure, to having killed or ordered the deaths of multiple individuals, mostly rival gang members. These killings are symbolically represented by three tattooed tears underneath his right eye—the gang equivalent of a "stripe" for eliminating a rival. Tattooed on his eyelids are the letters "W" and "F." Beneath the slogan on his shoulders, a mural of tattoos on his torso and arms depict the gang's ethos, a visual creed composed of female genitalia, gang "homies" dressed in the "cholo" style, and marijuana leaves, as well as the skulls, graves, and flames that represent his gang "matrimony." But now JJ's tattoos speak differently than they used to. Today they speak of a former life—one that ended three years ago when JJ took the dangerous step of leaving the gang for good. JJ is an *ex*-gang member.

When I first met JJ it was at his new place of employment, a computer hardware wholesaler located on a main thoroughfare of Guatemala's upscale “Zona Viva.” Our meeting had been arranged by cell phone through the recommendation of a former member and cell leader of the gang, *Mara Dieciocho*, Antonio “the Bread Maker.” Antonio's brother, also a former gang member, had been killed only two months earlier by the opposing gang, *Mara Salvatrucha*. JJ himself had warned me over the phone that we would have to conduct the interview at his place of work since he recently received a death threat and could not venture outside the warehouse compound except to go directly to his home in another area of the city. In his home neighborhood, he later informed me, he feels safe, but on public transportation or on the street, he always has to keep an eye out.

In the taxi on the way to the meeting, I worried about what to expect. My wife, like most Guatemalans, fears gang members, “reformed” or not, and worried that I had not taken enough precautions this time in vetting the interviewee. She insisted that I call just before and immediately after the interview to let her know I was safe. While most of my interviews with ex-gang members so far had been arranged through trusted gatekeepers, through professionals in substance abuse, or at rehabilitation centers or tattoo-removal clinics, this meeting had been set up after a short telephone conversation in which JJ, in his husky voice and direct manner, asked about my study and what kind of questions I wanted to ask and then told me to meet him at work on the following day. When I arrived at the warehouse and inquired at the security gate, a small, thin man emerged from the building wearing long sleeves under his dark company polo and a hat pulled low over his eyes. Although his coworkers are aware of his past and treat him cordially, JJ wears a baseball cap and long sleeves whenever he leaves the home in order to hide his tattoos and reduce the risk of being spotted by a former enemy or by off-duty police officers. He wants to avoid the fate of so many other ex-gang members, killed on account of decisions made in a former life. The company manager, upon learning of the nature of my interview had offered the use of a plush boardroom to carry out the interview. The boss, a soft-spoken Guatemalan about JJ's age but with lighter skin and a degree in engineering, had hired JJ six months earlier because he is a rare businessman who believes in giving ex-gang members a second chance. In the boardroom, JJ began to tell the story of his life in the gang—a story alternately dramatic and tragic, all too common in the barrios of Central America. He spoke slowly at first but after a time he began to relax, demonstrating eloquence well beyond his three years of formal schooling:

> I entered the gang not because anyone told me to join but because my family was so poor that they could not provide me with an education, shoes, or clothing. And in addition to being poor, they treated me horribly. My mother would beat me. My brother would kick me. They would torture me—a six-year-old—and it made me look to the streets for refuge.

Of his immediate family members, JJ spoke well only of his father, who was killed by poisoning when JJ was only eight years old. When that happened, "It was as if everything had died," he said. "I saw him, dead on December 25, 1989 and I got on my knees and promised that I would avenge his death. It was a promise I made to myself." It was a promise that the young gang member would fulfill only a few years later. Originally from Escuintla, a rough-and-tumble industrial town about an hour south of Guatemala City, JJ moved with his abusive older brother to the capital after his father's death. There he hoped to finally be able to go to school and "become someone—maybe a doctor or a lawyer." But the abuse continued and even worsened. "My brother wore cowboy boots and he would kick me in the face until my forehead bled. I couldn't stand it so I took to the streets. There I found friends, companions who listened to me. They would say, 'Yeah man. What a jerk. Why don't you hang out with us?'"

But their moral support also carried an expectation. When JJ was nine, a group of older gang members asked him to "prove" his loyalty by robbing a corner store using a.38 revolver. Although the request appears to have been as much a dare as an assignment, JJ nevertheless decided to take the opportunity to show his mettle. He burst into the store, aimed his gun at the young man behind the counter, and told him to give him the money in the cash register.

> "Hey you, this is a stick-up!" I said. "Give me your money please, but right now!" The guy started to laugh. When he started to laugh, all at once I saw in his face the face of my brother and then I snapped and started shouting, "I'm going to kill you! I'm going to kill you!" I'm not sure what he saw in my face but right then he opened the drawer and gave me the

> money and told me, "Get out of here but don't kill me." I went back to the gang and that's when they knew I had potential. They started taking me with them to rob other places and pretty soon they didn't do the robbing any more. Instead they would send me in to do it. I worked for them. But through this I started catching the vision of the gang.

In the experience of the armed robbery and through the ensuing crimes, JJ was learning how to translate shame from childhood abuse into anger, and anger into intimidation and violence. He was capturing the "vision" of the gang. During the next decade and a half, JJ dedicated himself to expanding this vision. When "Skinny," the local cell leader who had recruited him was killed, JJ saw his chance to become the new leader or *ranflero*. He called a meeting where he presented his "credentials" as the man for the job.

> As a new *ranflero* I laid out my vision of making my clique the worst of all cliques—the most subversive, the most evil, the most powerful, the most murderous, the one that moved the most drugs and had the most power in prison, the most respected on the outside by all Guatemalans.

By then JJ's resume was long. He had proven his ability to handle weapons and move drugs. Unimpeded by anyone else, he took the position and immediately began recruiting. Under his charge the cell grew to thirty-four gang members in his own neighborhood and fifteen in a start-up cell in Escuintla. "I started bringing in more people and they weren't coming in because I was forcing them. The same thing was happening to them that happened to me. They were being abused too. They were looking for attention and they found it with me. I gave them attention and took an interest in them." He also gave new names to incoming members—English nicknames with an oddly affectionate ring. A young girl with striking good looks he called "Baby." A young boy known for his cleverness he called "Flipper" after the dolphin in the television series.

But as the gang grew so did JJ's reputation, and his growing notoriety made him a target to both other gangs and the police. His list of enemies grew and the police began arresting him for more and more serious crimes. In prison he continued to direct gang activities and his "homies" brought him news, money, and drugs. After spending several years in and out of juvenile detention and then prison, JJ began to suffer from lung dysfunction due to regular consumption of marijuana and cocaine. Meanwhile his growing list of enemies was making it almost impossible to sleep at night. "I would sleep with three or four weapons by my side. One in my belt, one under my pillow, another under the mattress and sometimes even one in my hand." Even his mother's concern had turned to fear. "My mother came to fear me greatly. Greatly. And she decided not to speak to me anymore. She would just give me whatever I asked for and then some." By the time JJ reached his twenties he had succeeded in establishing "respect"—he was feared by many—but only at the price of trust. Unable to trust or be trusted by anyone, his "marriage to death" had made him the ultimate outsider, cut off from everything but the gang and connected to that institution only through his weapons and his tattoos.

CONVERSION: THE MOVE TO ANOTHER PLANET

JJ's descent into criminal violence tracks the wider phenomenon of gangs in Central America in the 1990s. The "White Fence" to which he belonged is a lesser-known group compared with the far more prevalent *Mara Salvatrucha* and the *Mara Dieciocho*, but like these gangs, the White Fence traces its roots to the immigrant communities of Southern California (Vigil 1988). These gangs became established and powerful in Central America after a series of deportation initiatives by the Los Angeles Police Department brought thousands of immigrant youth with criminal records back to Central America (Arana 2005; Quirk 2008). The increasing availability of drugs and weapons coupled with minimal social spending and a weak and corrupt police force allowed the gangs to grow exponentially during the 1990s while forging transnational ties through the increase of cell phone communication and migration. This growing efficiency and organization was accompanied by more rigid rules regarding membership. The slogan etched on JJ's body illustrates one of the major themes characterizing these new "transnational" gangs of Central America—a rule I heard so often that I came to call it "the morgue rule." Most gang members are told when they join one of Central America's transnational gang cells, that their new commitment must last *hasta la morgue*—that is, "all the way to the morgue." And many Central Americans, both gang members and onlookers, have concluded that the morgue rule is true, believing that "once a gang member, always a gang member." And yet, here was JJ, fully tattooed and looking very much like a gang member but working, paying bills and helping other youth to leave the gang or stay out altogether. Is it possible to truly leave the gang with no strings attached—to remain safe, leave drugs and violence, find work, start a family, and start over again?

Many would say no. Father José "Pepe" Morataya of San Salvador, a Spanish Salesian who goes by "Padre Pepe" is one of them. Although he has helped a number of gang members leave the gang in the past by teaching them trades such as bread baking or metalwork, he made it very clear to me that he believes that the Salvadoran gangs of today no longer allow for deserters. At best they allow gang members to become what some call *pandilleros calmados,* or "settled-down gang members" who reduce their criminality and seek reintegration but continue to hold allegiance to the gang and often are expected to continue paying dues for weapons or to help out in the event of a major operation. But for Padre Pepe, severing all ties with the gang by becoming an "ex-gang member" is not an option for the gang youth today. Other experts are nearly as skeptical. The well-known Jesuit sociologist Ricardo Falla likens the gang to "a prison cell with many bars." Many gang members are trapped by the threat of physical death from the homies who view the exiting gang member as a traitor as well as the threat of a "social death" at the hands of a society that loathes him for what he represents (Cruz and Portillo 1998). For who can trust a gang member who has taken an oath of solidarity, burned his allegiance onto his body, and "married death"? In fact, when I asked a Guatemalan psychiatrist who treats incarcerated gang youth what can be done to help a gang member leave his gang and reintegrate into society, he shook his head in silence for several moments and finally offered a suggestion: "Take them to another planet."

With a few exceptions, the only alternative "planet" that governments have offered gang members like JJ as an attempt to persuade them to leave the gang is that of the prison. Police and military forces have taken to conducting neighborhood sweeps, which have led to massive arrests often based on little more than the presence of a tattoo. But in Central America's overcrowded and underfunded prisons, gang members have simply congregated, honing their skills, networking with drug dealers, and directing operations with their homies on the outside. Instead of "corrections" or reform, the prisons have become "graduate schools of crime" where homies enhance their skills and "earn their stripes" by doing time for the gang. Understandably angry about the government's inability to arrest the spiraling crime in the region, many Central American's have concluded that the best way to "deal with" the violent and incorrigible gang youth like JJ—especially given his vow of lifelong commitment to the gang—is simply to eliminate them. Evidence of "social cleansing," or extrajudicial killing of gang members by off-duty police or hit men associated with the military, has begun to mount as bodies of gang members appear daily on the streets, often bearing the marks of torture that hearken back to the political violence of an earlier time (Moser and Winton 2002; Payne 1999; Ranum 2007). In Guatemala, a national newspaper reported in 2007 that 60 percent of Guatemalans polled supported social cleansing as one means of dealing with gang violence (R.M. Aguilar 2007b). Supporters of social cleansing seem to believe in effect, "If the gangs are so enamored of death, then why not let them have it?"

But despite the pessimism on the part of the government, the media, and even some social scientists, and despite ominous warnings from their erstwhile gang mates, JJ and hundreds of others like him have indeed managed to find a way out of the gang leaving violence and drugs behind, land a steady job, and start over. Despite his tattoos and his criminal record, and in spite of the "morgue rule," JJ has managed to live down his tattoo by "falling in love with life." But in order to do this, he has done the next best thing to "moving to another planet"—he has become an evangelical Christian. To listen to JJ today is to hear the voice of an old-fashioned *evangélico* who has thoroughly adopted the identity of *un hermano*, or "brother in the faith," in place of his homie identity. He peppers his speech with Bible verses and thanks the Lord for everything. He has begun a ministry out of his home called "Freed by Christ" aimed at convincing gang members to leave the gang and join the church, and he speaks at evangelical and charismatic Catholic revival meetings for youth. Even his hair is combed in the decidedly old-fashioned evangelical manner, parted on the side instead of slicked back as it used to be. JJ took the long route in leaving the gang by going in a very short time from the decidedly rough and hyper-macho homie to the domesticated *hermano*.

On the face of it, JJ's approach to leaving seems both easy and unlikely. On the one hand, joining a church is uncomplicated. What could be easier than running into the open arms of the spiritualistic, conversionist Christianity of the Central American *evangélicos*? On the other hand, succeeding as a member of an evangelical congregation, with its teetotaling moralism and "cold turkey" expectations for lifestyle changes seems less than likely. Evangelical congregations do not seem to present much in the way of attractions for the hyper-macho male gang member accustomed to trading female partners, toting weapons, and generating instant and sometimes plentiful income through theft and extortion. What on earth could make possible such a drastic reversal of identity and what would cause a gang member to opt for what seems like the most unlikely of identity transformations?

This book is a sociological exploration of the transformation that many gang youth take from "homie" to evangelical *hermano*.[4] What makes a gang homie trade in his gun for a Bible? And what does the trade teach us more broadly about the nature of youth violence, of religious conversion, and of evangelical churches in Central America? To answer these questions I interviewed a total of sixty-three former gang members, fifty-nine men and four women, in all three countries of the "Northern Triangle" of Central America—Guatemala, El Salvador, and Honduras—the only countries with high concentrations of gang members and gang violence.[5] I first learned of the phenomenon of conversion as a pathway out of the gang when reading a chapter written by Ileana Gomez and Manuel Vásquez (2001) on Salvadoran ex-gang members and evangelical ministries. As I read further in the fledgling literature on Central American gangs, the claim about evangelical conversions out of the gangs kept on surfacing, whether cited by skeptics as a naïve rumor (Foro Ecuménico por la Paz y la Reconciliación 2006) or noted in passing by researchers recounting interviews with residents of gang-controlled neighborhoods (López 2004; Winton 2005). Because I wanted to know whether the phenomenon was an overreported rarity or a relatively frequent occurrence, I contacted and interviewed ex-gang members in a variety of settings including evangelical and Catholic-sponsored organizations and nonreligious nongovernmental organizations, as well as prisons and dry-out centers. I contacted some of the ex-gang members via "snowball sampling" using interviewees to generate new contacts. Others were contacted through trusted gatekeepers such as priests, pastors, and government rehabilitation officers. Generating a random sample was out of the question, since no gang membership lists exist, much less a list of ex-members. But by interviewing all ex-gang members who sought services at a walk-in tattoo-removal clinic over the course of several weeks, I was able to improve my sample by reducing the odds of encountering only ex-gang members who had been preselected on the basis of their life history or because of their "success" after leaving the gang. While none of these measures guarantees that the ex-gang members I interviewed are representative in a statistical sense, both the variety of geographic contexts and the stories I encountered allow me a certain confidence in trusting that the sample is not overly biased toward religious ex-gang members.[6] After all, I wanted to hear more than just conversion stories. I wanted to compare these stories with the critical and comparative perspectives of those ex-gang members who left the gang *without* converting.

In addition to my interviews with ex-gang members themselves, I interviewed more than thirty experts and practitioners working at twenty-seven organizations and ministries aimed at reducing gang violence. These interviews proved invaluable in helping me to understand the broader social context affecting gang exit. Because many of these experts knew the ex-gang members I interviewed, they were able to verify some of the incidents and experiences reported by the ex-gang members themselves. Finally, in addition to the interviews with ex-gang members and experts, I took field notes during trips to prisons, pastoral visits, excursions in "red zone" neighborhoods, and an evangelistic campaign aimed specifically at "winning" gang members to evangelical faith.

RELIGION AND THE PROBLEM OF GANG VIOLENCE

My interest in the role of religion in Central America began in the early 1990s during a semester of cross-cultural study in Guatemala City. In a region marked by crippling foreign debt and political violence, we studied issues of poverty and war in the nascent democracies of the region. I returned to Guatemala shortly after the close of the civil war to live and work as a member of the Mennonite volunteer corps, leading cross-cultural seminars dealing with violence, poverty, and culture in that country and its neighbors. During these years, the central issues facing Central Americans of the "Northern Triangle" of Guatemala, Honduras, and El Salvador began to shift perceptibly from land reform and political violence to fighting political corruption and addressing rampant crime. Today, when Central Americans in these nations are asked to rank their most pressing concerns, addressing street crime is usually at or near the top (Latinobarómetro 2010; Pew 2002). During six years of working and living in Guatemala City, I watched and listened as the gangs became a daily topic of conversation, and a political and media obsession. Gang graffiti grew more and more common, the murder rate rose, and by the early 2000s it seemed that no evening news report was complete without footage of police officers parading "captured" gang members into the back of a police pickup—tattoos and hand signals flashing, and heads held high for the cameras. In Honduras and El Salvador, conservative presidential candidates promising "iron-fist" polices rode a wave of anti-gang sentiment into office. Meanwhile, in Guatemala, the infamous Guatemalan army had found a new *raison d'être* in the "joint" military/police forces dispatched to combat gangs by patrolling the streets from pickup trucks mounted with gun turrets and automatic weapons. Avoiding assault by a gang member had become a daily concern for anyone riding public transportation to and from a neighborhood "controlled" by the gang. By the time I left the region in 2003, gangs were collecting thousands of dollars in "war taxes" through mafia-style extortion of bus drivers, homeowners, and small business operators. Though the masterminds behind the far more lucrative bank robberies and kidnappings continued to be the organized crime bosses, gang members' low social class and high visibility made them easy targets for politicians and other "moral entrepreneurs" seeking a scapegoat. *Las maras* (the gangs) had become public enemy number one.

But my interest went beyond the gangs and gang violence. I was also intrigued by the role of religion in an increasingly violent society. My work in Central America had been at a Mennonite seminary with a deep commitment to nonviolence and a "holistic" gospel of social and spiritual liberation. My colleagues on the theological faculty strove to "wake up" pastors and lay leaders to the realities of structural and political violence around them and a key concern in many of the courses was to counter the emotional, Pentecostalist tendencies increasingly apparent in many of the congregations of the denomination. For some among the faculty, the emotionalism of amped-up religious services and the emphasis on spiritual conversion smacked of escapism that could easily get in the way of the "real work" of teaching the faithful to practice justice and promote peace. And yet the Pentecostalized churches that made up many of our constituent congregations seemed mostly to be thriving among Mennonites as well as other historic Protestant churches of the region (Chesnut 2003; Smith and Higueros 2005). The members of these congregations often seemed more interested in a spiritual or emotional liberation than in liberation of a political nature. Some of these congregations were very involved in addressing the nagging social problems of their local communities. But invariably they used spiritual language to frame such involvement. Thus, my entrance into graduate school back in the United States came by way of the sociology of religion and an attempt better to understand the intersections between religion and society in violent, impoverished communities. Does religion in contemporary Central America make any difference now that the energy of Pentecostals and charismatics has eclipsed that of the liberationists? Specifically, what do the churches in Central America—evangelical and Catholic—have to say or do about the gang violence that now scourges their neighborhoods?

STRUCTURE OF THE BOOK

In Chapter 1 (in this volume) I give a brief overview of the current research on the Central American gangs, much of it published by scholars in the region, especially from the Jesuit Universidad de Centroamérica in San Salvador. By reviewing the findings of much of the empirical literature to date, I set the gang phenomenon in its sociohistorical context and briefly explore some of the key social and political factors that contributed to the emergence of transnational gangs in northern Central America.

It is clear that the Central American gangs of today are not the mildly delinquent street gangs of a generation ago. Nor are they the same as their counterparts in the United States, where most gang members are expected to "age out" of the gang by early adulthood. The influx of narco-business brought on by the squeezing of the traditional drug routes of the Caribbean in the early 1990s has vastly increased the income-generating opportunities for the gangs and helped them to acquire increasingly sophisticated weapons. In addition to providing opportunities for income through drug sales, many gangs have taken "turf protection" to a new extreme by levying "war taxes" on neighbors, bus and taxi drivers, and small business owners in their own communities, forcing them to pay hefty extortion fees or face the threat of death or abduction. In Guatemala alone in 2008, there were eighty-five murders of bus drivers, many alleged to be ordered by a single gang boss of the Mara Dieciocho (Notimex 2009). The income from drugs and extortion allows gang leaders to buy off woefully underpaid local police and gain a measure of impunity, at least for a time. It also makes recruiting and keeping youth much easier by allowing them to offer "real money" to active members.

Chapter 2 turns the attention to evangelical religion. Here I introduce the concept of "barrio evangelicalism" to describe the evangelical-Pentecostal congregations of small to medium size which populate the working-class and marginal neighborhoods of Central America. These congregations share the social space occupied by many gang cells and they are the congregations to which many of the converted ex-gang members I interviewed now belong and where they participate actively. While I found no evidence of an illicit connection or relationship between gangs and churches, I point out similarities between the social structures of evangelical churches and transnational gang cells, including their franchise-like organization and their entrepreneurial growth model. But the differences between the two social phenomena are considerable and these differences are clearest when examining the value systems of each. While the gang promotes a hedonistic vision of pleasure pursuits, evangelicals, especially the pietistic *hermanos* of barrio evangelicalism, promote strict moralistic prohibitions aimed at eliminating alcohol and tobacco use and curbing and domesticating sexuality.

Chapters 3 and 4 (in this volume) shift focus back to the gang, but this time at the micro-level of everyday experience. In Chapter 3 I mine the stories of ex-gang members for clues as to why Central American youth join the gang in the first place. To date, most research on gang entrance in Central America has identified the "usual suspects": poverty, unemployment, and dysfunctional or abusive families. These explanations are not untrue, but they do not explain enough. I employ the tools of symbolic interaction theory and the sociology of emotions to more carefully specify what it is about the experience of poverty or abuse that "pushes" youth toward the gang and what it is about the gang that "pulls" them toward becoming a homie. Drawing heavily from testimonies of ex-gang members, I argue that joining the gang is not a one-time, momentary decision but an interactive process in which youth "try on" the gang member identity by becoming a gang "sympathizer" and spending time with the gang, learning about its rituals and symbols. Although not all sympathizers eventually join, those who do often reported "feeling good" when they experienced violence, even when it was directed at their own person, as in the jumping-in ritual called a "baptism." Borrowing from Thomas Scheff's work on shame as a key factor in human interaction (Scheff 1988, 1991, 2004), I argue that disenfranchised youth are drawn to the gang because it offers the opportunity to avoid acknowledging feelings of shame, "bypassing" shame through the experience of violence, "adult" pastimes such as sex and drug abuse, and solidarity from feeling part of a group.

But the "good feeling" experienced through participation in crime and violence tends to wear off after a while and can in fact become a new source of shame. Chapter 4 examines what happens when the violence of the gang begins to "catch up" with the homies and the gang tattoos start to feel more like a "stain" than a source of pride. I examine the various motivations that ex-gang members reported began pushing them to consider leaving the gang, as well as the enormous obstacles standing in the way of their following through on that desire. Remarkably scant research has been published on the matter of gang exit since most studies of Central American gangs have instead examined the factors causing gang members to join. This emphasis makes sense up to a point. After all, if the object is to arrest the growth of the gangs, then the old adage applies: "An ounce of prevention is worth a pound of cure." Unfortunately, the focus on prevention means that we know very little from empirical research about why and how some youth manage to leave the gang and what factors stand in the way of their doing so.

In spite of the oft-repeated warning that joining the gang commits youth "all the way to the morgue," more than a few gang members have made successful exits. Among the sixty-three former gang members I interviewed for the study, I know of only one so far who was unable to overcome the first obstacle, that of staying alive. Among the other sixty-two, many are thriving, while others are getting by through help from family or friends who encouraged them to leave the gang in the first place. A majority of the ex-gang members I interviewed reported experiencing a religious conversion during or soon after leaving the gang. Like JJ, they found in evangelical religion an effective means for addressing the obstacles to leaving and starting over outside the gang. Chapter 5 examines the nature of these religious conversions and explores how ex-gang member converts found evangelical religion to be both advantageous and effective. The story there is both surprising and instructive. Multiple informants in all three countries told me that many gang leaders extend a "pass" to members who report a conversion or have joined a church, though the self-described convert will be observed to make sure his conversion was not simply a ruse to escape the morgue rule. Since nearly all evangelical churches, especially the small evangelical-Pentecostal congregations of the Central American barrios where gangs are common, practice teetotalism, restrict sexuality, and require frequent attendance at worship, ex-gang member converts possess a relatively simple—if not particularly easy, given its strict behavioral standards—means of "proving" the genuineness of their conversion. Although some ex-gang members reported avoiding the morgue rule by other means than evangelical conversion, no exception was as widely referenced as the evangelical exemption.

But evangelical conversion offers more than a "pass" on the morgue rule and a means of proving one's sincerity. The converted ex-gang members reported a variety of other benefits, both social and psychological, such as helping them to find work, reorder their priorities, and rebuild networks of trust after the gang. Thus, my research builds on the work of others who have found that evangelical religion provides a resource for Latin American men who struggle with addiction, violence, and chaotic relationships by helping them to establish healthy routines through the social support and accountability of a small congregation with strict behavioral guidelines and an emphasis on the domestic sphere (Brusco 1995; Burdick 1993; Smilde 2005). My research adds depth to the field by exploring the role of emotion in the process of conversion and identity reconstruction. I argue that the emotional experiences of conversion reported to me by several ex-gang members worked in part by allowing young men to acknowledge and effectively discharge chronic shame in a public setting, thereby escaping the vicious shame spiral underlying their attachment to the gang and its violent code of *respeto*. Although emotion-laden conversion experiences tended to be brief and were usually followed up by months if not years of identity work, their power in engendering attachment to evangelical religion and to forging new lines of action and new identities was difficult to ignore.

All of this adds significant depth to our understanding of the role of evangelical religion in Central America but there is more to learn. Chapter 6 begins with a discussion of the religion-inspired initiatives aimed at gang violence reduction in the region. Neither the Catholic nor the evangelical churches have launched massive programs or created large organizations for arresting gang violence. But within each, congregations and parishes, as well as priests, pastors, and lay workers, have made impressive attempts at addressing the issue. Catholics have tended to found programs and invest in approaches that promote gang *prevention* through social programs and community development, while evangelicals have tended almost exclusively toward promoting gang *exit*, especially by means of religious conversion. Each of these approaches fits both the theology and the social shape of the tradition to which it belongs. Interestingly, not a single gang member in the sample of sixty-three participants I interviewed chose to embrace Catholicism as a means of addressing the challenge to *un*becoming a homie. Perhaps this finding should come as no surprise since Catholic gang exit initiatives are relatively few. Yet, even youth who passed through one of the few Catholic-affiliated gang exit programs were often evangelical converts themselves.

I conclude the book by summarizing my findings regarding gangs and religion and briefly suggesting broader strategies for arresting gang violence. One point I must make very clear. I do not by any means wish to suggest that a religious conversion is exactly what is needed for dealing with the violence of gangs in Central America or anywhere else. If a surprising number of aging gang members have found a refuge of last resort in the evangelical churches of the region, this fact hardly means that religion, evangelical or otherwise, is the antidote for Central America's struggle with gang violence. I would not be a sociologist if I did not believe that the principle factors leading to profound social problems such as the growth and hypermilitarization of the transnational gangs were linked to historic patterns of structural violence. The religiously inspired gang prevention advocates and *promotores ambulantes* (walking neighborhood gang-exit promoters) are playing a courageous and important role in helping aging gang members find nonviolent pathways toward social reintegration. But these programs are a single component of a much larger effort necessary for controlling, reducing, and, someday, eliminating gang violence. Arresting gang violence must be an effort that is both deep and wide, including local, national, and international efforts to undermine the structures that produce the conditions for shame among thousands of youth in the impoverished barrios of the region while severely eroding access to the weapons and drug money that provide these youth with a quick and easy route to bypassing shame. Congregations and parishes can and should increase their efforts to provide nonviolent pathways out of the gang, but religious institutions will be hard-pressed to provide long-term solutions that keep children from viewing the gang as an attractive alternative in the first place.

Still, it is hard not to be impressed by the impact of conversions in the lives of ex-gang members themselves and of their families. One year after I first met JJ, I received an invitation to a wedding. This time the wedding was a real one and the bride was not the gang but rather JJ's long-time partner and mother of his young son. Even though JJ had given up womanizing along with drugs, weapons, and the rest of *la vida loca,* as an evangelical Christian, he felt the need to "formalize" his conjugal relationship with a church wedding that included a long guest list and cake, a *tamal,* and a Coca-cola for everyone. The wedding service was long and included the required legal marriage ceremony followed by a festive religious program, complete with a sermon from the Bible's most romantic book, the "Song of Songs." By the end of the ceremony, JJ had wept several times, soaking the tattooed tears with his own and shedding any scrap of gang pride he had left. His marriage to death had been permanently annulled.

1

From *Pandilla* to *Mara*

Back in the 70s and 80s we had *pandillas* but not *maras*. That's a new phenomenon and it came imported. It is not from here. In 1992 the U.S. started sending gang members back to El Salvador. . . . And my hats off to the U.S.—at least they waited until the war was over to start sending them back!
—Fr. José Morataya, Director of Gang Prevention Center

Shit homes! I've never been here. I mean, I know I'm from here, homes, but I've never been here.
—Deported Salvadoran Gang Member (from Zilberg 2004)

Enrique was thirteen years old when he first met Ninosa. The year was 1993 and the ink on the Peace Accords, signed between the Salvadoran government and the guerrilla group, the Farabundo Martí National Liberation Front, was barely dry. In an interview, Enrique, a young, well-dressed Salvadoran, recalled to me how his father, a laborer, had been killed in a workplace accident when Enrique was seven, and how his mother struggled to feed and clothe her five children. Nor could his mother depend on extended family. Two of Enrique's aunts had been killed in the war several years earlier. Like many young Salvadoran children coming of age in a postwar society, Enrique remembered casting about in search of a sense of security and identity.

> You're left in orbit, without anyone. It was only by sheer strength that mom was able to keep us going, you know? And [as a kid] you just want something to get your mind off it all. And so this guy named Ninosa shows up with a [gang] structure from the United States and wants to set up shop here and he's telling us all about it. And what do you do? You join up.

Ninosa's arrival in San Salvador was not a random event. That year the Los Angeles Police Department had begun a major effort to deport young Salvadoran men like Ninosa—gang youth with a criminal history and precarious legal status—by the thousands. Like many other deported youth, Ninosa began organizing young males in the neighborhood, teaching them about survival and ethnic rivalries developed on the streets of a mega-city thousands of miles away. Although Enrique was already "hanging out" with a local street gang, he described how Ninosa had "schooled" Enrique and his friends in the ways of the new gang:

> Back then there were [local] gangs like *la mara gallo* (the rooster gang), *la mara chancleta* (the sandal gang). There was no such thing as *la Mara Salvatrucha*. We had already formed our own group when this guy, Ninosa, comes along and starts feeding us the line. He's like, "No, it's not about that. Here it's all about the *Mara Salvatrucha*, the *Salvadoran* gang. They hate us over there [in Los Angeles]. The blacks hate us . . . and they don't want us up there and so we have to be strong." He told us that illegals suffer there and that they destroy them (*los hacen pedazos*) and of course we believed him. They sow hatred in you like that because they come down with this hatred from being deported and mistreated.

Enrique remembered being intrigued by the stories of racial-ethnic conflict in the United States and in the Los Angeles gangs. Ninosa told of being beaten and mistreated in prison and of the need to defend oneself against Mexican-Americans. He also described the discrimination and deportation of Central Americans and of the need to oppose Mexican-Americans. "We had to be against the *Dieciocho* [Eighteenth Street gang] because they're Mexican and the Mexicans hate Central Americans. So my friends and I thought a lot about it. 'Why would they deport people like this?'" For young men in the San Salvador barrios, the hatred was contagious. Soon, he and his friends began affiliating with the "new gangs," some on the side of the *Dieciocho*, but most with the *Salvatrucha*. Indeed, Ninosa found fertile ground for recruiting. "He had been in prison up there but here arrived free, and he started laying the groundwork. He raised up many *clicas* (cells or "cliques")."

I asked Enrique if Ninosa was still alive today. "He was killed by the *Sombra Negra* (Black Shadow). That's what they called themselves, but in the end it was the government. The death squad was breaking all of the leaders." Indeed, the *Sombra Negra*, a secretive death squad allegedly composed of police and military officers, claimed to be involved in "cleaning up" society by eliminating gang members and other "undesirables." In a note sent to the press, the group claimed responsibility for the deaths of seventeen gang leaders in 1994 alone, many of them killed in symbolic death squad fashion with a bullet to the skull at close range. Although several high-profile arrests were made in 1995, including members and officers of the police, all those arrested were either released or eventually found "not guilty" for lack of evidence. In the years that followed, other copycat death squads would make similar claims (Payne 1999).

But if the death squad killings were meant to snuff out the gangs by intimidation and through the "strategic" elimination of gang leadership, their impact was just the opposite. Enrique and his friends, until then only marginally associated with the *Salvatrucha*, took to the streets to threaten revenge, their loyalty now solidified. "We went crazy. We started calling the media to try to make our presence felt. Some of us even went out into the streets with grenades in hand. We wanted to make our presence felt. We thought we were going to put an end to the *Sombra Negra*. We didn't know what we were talking about." Nor did the new recruits have to look far for new leaders. I asked Enrique what happened in the wake of their new leader's death. "A new leader arrived," he said. "There was always someone else waiting. And here too, we were starting to rise through the ranks."

DEFINING GANGS IN CENTRAL AMERICA

As one of the oldest former members of the Salvadoran gangs I interviewed, Enrique's account illustrates some of the most important features of the emergence of the Central American transnational gangs. Poverty, precarious family structures ruptured by war and deportation, the prison-ghetto connection, and the rise of "social cleansing" all played a role in the emergence of the transnational gangs of Central America. For while it is true that Los Angeles is the "birthplace" of the transnational gangs, it was in San Salvador that the gangs grew and evolved toward the violence that characterizes them today—a violence that grips hundreds of urban neighborhoods across northern Central America. My aim is to sketch the demographics and characteristics of the gangs while critiquing some of the more exaggerated and unfounded claims about the power and reach of the transnational gangs. I rely heavily on the work of a number of Central American social scientists who have produced a growing body of scholarly literature on the transnational gangs. These researchers, many of them associated with the Center for Public Opinion at San Salvador's Jesuit Universidad de Centroamérica, have completed empirical work that provides a basis for understanding the emergence and growth of the gangs in recent decades. In addition to citing current research, I use press reports and excerpts from my own interviews to illustrate a number of points. Of course, gang life in Central America shares many similarities with life in a typical street gang in the United States, where members are predominantly male, from the lower economic rungs of urban society, and, many, from precarious family backgrounds (Decker and Van Winkle 1996; Moore 1991). And yet the gangs of Central America have institutionalized in ways that set them apart from most youth street gangs in the United States. Understanding the nature of the transnational gangs is essential to grasping why leaving the Central American gang presents such a unique set of challenges to gang members—and why religion provides such a popular pathway out of the gang.

International gang scholars Malcolm Klein and Cheryl Maxson offer a widely accepted definition of the term "street gang" defining it as "any durable, street-oriented youth group whose involvement in illegal activity is part of its group identity" (2006:4). Their definition is based on a consensus among many researchers who study gangs in the United States and Europe, but its minimalism allows application to contexts such as Central America (Medina and Mateu-Gelabert 2009). Although it hardly begins to describe the many characteristics shared by most Central American gang cells, the definition offered by Klein and Maxson distinguishes conceptually the transnational gangs from other groups sometimes inappropriately confounded with them. For example, middle-class *góticos* (Goths) roam the upscale shopping malls in Guatemala City or gather to experiment with drugs, alarming their parents with their clothing and piercings, but they do not engage in violence or spend their afternoons in *la calle*. Nor are the gangs to be confused with *roqueros* (hard rockers), groups of working-class youth who listen to heavy metal and engage in mildly delinquent behavior and drug abuse for pleasure. Teenage *roqueros* are a source of concern for neighbors and police, but if and when they engage in illegal activity, such "entertainment" only occasionally rises above the level of random delinquency and usually does not contribute to the group's core identity. At the other end of the spectrum are the drug cartels that have grown in power and influence, especially in Mexico. Although the press sometimes refers to them as "drug gangs," these groups are not youth-based, nor is their violence intended to elevate a particular identity. They represent a form of organization, discipline, geographic reach, and access to resources well beyond the scope of the gangs of Central America. Finally, a crucial distinction must be made between the street gangs, made up of youth from marginal barrios, and the organized criminal rings that have taken shape in Central America during recent decades. The latter involve shadowy networks of individuals from the middle class and elites who wield considerable political and economic power and who mix legal business and illegal activities (including money laundering, drug trafficking, kidnapping, and tax fraud) in order to acquire and maintain considerable wealth (Torres-Rivas 2010). Although it is well-known that organized crime rings can and do draw recruits from the gang when in need of foot soldiers for carrying out the "dirty work" of kidnapping and score settling, politicians and the media have a tendency to conflate the two, thereby setting up a convenient smokescreen allowing them to ignore tax reform and turn a blind eye to political corruption (Martinez Ventura 2010).

Nevertheless, as U.S. gang scholar John Hagedorn (2009) has pointed out, gangs are not static but dynamic institutions, able to change and adapt to their own unique set of circumstances. This capacity to adjust and grow is especially apparent among the gangs of northern Central America, where weak state institutions and porous borders have allowed the emergence of an institutionalized gang culture that is best described as "transnational."

EXPORTING VIOLENCE: THE ORIGINS OF TRANSNATIONAL GANGS

Enrique's "on-the-ground" account of the proliferation of the *Salvatrucha* in El Salvador makes it clear that it is impossible to talk about the gangs without starting earlier, in the civil wars of the 1970s and '80s. These wars set the stage for the rise of the transnational gangs by sending tens of thousands of Central American refugee families fleeing to the United States for safety. In El Salvador, where by the late 1980s civil war had enveloped most of the country, even reaching the outskirts of the capital, the emigration flow was especially intense. By 1990 the U.N. estimated that approximately 700,000 Salvadorans were living in the United States, primarily in Los Angeles but also in the D.C. area and in New York City (Hayden 2004). This figure represented considerably more than one-tenth of the tiny country's entire population. Lacking a strong formal education, useful network ties, or clear prospects for employment, hundreds of Salvadoran youths joined local Latino gangs, especially the Mexican-American 18th Street (*Dieciocho*) gang. Many other young Salvadorans found the local gang territory hostile, and formed their own groups, especially in the Pico Union area of Los Angeles (Vigil 2002). These Salvadoran immigrant gangs eventually took the name *La Mara Salvatrucha*. Meanwhile, a thriving underground economy, buoyed up by surging demand for crack and other illegal drugs, had provided U.S. gangs with increasing economic opportunities (Jankowski 1992; Venkatesh 2000). Such opportunities were especially attractive to Central American youth, particularly those who lived in constant fear of being arrested and deported. For young, undocumented immigrants, it "made sense" to look to the street for income rather than to risk being detained while trying to produce false papers for a job interview.

In 1992, riots shook Los Angeles following the innocent verdict in the Rodney King trial. When Latino gang youth were accused of playing a major role in the looting that accompanied the chaos, the Los Angeles Police Department (L.A.P.D.) spearheaded a campaign to arrest and prosecute gang members, even minors, as felons, and initiate deportation proceedings. The signing of the Peace Accords that same year ended El Salvador's civil war and gave the L.A.P.D. further justification for its massive round-up and deportation under a now-defunct program called CRASH—Community Resources Against Street Hoodlums. Thousands of Salvadoran youth and young men, many of whom had lived most of their lives in the United States, were arrested, prosecuted as adults, and deported to their "home country." Nor were local authorities provided with information regarding the criminal background of the young men arriving in their communities. Set adrift in a context they barely knew and with even fewer prospects for legitimate employment, these young gang members set about organizing and recruiting a local youth population that treated the deportees with a combination of fear and reverence. For youths facing bleak circumstances in the impoverished marginal neighborhoods of San Salvador, tattooed young deportees like Ninosa, who often spoke English far better than they spoke Spanish, displayed a worldly wise self-confidence that was magnetic in the Central American barrio.

Gang developments in Guatemala and Honduras followed a similar path. Altogether, more than 50,000 Central Americans with a criminal record were deported by the United States in just over a decade from 1994–2005 (Kraul, Lopez, and Connell 2005). Although far fewer gang youth were deported to Guatemala and Honduras, thousands returned to these countries with gang knowledge and experience, often acquired during a prison sentence before deportation. Just as important, Salvadoran gang members began traveling to Honduras and Guatemala in the mid-1990s to organize gang cells there and to flee authorities seeking them in El Salvador (Loudis, del Castillo, Rajaraman, and Castillo 2006; Sibaja, Roig, Rajaraman, Caldera, and Bardales 2006). Taking advantage of porous borders and minimal information sharing between police, these gang organizers expanded their network of gang cells throughout the three countries of the Northern Triangle. By the late 1990s, two major gangs, the *Mara Salvatrucha*, also known by its abbreviation, MS-13, and the *Mara Dieciocho*, similarly represented by the abbreviation M-18, had obtained a clear position as *the* dominant gang rivals in the region. They accomplished this not only by recruiting disenfranchised youth in the impoverished urban neighborhoods of the Northern Triangle but also by co-opting nearly all of the already-established local street gangs. Due to a combination of loose networks, access to weapons, and the thrill of belonging to a gang whose experience and connections stretched all the way to Los Angeles, the Salvatrucha and Dieciocho organizers were able to replicate these local gang cells by the hundreds in *clicas*, or "cliques."

Other social and economic factors played a role in the expansion of the Central American gangs. The sheer size of the young, urban population—Enrique's family of six was typical—placed enormous strain on already-underfunded public schools and hospitals. More important, the burgeoning youth cohort expanded the audience of adolescents, curious about the new gangs and their connections to *el Norte*. In 1990 approximately one-fifth of the population in each country were between the ages of fifteen and twenty-four, and the balance of the population was shifting, from majority rural, toward becoming majority urban societies.[1] Each year, thousands of Central American youth moved with their parents to the marginal neighborhoods and satellite towns of the growing cities where they witnessed firsthand, many for the first time, the steep economic pyramids that characterize urban Latin America. Public security was even less able to keep up with the demands of the population. In El Salvador and Guatemala, police had earned the distrust of the people by collaborating with the military in their dirty wars and in all three countries many viewed (and continue to view) the police as corrupt and inept. While a major overhaul of the police force in El Salvador was able to restore a modicum of trust and professionalism in that force, Guatemala opted to recycle most of its wartime police force, leaving the entire command structure intact. The tiny police force in Honduras, also accused of corruption and participation in the civil violence of the 1980s, fared no better. In all three countries, local security forces were ill-equipped, poorly trained, and unmotivated to provide effective security for the densely populated barrios where the gangs were establishing a foothold. While the rich and the middle class barricaded their streets and contracted private security firms to keep them safe, the gangs offered "protection" to their own neighbors—and also charged a fee.

Finally, in addition to the migration-deportation cycle, poverty, a burgeoning urban youth cohort, and an inept and underfunded police force, one other social factor contributed to the growth and evolution of the gangs—the "war on drugs." Following the relative success of the U.S.-led drug war in shutting off drug routes from Colombia to Miami via the Caribbean, the unflagging demand for illegal drugs led to the establishment of new Central American routes now under the control of the Mexican cartels. As the drug shipments made their way northward across the isthmus, some of the product became locally available—indeed, the drug cartels often used drugs as payment for services rendered—and the gangs took advantage of the opportunity to sell cocaine and marijuana in their own neighborhoods, creating new demand where there had been little of it. With drugs came weapons and over time the gangs established networks for acquiring and trading in weapons, using them to protect their increasingly valuable "turf" and to conduct "missions."

All these factors played a role in the transformation, or "evolution" of the Central American gangs in the 1990s. In effect, the gangs became institutionalized in Central America due in large part to the weakness of state and local institutions, ravaged by years of civil war and weak economic growth and unable to keep up with a rapidly growing population due to cutbacks in social services from successive neoliberal administrations. The institutional vacuum was most severe in the densely populated marginal neighborhoods of the major cities, where young families came fleeing the violence of the countryside (in El Salvador and Guatemala) or flocking to *maquiladoras* (clothing assembly plants) and the promise of an income (in Honduras). In these neighborhoods, the gangs were able to carve out what Hagedorn (2009) calls "defensible spaces" for conducting business and building camaraderie based on a brotherhood with international reach.

WHO ARE THE GANGS?

The institutionalization of the gangs was accompanied by a change in terminology. During the late 1980s and early '90s the term "mara" came to stand for a street gang in Central America. Youth street gangs like the "Rooster Gang" to which Enrique referred, had been around at least since the 1970s in places like Guatemala City and San Salvador, but they received little attention, and were referred to with the term "pandilla," which translates roughly as a "band" of youth. As the gangs grew in size and came to be associated with criminal violence, the press began referring to them as *las maras*, perhaps in reference to the *marabunta* ants which overcome their victims by attacking in swarms (Smutt and Miranda 1998). The most common gangs by far are the Mara Salvatrucha, which uses the initials MS-13 or simply "MS," and the Eighteenth Street Gang or Mara Dieciocho, which uses the shorthand M-18 or simply "18" to describe itself. Many gang members sometimes refer to themselves as belonging simply to *las letras* (i.e., the letters MS) or *los números* (e.g., the number 18). Other gangs exist, but in the Northern Triangle of Guatemala, Honduras, and El Salvador, the MS-13 and the M-18 have come to dominate the youth gang culture. In fact, as I learned from the young men and women in my interviews, many local *clicas* have taken names that do not immediately identify them with the larger gangs. But at least by the early 2000s, nearly all of the local *clicas* had affiliated with one or the other of the transnational gangs. In a few cases, other gangs with international ties managed to survive by brokering an informal truce with either the M-18 or the MS-13, thereby earning default enemy status with the transnational rival. The White Fence, an L.A.-based gang with roots reaching back at least to the 1950s (Vigil 1988), is one such gang.[2] The gang, which developed several *clicas* in satellite neighborhoods of Guatemala City in the 1990s, had been all but swallowed up or eliminated by the MS-13 by the mid-2000s. In Honduras, a few neighborhoods developed several cells of the *Vatos Locos*, a gang with origins in Chicago and represented by the initials VL or BL. Like the White Fence *clicas* in Guatemala, the Honduran *Vatos* have all but disappeared in recent years. Thus, while a few other gangs have occasionally made headlines in the region, the Salvatruchas and the Eighteenth street gang have come to dominate the street wars using a mixture of conquest and co-optation and their presence in all three countries as well as the United States has given them international status. Over half of the youth interviewed for this study formerly belonged to one or the other of these two transnational gangs.

What made the gangs transnational was a combination of social and political factors deriving from the late-twentieth-century forces of globalization, especially those of mediated communication and international immigration patterns. If the Central American gangs were simply characterized by small pockets of street gangs sharing a name and symbols across two or three countries, the "transnational" descriptor might be unwarranted. If a gang has active cells in Los Angeles and Toronto, this fact does not warrant the use of a new term or concept to describe it. And yet the MS-13 and the M-18 display a variety of characteristics that both set them apart from earlier manifestations of street gangs and reveal a surprising level of international communication and intercultural hybridity giving rise to the transnational qualifier. Indeed, it was the experience of international migration and coming of age in a new country that accompanied the birth of both gangs in the first place. Furthermore, police records as well as empirical studies show evidence of significant MS-13 and M-18 presence in at least four countries—from Honduras to the United States—leading to membership and income-generating crime in each country (J. Aguilar 2007a; Loudis et al. 2006; Sibaja et al. 2006). Nor do the gangs limit themselves to simultaneous international expansion. An array of studies have demonstrated at least some international communication, by cell phone and through well-traveled migration routes, taking place between *clicas* and their leaders, called *ranfleros* (Arana 2005; Kraul et al. 2005; Ribando 2005; Vigil 2002). One aspect that sets the MS-13 and M-18 apart from other multinational gangs such as the White Fence or the Vatos Locos is their cross-border network savvy.

In choosing the term "transnational," I have avoided other proposed terms. For example, some U.S. criminologists and military sociologists call the Central American *maras* "third-generation gangs." Based on data gathered from archives and interviews with Salvadoran National Police, military sociologist Max Manwaring argues that the Salvatrucha and Dieciocho represent a "new insurgency" of "urban guerillas" who desire nothing less than the overthrow of local and even national governments in order to enlarge their territory for extracting resources from the population (Manwaring 2005). For Manwaring, the gangs ultimately seek power and enrichment through crime and thus engage the legal political structures in "political war" with the intent of promoting the failure of state sovereignty. Manwaring borrowed the term "third-generation street gangs" from John Sullivan, a California gang researcher and member of the Los Angeles Sheriff's Department who considers members of the Dieciocho and Salvatrucha to be "non-state soldiers" involved in transnational criminal organizations on par with international organized criminals and terrorists (Sullivan 2002). Sullivan's term is part of a larger strategy aimed at calling attention to all manner of "non-state actors" such as warlords and mafia and other "transnational networks of crime" that are changing the "rules" of international warfare. In my view, his inclusion of gangs and gang leaders in this list is a stretch. For while it is undeniably true that the MS-13 and M-18 have become far more violent than their local, territorial predecessors, theirs is a violence aimed largely at the poor and those at society's margins. Far from a war for geopolitical dominance, the violence of transnational gangs is largely, as one Catholic priest put it, "A war of the poor against the poor about which the state could care less" (Munaiz 2005). In short, while the transnational gangs have clearly evolved in ways both economic and violent, the data from the best empirical investigations simply do not support the view that a high level of sophistication exists, or that gang leaders manage *clicas* via tightly streamlined vertical structures like those of an army or mafia (Aguilar, Carranza, and Instituto de Opinión Pública Universidad Centroamérica 2008; Barnes 2007). Even the head of the FBI's special unit dedicated to tracking and countering the MS-13 conceded this fact in 2007:

> We tried to uncover a vertical structure but we couldn't. What we see are different *clicas* or cells that operate in different parts of the United States and Central America using similar methods. (Boueke 2007a)

Although some of the ex-gang members I interviewed reported that local cells and cell leaders do maintain contact with higher-ups and "pay it up," especially when securing weapons for local turf wars, I also found interviewees reporting a wide variety of rules and policies from one cell to the next. Respondents reported that much of the rule structure was a result of the local leadership. From an organizational standpoint then, it may be more helpful to think of the transnational gangs as functioning more like a franchise than a single, monolithic entity. In the franchise model, transnational gangs offer local *clicas* and ranfleros—"franchisees"—incentives for affiliating with the transnational "brand" of MS-13 or M-18. Affiliates in turn receive a recognizable logo, access to weapons, and a proven method for attracting "clients" and generating income. Thus, any youth with enough chutzpah and daring may create a local affiliate as long as he remains clear of other local leaders—or manages to depose them. But as franchisees, *clicas* maintain local autonomy as long as they do not grossly violate the norms of the "franchise." Understanding transnational gangs as franchises sidesteps the debate between the sensationalism of those who cast the transnational gang as a global criminal organization and those arguing that the communication between gang cells does not warrant such a conclusion, but who appear to underestimate the reach and role of the gangs.[3]

GANG MEMBERSHIP: WHO BELONGS?

No one knows for sure how many youth belong to the transnational gangs. Their loosely networked, entrepreneurial structure and secretive nature would make quantifying membership difficult even for a well-resourced intelligence apparatus. Although at least two studies have attempted to conduct a gang "census" for a single metropolitan area using gang member or ex-gang member informants (Bardales 2007; Giralt and Cruz 2001), a nationwide or regionwide census would be difficult if not impossible. Instead, we must piece together membership estimates from a variety of studies that use a variety of methods. Table 1.1 shows some of the membership totals often cited by those who study the gangs.

With some exceptions, most authors in the mid-2000s seemed to agree at least broadly on the size of the gangs, arriving at a total membership of about 70,000 in the entire region of Central America. But the overlap appears to have resulted from analysts getting their figures from the same source—the Salvadoran National Police. Although some estimates reach as high as 180,000 for the MS-13 gang alone (Spinelli 2006), such wild variations in reporting often result from the motives of police officials, politicians, or nonprofit workers who use the estimates for the purpose of generating electoral support or for accessing national and international funds for their work (Ecumenical Forum for Peace and Reconciliation 2006). More important, what constitutes "membership" in the gang can vary greatly by one's perspective. Many youth who wear

TABLE 1.1. Estimates of Gang Membership by Country and Source

	USAID (2006)	*Bruneau (2005)*	*FEPAZ (2006)*	*Arana (2005)*
Guatemala	14,000–165,000	14,000	13,450–170,000	
Honduras	36,000	36,000	31,000	40,000
El Salvador	10,500	11,000	10,500	10,000 (core) + 20,000 "young associates"
Costa Rica		2,700		
Nicaragua	2,201	4,500		
Reported Total (for all of Central America)		69,145		70,000–100,000

tattoos are not jumped-in members of the gang but rather seek to emulate the power and identity possessed by the local gang members. Sometimes called *simpatizantes* or "sympathizers," some but not all of these youth eventually join the gang after a period of *chequeo* or "check-out." Other *simpatizantes* simply spend a year or two of their youth enjoying the thrill of keeping company with gang members but eventually choose not to join. Thus, estimates of local or national youth belonging to the gangs depend largely on the choice of whether or not to include the younger sympathizers, many of whom have only minimal criminal engagement.

My own research led me to be wary of the higher estimates of gang membership, especially when cited by analysts who have a stake in impressing the public with the nature and impact of gang violence.[4] Informants with the most firsthand knowledge of the gangs tended to produce lower estimates of gang membership. Nevertheless, regardless of the wide disparities in estimates, there seems to be evidence that Honduras had especially high rates of gang membership in the early 2000s and that transnational gangs have made little impact on countries outside the Northern Triangle. To the South, Nicaragua's smaller gang population consists of local neighborhood gangs rather than the

Salvatrucha and the Dieciocho. While Nicaragua also underwent a war and protracted violence in the 1970s and '80s, Nicaraguan immigration patterns involved Costa Rica and Miami, where Latino gangs do not have a major presence. Meanwhile in Mexico, although some police insist that the transnational gangs are growing, there is little evidence to suggest that the transnational gangs have gained a foothold in any major city. Despite its strong Mexican-American heritage, the Eighteenth Street gang is not a major presence in Mexico. Among the reasons cited for the absence of the transnational gangs in that country are the strength of the drug cartels in monopolizing underground economic activity, stronger state and local institutions, and a wider array of positive, identity-enhancing opportunities for Mexican youth (Barnes 2007).

GANG DEMOGRAPHICS

Young men and adolescent boys dominate the gang. Although one recent study made waves by claiming that female gang members make up as many as 40 percent of the gang rolls (Lacey 2008), most studies estimate female membership to be between 5 and 10 percent (Aguilar et al. 2008; Bardales 2007; Foro Ecuménico por la Paz y la Reconciliación 2006). Female gang members, called *jainas* (HI-nuhs) in the language of the gang, carry out a number of tasks in the gang. Early research suggested that young girls are recruited to the gang for sexual purposes and my own interviews indicated that, indeed, many female gang members provide sex, forced or consensual, for the male membership of the *clica*. Informants of both sexes reported to me that a girl can avoid becoming the sexual partner of the rest of the men if she becomes the girlfriend of a male gang member, preferably a leader.

However, not all young women in the gang serve as the sexual servants of the male population. Some girls and young women perform strategic tasks for the gang, though they rarely take part in planning or decision making at a higher level. Because they are less likely to be suspected for crime by the police, the female gang members carry out important missions such as collecting extortion fees (Lopez 2005) or carrying weapons or drugs. Ester, a Guatemalan ex-gang member, recalled that selling and transporting weapons for the gang was by far the most important work she and her female companions in the gang carried out. "The police always looked for the men, so we, as women, minors, they couldn't touch us, right? They [the police] had no right to touch us [unless] there were female officers present." Ester remembered the exhilaration of firing handguns with her young friends as a fourteen-year-old. Another female member recalled being arrested after a police sweep of a local home turned up a homicide-linked weapon with her fingerprints on it. The girl had been asked to "store" the gun at her home and only later realized she had unwittingly "cleaned" the weapon of its owners' fingerprints. In this sense, the gang reproduces the patriarchal structure of Central American society.

The *Mara Salvatrucha* appears to have the highest membership of the two major gangs, with estimates ranging from 65–85 percent of all gang members in the region (Bruneau 2005; Loudis et al. 2006; Thompson 2004). The *Mara Dieciocho* is significantly smaller. Other local gangs such as the *Vatos Locos* (Honduras) or the White Fence (Guatemala) have followings in certain cities and regions but account for only a small minority of the gangs in the northern countries. Research in the early 2000s suggested that the median age of gang members at the time was nineteen (Arana 2005) and most experts estimate that typical gang members range in age from twelve to twenty-five years. Recent evidence suggests that the average age of gang members is rising, either because of a smaller cohort of entering adolescents or, as seems to be more likely, because "aging out" of the gang has become increasingly rare (Aguilar et al. 2008; Bardales 2007; Boueke 2007b; Ranum 2007).

Race is an enormously important factor running through Central American politics and national identities (Miller 2004). A "pigmentocracy" exists in Central American society, legacy of the Spanish colonial period (Anderson 1991; Cojtí 1999; Pelaez 1998 [1970]), whereby light skin and hair along with tall stature and European facial features carries social and economic privileges. Guatemala represents a partial exception due to its unique history and demographics, including a large Mayan population that continues to speak their indigenous language and wear indigenous clothing. In that country a two-tiered social hierarchy exists in which the politically and economically dominant Spanish-speaking *ladinos* (mestizos) have managed to keep the Mayan majority in a subordinate status (Taracena, Gellert, Castillo, Paiz, and K. 2002). In El Salvador, a massacre of indigenous peoples in 1932 all but erased the population of indigenous peoples who openly embraced their ethnicity. In Honduras, in addition to small pockets of indigenous communities and a majority mestizo population, a sizable Garifuna population of Afro-Caribbean descent lives on or near the northern coastal region, changing the race dynamics in that region. But even in Honduras, as anthropologist Adrienne Pine has noted, the "Indian character" gets blamed for all manner of weakness and sloth (Pine 2008). In all three countries the resulting racial ideology is the same: Spanish-European "blood" is assumed to carry superior inner character traits of civilized bearing and self-control while indigenous "blood" is associated with irrational behavior, drunkenness, and unpredictable rage.[5] Although we have no statistical data regarding the racial-ethnic composition of the gangs, by taking notes on phenotype during my interviews I was able to anecdotally confirm what others have already suggested—that the majority of youth who enter the gangs have mixed (mestizo) features tending toward darker skin and short stature. Very few of the sixty-three ex-gang members I interviewed had clearly indigenous Mayan features and none were black, but several of the young ex-gang members I interviewed were in fact tall and fair-skinned. With only one exception, the lighter-skinned ex-gang members had been leaders in the gang at the local if not regional level. My observations suggest that the gang reflects the pyramid of privilege typical throughout Central American society.

GANG VALUES

Just as the gang's racialized hierarchy and sexist power structure mirror the power arrangements in formal society, many of the values of the gang present little contrast with those of the barrio itself, or, for that matter, with youth from the United States. Gang youth value friendship, camaraderie, solidarity and, *el vacíl*, which loosely translates as "kicking it." Drugs, alcohol, and fighting, especially with weapons, are some of the common means of "kicking it." Colombian sociologist Mauricio Rubio has argued that early and abundant sex is one of the most attractive features of gang life, especially for young boys (2007), and my interviews with ex-gang members lend credence to this observation.

But the values of the gang go beyond the typical notions of camaraderie amidst temporary, innocuous rebellion among teens. For the gang, danger and risk taking are dominant themes. Many interviewees spoke of the ability to *rifar* (i.e., to gamble or take chances) as the ultimate measure of one's commitment to the gang and its values. Demonstrating one's ability to take chances or rifar by engaging in violent crime is the most direct pathway to gaining *el respeto* (respect) and the leadership that goes with it. Many gang members refer to the lifestyle of the gang as *la vida loca*. Gang leaders who have demonstrated their prowess at taking risks without getting caught are often bestowed with the English title "Crazy" or "Little Crazy" and many *clicas* adopt English monikers such as "Crazy Gangsters."

Violence is a common pastime in the gang and access to weapons has turned the fistfights and stabbings of an earlier era into the bullet-ridden street warfare of today. While in the late 1990s many local *clicas* fabricated their own weapons called *chimbas* (Honduras) or *hechizas* (Guatemala), today handguns are plentiful and semiautomatic weapons are far from rare (FLACSO 2007).[6] Santos, a long-time gang interventionist in a tough neighborhood of San Salvador told of seeing a weapon that surprised even him:

> The other day I saw a Salvatrucha with a grenade-launcher walking down the street. Imagine that—a grenade launcher. Now where are you going to get one of those? The military is the only place to get a grenade launcher. It had to be borrowed from an army member. And think about a weapon like that in a [densely-populated] neighborhood like this.

Santos reported that the young men did indeed fire the weapon later that day, hitting a weld shop that was, mercifully, unoccupied at the time. Such "recreation" reveals the role of violence and violent weapons in creating a mystique and a sense of empowerment in the gang. But power, weapons, and la vida loca are not the whole story of the gang values. Loyalty to the neighborhood and the gang presents perhaps the single most important value in the gang. Indeed, gang members use the word "barrio," which means "the neighborhood," to refer to both the neighborhood itself *and* to the gang. When interviewees spoke of "defending the barrio" it was often unclear whether they were referring to their neighborhood, the gang cell, or the transnational "barrio" of the MS-13 or M-18. Such ambiguity is probably intentional for the young men who see the transnational brotherhood of the gang as simply an extension of the neighborhood.

Loyalty can take many forms. Upon initiation to the gang, new recruits must undergo a short period of beatings at the hands of their "homies"—here, again, the English gang term is used. During the thirteen or eighteen "seconds" of beating—seconds are not timed but counted out slowly—the new members may not strike back or protect themselves except for covering the face or genitals.[7] Honduran gang members call this ritual the *calentón* or "warm-up." Thus, new members "prove" their ability to "take heat" for the gang. Furthermore, even before the "heat-up," new recruits and sympathizers must spend three to six months in chequeo, a "checkout" period during which time they conduct missions for the gang. Clearly, risk taking for the sake of the gang provides a sure sign of loyalty and solidarity. Sympathizers who wish to shorten their term of chequeo can volunteer for an especially dangerous or violent mission.

Gang members display their loyalty not only with actions but on their bodies via dress, hairstyle, manner of walk, and tattoos. Tattoos are the most obvious form of embodied loyalty. Typically, the more visible a tattoo, the more respeto accorded the wearer. Tattoos have become especially controversial in the wake of the "zero tolerance" programs aimed at incarcerating and punishing gang members, sometimes with little or no solid evidence linking them to actual crimes. If the tattoo has become the mark of courage inside the gang, many on the outside regard it as a kind of "mark of Cain." Whereas in the United States tattoos are merely a symbol of individual expression, in Central America they have come to be associated almost exclusively with the gang and criminality. Tattoos make gang members easy targets for opposing gangs, police, and local vigilantes and many employers refuse to hire an applicant with a tattoo. Now more than ever, wearing a tattoo in a highly visible place on the body such as the face, neck, or hands represents a permanent withdrawal from non-gang society.

Major distinctions between the two main transnational gangs are difficult to verify, but a few differences came up frequently enough to be mentioned here. The MS-13 has the strongest nationalist identity. Indeed, the word "Salvatrucha" is a combination of *salvadoreño* (Salvadoran) and *trucha* (trout), a persistent, migratory fish with a knack for "slipping away" from its pursuers. While the Salvatrucha has the strongest presence in El Salvador and Los Angeles, the gang appears to dominate numerically in Guatemala *and* Honduras despite a history of national rivalry between Honduras and El Salvador. In spite of, or perhaps as a result of the MS-13's higher numbers in the region, some members of the M-18 insist that theirs is a gang with stricter requirements than those held by the rival Salvatruchas. Several ex-members of the M-18 reported with pride that their (former) gang was not a gang of the masses but a selective one that preferred smaller numbers and greater commitment. As for its identity, the Dieciocho has a Mexican-American character rooted in the "cholo" culture of second- and third-generation Mexican-American immigrant experience of the 1950s and '60s (Vigil 1988). The Virgin of Guadalupe figures prominently in many M-18 murals and tattoos, and some members of M-18 wear the rosary.

TRANSNATIONAL GANGS AND CRIME

Central American politicians and U.S. criminologists emphatically proclaim the criminal nature of the transnational gangs, and documentary films such as National Geographic's *World's Most Dangerous Gang* virtually equate gang membership with involvement in murder and mayhem. In some respects, this perspective is understandable. Gang members like Enrique went out of their way to actively promote the violent image of their gang, and homicide and violent crime soared in the Northern Triangle during the years of the rise of the MS-13 and M-18. Figure 1.1 displays the homicide rate in all three countries of the Northern Triangle, which remains two to three times higher than the rate of any of the neighboring countries where transnational gangs have not established a presence.

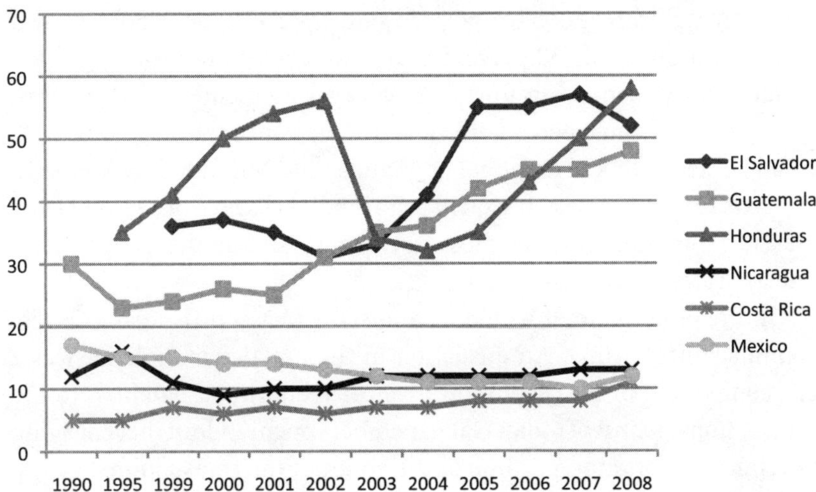

FIGURE 1.1. shows the number of homicides per 100,000 inhabitants in Mesoamerica and the United States during select years from 1990 to 2008.
Source: Observador Centroamericano de Violencia 2009; Instituto Ciudadano sobre la Inseguridad 2010

When high-profile arrests of heavily tattooed gang members are televised on the evening news, the connection between gangs and spiking crime rates seems even more indisputable. But laying the blame for stratospheric homicide rates at the feet of the gangs is a mistake. High homicide and reported crime rates do not correlate neatly with cities or neighborhoods where gang membership is highest. An analysis of high- and low-crime neighborhoods in three Salvadoran cities found no statistical correlation between reported crime levels and reported presence or prominence of gang activity (Cruz, Carranza, and Giralt 2004). In Guatemala, the provinces with the highest homicide rates in 2006 were rural or small-town regions with little if any gang activity but considerable narco-traffic (Barnes 2007; Leggett 2007; Ranum 2007). Nevertheless, officials for the national police in both El Salvador and Guatemala have consistently and without evidence blamed gangs for "60 percent" of all homicides in both countries (Kraul et al. 2005; Ranum 2007). Such figures get reproduced in the popular media and provide justification for draconian laws and heavy-handed police tactics. But as

Salvadoran researchers have pointed out, the Salvadoran police's own records attribute only 30 percent of the homicides to the gangs. Other organizations such as the Institute of Legal Medicine report a much lower figure—from 8 percent in 2003 to 13 percent of homicides in 2005 could be clearly linked to the gangs (Aguilar and Miranda 2006). Finally, Mexico's recent increase in violent crime in the absence of a strong gang presence provides further cause for skepticism in the gangs-drive-murder-rates hypothesis.

On the other hand, it would be a mistake to assert that gangs rarely commit violent crime. An escalation in the practice of violence was a key component of the "evolution" from neighborhood *pandillas* to the transnational *maras* of today. Gang members openly admit that engaging in crime is a common pastime of the youth of the transnational gangs. In a census of the gang population of greater San Salvador in 2001, half of all gang members interviewed reported owning a firearm. One of five reported having committed at least one homicide (Santacruz and Concha-Eastman 2001). In a similar census conducted in San Pedro Sula, Honduras, over 91 percent of 1,426 gang members interviewed admitted to having committed a crime (Bardales 2007). While there are many sources of Northern Central America's alarmingly high crime rates, it is beyond dispute that armed violence has become a part of the vernacular of the Central American gangs. As firearms became more accessible and as local drug sales became more lucrative and inviting, armed violent crime overshadowed street delinquency in the transnational gangs. Furthermore, cell-to-cell networks and information sharing in prison made possible the transfer of criminal experience from one context to another. Beto, a Honduran who formerly belonged to the M-18, recalled that many of the local gang population in his own urban satellite neighborhood were either displaced or emigrated after the devastation caused by Hurricane Mitch in 1998. When some of these youth returned or were deported in 2000, they brought knowledge and self-confidence that emboldened them to promote more serious, economically strategic forms of delinquency:

> In the beginning it took some getting used to because they outlawed some of the things we were used to like petty crime. They had come back stronger and they established strict rules with more respect. Now we had

> to take care of the name of the barrio [M-18]. We had to uphold our image. "No more of this business of stealing chickens and ducks," they told us.

Rather than taking small animals from their neighbors' backyards, Beto and his friends were told to do their stealing in other neighborhoods and to prioritize the acquisition of large-caliber weapons. Thus, by stockpiling weapons and bribing local police, many *clicas* have been able to create "defensible spaces" within their communities. Within these contexts, the gangs may sell drugs to other low-income youth in their neighborhoods and collect *la renta*, a monthly extortion fee, from local business owners and bus and taxi drivers. Antonio, a Guatemalan ex-member of the M-18, recalled collecting weekly "rent" from families and businesses in his community. He described the logic of the "rent" system with unusual forthrightness:

> [T]he gang needs to survive and looks for the easiest way like we all look for the easiest way to survive, right? [They do it] charging people "rent" (*renteando a la gente*) and if people don't pay rent, they kill them so that other people will understand how it works and pay up because what is the rent money for? To buy weapons to defend yourself so they don't kill you. In other words it's a circle.

Antonio's comment reveals the way gang violence in Central America is linked to both acquisition and survival. In recent years some homeowners have even been forced to pay *la renta* or sell their homes at a loss, often to the gang itself, when the payments become too burdensome. Thus, turf wars and "protecting the barrio" from other gangs seeking to gain real estate are important means of preserving and expanding the gang's source of income, not just pride in one's neighborhood. This fact explains why gang members sometimes refer to la renta as *el impuesto de guerra*—the war tax. One of the more tragic examples of gang violence came in early 2011, when a car bomb exploded on a rush-hour packed urban bus in Guatemala City, killing nine civilians, among them several children. Subsequent investigations revealed strong evidence that an imprisoned leader of the Guatemalan gang cell "Little Psychos" had arranged the bombing from his prison cell after the bus company refused to meet his gang's demands to increase their weekly war tax contributions (Gonzàlez 2011).

In light of such atrocities, equating the transnational gangs with "urban guerrillas" could almost make sense. But that logic implies that such local extortion practices are part of a vast "insurgency" campaign or ideological warfare comparable to the civil wars of the 1980s when in fact the gangs have not established broad and clearly articulated chains of command of national or international scope. In one of the most extensive empirical studies yet available, researchers from several countries concluded that although the transnational gangs are indeed "a serious public security problem" in Northern Central America, they have yet to match the level of organized sophistication exhibited by organized crime and the drug cartels. The group reported that

> [W]hile gang-related violence is a problem, it is not tightly linked to narco-traffic and organized crime. Additionally, within all the countries, the primary victims of youth gang-related violence are other youth, both gang and non-gang involved. (Barnes 2007:2)

The report drew its conclusions from a written survey of incarcerated gang members, noting that, "only a small minority of gang members in El Salvador, Honduras and Guatemala, possess transnational ties with other gang members, or ties with organized crime and/or narco-trafficking" (Barnes 2007:2).

Although one could argue that only a handful of gang leaders actually *need* to possess transnational ties in order to orchestrate international cooperation between *clicas*, the point stands and my interviews with ex-gang members support the finding that most local *clicas* are not taking part in a vast conspiracy to destabilize the region.

RESPONSES TO THE GANGS

The responses of national governments in the Northern Triangle have ranged from erratic to extreme and excessive. In all three nations, the gangs and fear of gangs have given rise to widespread desire for the "strong-armed" populism of an earlier era. Honduras responded first after Ricardo Maduro, a successful business owner whose son had been kidnapped and killed by gangs in the 1990s, campaigned for president and won on a *mano dura* (iron fist) approach to crime and gangs. Legal reforms like Article 332, known as "the anti-gang law," made it possible for courts to prosecute youth for merely belonging to a gang. International institutions including the United Nations protested that the law violated Hondurans' civil and human rights, especially those of minors, and some judges refused to apply the law regarding it as unconstitutional. Nevertheless, arrests and incarcerations of gang members soared, overcrowding prisons and jamming the courts. Meanwhile, a rising death toll of Honduran minors led some institutions to accuse the government of providing tacit approval for "social cleansing"—the extrajudicial execution of gang members and other "undesirable" youth (Casa Alianza 2009). Their accusations gained further credibility when two separate prison fire incidents in 2003 and 2004 resulted in the burning to death of over 160 gang members, all of whom were being held in special gang-only blocks of Honduran prisons.

El Salvador's conservative ARENA government unleashed its own get-tough approach in the form of a raft of legal and policy packages including the *Plan Mano Dura* in 2003 and the *Plan Super Mano Dura* in 2004. The policies included lowering evidentiary standards for arrest and incarceration of gang members, lowering the age at which minors can be prosecuted as adults, increasing spending on police, allowing military participation in joint army-police patrols, and, eventually, providing limited funding for rehabilitation and resocialization for gang members and at-risk youth. The legal and policy reforms led to massive arrests. In the year following the changes in the legal code allowing arrest for belonging to a gang, police detained 19,275 people on that basis but released 91 percent of those detained (Thale and Falkenburger 2006). Nevertheless, such "sweeps," usually conducted in marginal urban neighborhoods, have swelled Salvadoran prisons such that by 2007, over 5,000 gang members crowded El Salvador's prisons, comprising nearly a third of its entire prison population.

So far Guatemala's presidential administrations have not fully embraced the anti-gang rhetoric. But gangs and the violence associated with them have provided the government with a convenient means of raising the profile of its discredited military regime. In 2004, under *Plan*

Escoba (the Broom Plan), Guatemalan army units were authorized to join civilian police in patrolling neighborhoods and making arrests. This move was a clear violation of the intent of the 1996 Peace Accords, which called for constitutional reforms reining in the army and limiting army activity to the patrol of Guatemala's borders.

In short, successive administrations in all three countries have promoted punitive security measures as the primary approach for dealing with gangs and gang violence and, in the case of Honduras and El Salvador, have criminalized gang membership itself even though abundant research shows that most gang members make the decision to join the gang very early in life, and most come from marginal communities and precarious or abusive families (PNUD 2009). Not surprisingly, the high-profile anti-gang campaigns have virtually solidified in the minds of the public the connection—indeed the equation—of gangs with violent crime. Poor, and without social networks to "respectable society," gang youth provide easy targets for moral entrepreneurs eager to upstage each other with their laments of moral decay. As Aguilar and her associates have shown, the release of both the *Plan Mano Dura* and the *Plan Super Mano Dura* were followed by spikes in anti-gang sentiment recorded by Salvadoran public opinion polls (Aguilar et al. 2008). Nor have the heavy-handed punitive policies resulted in a clear and sustainable reduction in violent crime. Although Maduro's more focused policies did coincide with a reduction in the murder rate in Honduras, that reduction has not been sustainable over the course of several years.[8] Meanwhile, in all three countries evidence for the police tolerance of, or participation in, social cleansing practices continues to mount.

CONCLUSION

I will leave it to other gang scholars to develop a detailed causal argument that explains the emergence of transnational gangs in terms of a specific, bounded set of social forces and political events. Doing justice to that topic would require writing a separate book. Here I am simply attempting to describe in broad terms what the gangs are, where they came from, and how their emergence has affected Central American society. It seems clear that the Central American transnational gangs have institutionalized by taking advantage of the weak institutional context of the Central American barrio. Ex-gang members and gang interventionists alike call this the "evolution" of the gang from *pandilla* to *mara*. The newer form of the *mara* has some of the characteristics of a franchise. It is neither the well-articulated and vertically integrated international "guerilla" organization that some criminologists sought to compare it with nor an innocuous local neighborhood affinity group. While there are many other sources of street crime and violence in the country, gang youth practice violence with real repercussions to many marginal neighborhoods and the families living in them. The franchise metaphor underscores the variation existing from one *clica* to the next even while it highlights the symbolic continuity across *clicas* belonging to the same transnational gang.

As a social phenomenon, the Central American gangs emerged in the midst of a particular set of social, economic, and historical shifts such as war and civil strife, migration and deportation, weak and corrupt security structures, and a bulging youth population. Though no one single social, political or economic factor can be said to have *produced* the gangs, a variety of macro-social forces set the stage for their growth by creating thousands of micro-situations—biographies—in which joining the gang became an especially attractive option. But before we begin exploring these biographies, we must take a detour into the other social institution popular among youth in the Central American barrio—the evangelical church.

2

"Christian, Not Catholic"

So far we have explored the emergence of the transnational gangs and what they look like today. But if we are to make sense of evangelical conversion among gang members, it is worth taking time to explore what evangelical religion in the barrio looks like in the twenty-first century. Where did it come from and how has it changed in recent decades?

Central American evangelicals have long considered themselves spiritual and cultural outsiders. Fully aware that they live in predominantly Catholic Latin American societies, these evangelical *hermanos y hermanas* (brothers and sisters in faith) embrace their cultural marginality as part of their spiritual identity. They are, as they see it, part of the remnant "true faith" which rejects the "idolatry" of images, the special status of the priesthood, and the veneration of the Virgin. Having been saved *out* of the Catholic faith, most Central American evangelicals equate being a Christian with being an evangelical *rather than* a Catholic. The importance of this distinction became evident to me one evening in the late 1990s as I sat down to dinner in the home of an evangelical family in Guatemala City's densely populated La Brigada neighborhood. Unsure of the spiritual credentials of another guest at the table, the host asked her if she was "Catholic or Christian." With a chuckle, the forty-year-old Honduran single mother responded, *Pues, las dos cosas* ("Well, both.") That her response surprised and perplexed her host illustrates just how taken-for-granted is the notion among evangelicals that their faith sets them apart as the "true" Christians.

And yet as the evangelical community grows, the notion of being a "faithful few" who occupy the cultural margins of society is increasingly difficult to sustain. Today, barely half of all northern Central Americans claim to be Catholic and approximately one-third claim some form of Protestantism as their faith—usually using the term "evangélico" to describe their spiritual identity. Furthermore, the rise of the megachurches and Neo-Pentecostalism has coincided with political campaigns, some of them successful, by outspoken evangelical politicians and strongmen. How did evangelical Protestantism arrive in Central America and how did it gain so much popularity in countries that were once part of the Catholic "stronghold" of Latin America?

THE ARRIVAL OF PROTESTANTS TO CENTRAL AMERICA

In 1882, a Presbyterian missionary named John Clark Hill was making plans to head to China when a very special delegation arrived to the headquarters of his mission board. The president of Guatemala, a liberal (in the nineteenth-century sense of the term) autocrat named Justo Rufino Barrios, was shopping for Protestant missionaries during a diplomatic trip to New York. Hill's plans quickly changed—after all, it is not every day that the president goes begging for missionaries—and the young missionary changed plans and headed to Guatemala. The president's motives were hardly pious. Frustrated with the cultural and economic influence wielded by the Catholic hierarchy in his country, Barrios had set about undermining the church's power by confiscating huge tracts of church lands, reforming the legal system to allow for non-Catholic burials, and mandating civil, rather than religious, weddings. In addition, Barrios cleared the way for freedom of religious expression, largely in response to the arrival of Lutheran immigrants from Germany who had settled in the north, attracted by the president's offer of cheap land and cheap labor for growing and exporting coffee. Clearly, the president hoped that the founding of a Protestant mission would further erode Catholicism and its cultural and economic might. Though he spoke very little Spanish, Hill went to work ministering to the political elites of Guatemala City. He built a church on land adjacent to the national palace and founded a Protestant school for children of the political class. Thus the Presbyterian mission became the first permanent Protestant mission in Northern Central America.[1]

Shortly after the arrival of the mainline Presbyterians, evangelical missionaries arrived, organizing a well-funded mission called Central American Mission, or CAM. Associated with the popular new dispensationalist theology of Dallas Theological Seminary, these missionaries arrived to all three countries of the Northern Triangle in the waning years of the nineteenth century. Other mission boards established missions in the early twentieth century as well: Methodists, Nazarenes, Plymouth Brethren, and the Yearly Meeting of West Coast Friends began work around the region, coordinating their efforts by carving up the geographic space like pieces of a pie. But converts came slowly and by the middle of the twentieth century only the largest, best-funded denominations could boast more than 1,000 members in any nation (Holland 2001, 2002, 2008).

Pentecostalism arrived only a few short years after the establishment of the mainline and evangelical missions. In 1904, a Canadian missionary named Frederick Mebius began ministering to impoverished coffee laborers on the slopes of the Santa Ana Volcano in El Salvador. Although his work began *before* the Azusa Street revivals in California made Pentecostalism famous in the United States, Mebius had already been influenced by one of Pentecostalism's founders, Charles Fox Parham, the spirit-filled reverend from Kansas (Anderson 2004). Despite his meager resources compared with the denominational missions, by the late 1920s Mebius had founded dozens of "Apostolic" churches in El Salvador as well as in Honduras and Guatemala with membership totaling in the several hundreds. Each autonomous congregation possessed an "apostle," a "prophet," and a board made up of women as well as men (though the number of female board members was not to exceed the number of males). Eventually, these congregations came to affiliate with the U.S. denominations of Assemblies of God and the Church of God (Cleveland, TN). Meanwhile in Guatemala, a Methodist missionary who had testified to receiving the gifts of the Holy Spirit, left the Methodists to affiliate with the Tennessee-based Church of God, bringing many of his former congregations with him (Smith 1991). By the middle of the twentieth century, the Pentecostal congregations, only loosely affiliated with the Pentecostal mission boards of the North, had come to rival the historic, non-Pentecostal denominations in membership if not in institutional resources. Nevertheless, Protestants—Pentecostal or otherwise—continued to represent a tiny religious minority, easily ignored by the Catholic hierarchy.

THE PENTECOSTAL BOOM

Protestant growth began in earnest in the 1960s. Guatemala saw the first significant "boom" in Protestant membership during the early 1960s, when Protestant religious membership reportedly doubled between 1960 and 1964 during a massive nationwide, multidenominational evangelistic campaign. By 1980, Protestant churches in Guatemala were reporting a combined membership of nearly 14 percent of the country's total population (Holland 2002). Growth continued in the 1980s but slowed considerably in the 1990s only to resume again in the 2000s. In 2006, a study by the Pew Forum on Religion and Public Life used data from a national survey to estimate a Protestant population of about 34 percent of Guatemala's 13 million citizens. Of these Protestants, 58 percent described themselves as Pentecostal and another 27 percent self-described as Charismatic (Pew 2006). In the race to evangelize the country, Pentecostalism, despite its weaker ties to North American mission boards and its reliance on local finances and leadership, had clearly won.

Protestants in El Salvador showed similar patterns of growth. Evangelical growth was steady from the 1950s through the 1980s and relied mostly on the success of the Pentecostal churches that had adapted a local model of leadership in which pastors could be ordained with little or no formal seminary training. According to national polling by the public opinion center at the Jesuit Universidad de Centroamérica, Protestants made up approximately 16 percent of El Salvador's population in 1988 but had reached over 29 percent by 2008 (Instituto Universitario de Opinión Pública 2008).

In Honduras, Protestantism grew slowly for most of the twentieth century. As recently as 1980, less than 10 percent of the population claimed to be Protestant. But rapid growth in the 1990s and 2000s has produced an enormous shift in the religious landscape such that by

2007, a nationwide poll conducted by CID-Gallup reported that a majority of Hondurans no longer claimed "Catholic" as their religious identity. While the Catholic Church, at 47 percent, continues to be the most popular religious tradition in the country, Protestants are not far behind. More than a third of Hondurans now claim Protestantism as their faith. Meanwhile to the south and to the north, Nicaragua, Costa Rica, and Mexico all currently report significantly lower rates of Protestantism and higher rates of Catholic identification than those reported in the Northern Triangle (Holland 2009).

Obviously, data from national surveys asking respondents to self-report on their religious affiliation cannot pinpoint with perfect accuracy the percentage of Protestants or Catholics in a given country, so these statistics should not be read as providing an exact count, or as evidence of which Central American country is "the most Protestant" in a given year. But the overall trend is clear. Protestantism continues to grow in Central America, and it is especially strong in the Northern Triangle. Largely as a result of this Protestant growth, rates of Catholic affiliation are in decline in the same region (Brenneman 2010). In effect, the trend in northern Central America is toward religious heterogeneity since nonaffiliation is also on the rise although at a more modest rate than the increases in Protestantism. But the growth of Protestantism, fueled mostly by the gains of Pentecostal and charismatic congregations, is startling since it has continued after the end of the civil wars and violent chaos of the 1970s and 1980s. Thus, it seems that the answer to the question posed by anthropologist David Stoll in his book published two decades ago *Is Latin America Turning Protestant* (1991) just might be, for northern Central America anyway, "Yes—and sooner, rather than later."

THE SHAPE OF EVANGELICALISM IN CENTRAL AMERICA

Although polling data usually employ the more technical term "Protestant" to refer to non-Catholic Christians, nearly all Protestant Christians in Central America—including Pentecostals—refer to themselves as *evangélicos*. There is considerable truth in this term, since nearly all Protestants in the region subscribe to a theologically conservative worldview that embraces the basic tenets of creation, sin, and redemption and promotes active evangelism through recruiting others into the faith. On the other hand, *evangélicos* demonstrate considerable variety in terms of religious expression and in their institutions. Except for denominational affiliations, I know of no agreed-upon classification system for distinguishing between evangelicals with distinct theological or liturgical affinities. But broadly speaking, scholars and church leaders often refer to at least three strands of religious and ecclesial expression within the evangelical community today: historic evangelicals, Pentecostals, and Neo-Pentecostals.

Historic evangelicals belong to congregations with roots in the historic missions like Presbyterian, Friends, Methodist, Baptist, Nazarene, Reformed, Lutheran, Mennonite, and CAM. While many of these congregations have adopted a charismatic worship style, most tend to downplay the exercise of the gifts of the spirit such as speaking in tongues and faith healing. Many among the clergy of these denominations possess at least some theological preparation, reflecting their stronger commitment to theological orthodoxy, and many congregations retain at least some ties to the North American denominations that helped to found them. Nevertheless, throughout the region, the historic evangelicals have never matched the growth of the Pentecostal and Neo-Pentecostal churches around them. Furthermore, since the 1990s many congregations in the historic evangelical tradition have responded to Pentecostal successes by adopting both the techniques and liturgy of their more charismatic neighbors. Institutional isomorphism—that is, the adoption by smaller "firms" of techniques and practices incorporated by the most successful firms (regardless of whether or not such techniques are responsible for growth)—is a common practice among religious organizations (Dimaggio 1998), and Central American congregations and pastors are no different in this regard. The pressures against appearing liturgically outdated and emotionally "cold" have forced many pastors of these traditional evangelical churches to "turn up the volume" on their worship services, adopting rock-band style music and, in some cases, making room for experiences of the gifts of the spirit.

Pentecostals make up the largest group of Central American Protestants. While the Pew study reports that 58 percent of Guatemalans self-describe as "Pentecostal," data distinguishing between Pentecostals and Neo-Pentecostals is difficult to come by in part because the latter term has only come into use in recent decades.[2] Phillip Williams estimated that Pentecostals made up three-quarters of Salvadoran evangelicals, but this figure probably includes Neo-Pentecostal groups. The Assemblies of God and the Church of God are the two largest Pentecostal denominations in the region and both maintain loose ties with corresponding denominational institutions and mission boards in the United States. A third major Pentecostal denomination, the Prince of Peace churches, was established by a Guatemalan in 1956 and spread throughout the region during the 1960s. Dozens of smaller Pentecostal denominations have emerged in recent decades, some with only a handful of affiliated congregations. In addition, many Pentecostal churches carry no denominational affiliation at all. Sociologist David Martin (1990) argues that one of the defining features of Pentecostal churches is their fierce independence and congregationalism, but this is not always the case among Central American Pentecostal churches. In some cases, national Pentecostal denominations maintain a tight organizational structure. In any case, the Pentecostal emphasis on the demonstration of the gifts of the spirit rather than theological training as the important credential for leadership mean that if an individual (usually, though not always a man) feels called by the spirit to found a church and can convince a handful of families in the neighborhood of the legitimacy of his calling, Pentecostal theology has little to keep him from splitting from his congregation and starting a new one.

Politically speaking, Central American Pentecostals vote in elections with about the same frequency as their non-Pentecostal Protestant and Catholic neighbors, and their votes do not typically cohere on the right or the left (Steigenga 2001). But few Pentecostals run for office and most are especially wary of involvement in partisan politics (Williams 1997).

The most recent development among Central American evangelicals today is the Neo-Pentecostal movement. In the 1970s, a handful of evangelical pastors and converts began stripping away much of the institutional and liturgical forms of traditional evangelical and Pentecostal religion. Meeting in middle-class homes as well as upscale restaurants and hotels, these religious entrepreneurs sought a spiritual experience that did not box them in to the starchy mold of traditional evangelicalism. After all, converting to evangelical religion still carried a negative stigma and converts in the more established middle and upper middle classes risked ostracism from friends and family who saw them as rejecting their cultural heritage in favor of an imported religion that smacked of anti-intellectual emotionalism. At the same time there was growing dissent among some middle-class urban Catholics, disenchanted with the clergy's "option for the poor" and the emerging liberation theology movement (Smith 1991). Many Neo-Pentecostal pastors adopted and adapted the prosperity theology of the popular new "health and wealth gospel" of U.S. preachers such as Oral Roberts and Robert Schuller, and combined it with charismatic worship services, media savvy, and a folksy, down-to-earth preaching style. The formula proved enormously successful, not only among the urban middle class but among tens of thousands of Central Americans *aspiring* to reach the middle class. By the mid-1980s, a handful of mega-churches had sprung up, each organized around a highly charismatic pastor with a knack for organizing and inspiring his members. While it is true that not all Neo-Pentecostals gather in stadium-like mega-churches, and some Neo-Pentecostal pastors do not endorse prosperity theology, large congregations and the gospel of health and wealth are strong tendencies within the movement and they continue to provide important distinctions with traditional Pentecostalism.

Like their religious counterparts in the United States, Neo-Pentecostal congregations utilize a cell structure in which small groups of members meet during the week for prayer, worship, and Bible study in each others homes, while joining together for large, carefully choreographed worship services on weekends. From the beginning, the mega-churches were less squeamish than historic evangelicals or Pentecostals when it came to getting involved in politics. The most notable example of this involvement was Guatemala's El Verbo mega-church which achieved notoriety overnight when in 1982 one of its members, Army General Efraín Rios Montt, was handpicked by the military to lead that nation. Ríos Montt's violent, erratic attempts to win the war and stamp out corruption cost him the presidency but won him a permanent place in the political life of his country. Several years later, Guatemalans elected evangelical minister Jorge Serrano to the presidency, and his tenure proved similarly disastrous. More recently, Harold Caballeros, former pastor of Guatemala's El Shaddai mega-church, made an unsuccessful attempt to run for president. In Honduras and El Salvador Neo-Pentecostals have also tended to be more active in politics than Pentecostals or historic evangelicals, but not to the same extent as in Guatemala and not always in alignment with the economic elites or in support of the status quo.[3]

BARRIO EVANGELICALS

Recognizing the diversity that exists among Central American Protestants, my primary religious focus in this book is on what I call "barrio evangelicalism." I use this term to describe the theologically conservative, liturgically Pentecostal, locally oriented congregations of the neighborhood or "barrio." Most of these congregations could be categorized as traditional Pentecostals, but a small minority would qualify as historic evangelicals. My research for this book draws heavily on informants from this religious context. Although I did conduct interviews with a handful of ex-gang members and ministers connected with Neo-Pentecostal mega-churches, the vast majority of former gang members and prevention ministries I encountered belonged to small- to medium-sized local congregations with tiny budgets, unimpressive facilities, and lively worship services. Some of the congregations had "Pentecostal" in their name, while others called themselves "evangelical," and some belonged to traditional denominations such as the Baptists or the Mennonites. But even the congregations belonging to traditional denominations had lively, emotional worship services, and some even encouraged practicing the gifts of the spirit. With the exception of one or two Mennonite churches, the theology of these congregations was not easily distinguishable from traditional Pentecostal congregations such as the Church of God, Assemblies of God, and Prince of Peace. By using the term "barrio evangelicals," I am highlighting the local orientation of these congregations, in contrast to recent trends toward participating in national politics among

Neo-Pentecostals. But I also use the term to describe a particular form of popular evangelicalism that has established deep roots in the region.

Four features stand out as core characteristics of barrio evangelicalism: theological conservatism, strong communal bonds, emphasis on healing and cathartic ecstasy, and strict piety. Other scholars of Latin American evangelicals have emphasized additional characteristics, but I believe these four features represent the most important elements of the typical "neighborhood congregation" of evangelical Central America.

Barrio evangelicals are not theological innovators. Most ascribe to a free-will brand of religious conservatism inherited from conservative missionaries and the seminaries they founded.[4] As Harvey Cox (2006) has noted, Pentecostals in general are not Calvinists. Rather than espousing divine election, in which God is the only actor with a role in salvation, most barrio evangelicals believe in a free-will orientation that places the individual believer and his or her choice—to convert or not to convert—at the center of the salvation equation. This conviction engenders a strong belief in the need to evangelize neighbors and encourage them to "respond to the gospel" by choosing to convert to evangelical religion. Furthermore, because salvation is precarious and depends at least in part on the convert's ability to sustain his or her commitment, pastors and members constantly monitor and encourage new believers in order to keep them from "backsliding" out of the church.

At the same time, barrio evangelicals are not dogmatists or theological fundamentalists who work hard to define and protect theological purity. For most Central American pastors, the experience of salvation and community far outweighs the ability to define and articulate Christian theological terms. The Pentecostal heritage and influence of most barrio evangelicals is especially apparent here. Virginia Garrard-Burnett has argued that part of the success of Pentecostal religion in Guatemala and beyond can be attributed to the congruence between Pentecostal and pre-Vatican II emphases on spiritual *experience* rather than rational theology (1998, 2000). Arguing in a similar vein, Andrew Chesnut calls the Pentecostal emphasis on ecstatic religious experience "pneumacentrism" (2003). But Pentecostal religious experience aims to provide more than just ecstasy. Barrio evangelicals, whose services are thoroughly shaped by Pentecostal worship practices, seek—and often find—healing in their worship services. This experience of healing is provided both explicitly, through formal services or times of healing, and informally, through emotional worship and dance. Detractors, like one Guatemalan Catholic priest I interviewed in 2007, describe the evangelical emphasis on lively, emotional evening services as *terapia del canto* (song therapy). In their view, song therapy is simply another form of what Karl Marx called "alienation." That is, the amped-up emotionalism of Pentecostal worship merely distracts religious people from their oppressed state. Whether or not barrio evangelicals are oblivious to social and political oppression is a question we examine later. The point here is that the Pentecostal roots and influence on barrio evangelicals lead them to emphasize cathartic experiences of emotional worship aimed at healing individuals in both a physical and psychological sense, and personal stories of experiencing such healing are abundant in these churches (Williams 1997).

A third characteristic of barrio evangelicals is their distinctly local orientation. As the term implies, "barrio evangelicals" worship locally, in congregations that tend to draw from a small area and focus their evangelistic and ministry efforts on the local community. Their working-class roots and membership mean that most members do not own a car, and, in any case, few churches can afford the luxury of a parking lot in a crowded neighborhood, much less parking security, which is a must in urban contexts. While some evangelicals from popular barrios take the bus to worship at a Neo-Pentecostal mega-church on the weekends, many still prefer worshipping with a local congregation in the barrio. Furthermore, there are organizational forces keeping these barrio congregations relatively small. Barrio evangelicals tend to split often, as pastors and members take advantage of an open religious market in order to try their hand at starting their own church. Dennis Smith, a knowledgeable Presbyterian missionary and social critic, calls this tendency to split often, "the amoeba school of church growth" (1991:131). Since these pastors are essentially called, chosen, or self-named on an ad hoc basis, most pastors of these congregations grew up in the community where they preach and therefore possess a native knowledge of the neighborhood population and its struggles. Denominational ties, while they do exist for some historic evangelical as well as Pentecostal congregations, tend to be weaker since denominational institutions lack the resources or structural rigidity of many denominations in North America.

Finally, barrio evangelicals emphasize personal piety. Both Pentecostal and historic evangelical congregations of the Central American barrio promote a strict code of personal ethics that creates a distinction between *los hermanos* (the saved evangelical brothers and sisters) and the Catholic majority. In Guatemala, this personalized moral code is captured in the evangelical-Pentecostal alliteration of "The Five P's." Evangelical congregations have traditionally promoted strict norms regarding five areas of life, each beginning with the letter "P": *pelo, pantalón, pintura, pelota, parranda.*[5] In a traditional evangelical church of the barrio—especially those in the Pentecostal tradition—women should not cut their hair (*pelo*), wear pants (*pantalones*), or put on makeup (*pintura*). Men should avoid playing in soccer leagues (*pelota*), especially on Sundays. Parties (*parrandas*) are off limits to all since they tend to involve alcohol and dancing, both of which are strictly forbidden in barrio evangelicalism. Since celebrations of national and local religious holidays typically involve alcohol as well as the veneration of Catholic saints, barrio evangelicals tend to steer clear of these *fiestas* as well as parties that are purely social in nature.

Clearly, not all evangelical congregations promote such strict behavioral standards. Many middle-class evangelicals tend to view the strictest norms as at least partially elective, and there is anecdotal evidence to suggest that even in the popular barrios, strict prohibitions against women's wearing pants, cutting their hair, or using makeup are becoming increasingly difficult to enforce. Nevertheless, many congregations in the urban barrio continue to use personal piety as a means of creating distinction and group solidarity. By dressing modestly and avoiding certain cultural activities widely shared in the barrio, evangelical congregations develop their "we-ness" as a recognizable community. Furthermore, pietistic religion goes hand in hand with respect for authority, especially that of the pastor. In an insightful ethnography of barrio evangelicalism in a Honduran barrio, Mark Baker, a long-time religious worker in Honduras, describes how evangelical and Pentecostal congregations promote and enforce strict standards of piety including, but not limited to, The Five P's. On the one hand, pastors employed the "carrot" of being named for a leadership role such as leading worship to encourage compliance. On the other, those who failed to live up to the standards found themselves subject to the "stick" of ostracism by fellow *hermanos*.

One young woman reported that when she started wearing pants rather than a skirt, her evangelical friends began referring to her as *amiga* (friend) rather than *hermana* (sister) thus questioning her personal faith and belonging in the church (Baker 1995).

That evangelical piety is highly gendered, with evangelical women facing stricter standards of dress than men, should come as no surprise given the patriarchal patterns of the barrio itself. At the same time, the proscriptions to drinking, smoking, and going to bars or dance halls called *discotecas* weigh especially heavily on men since it is precisely in bars and discotecas that young Central American men fashion a macho identity as *hombres* able to hold their liquor and woo young women. Thus, as anthropologist Elizabeth Brusco has shown, there is considerable contrast between the values of machismo and those of Latin American evangelicalism, and many evangelical women work actively to convert their husbands in the hopes of turning their attention as well as their allegiance from "the street" to the home (Brusco 1995).

CONCLUSION: COMPARING HOMIES AND *HERMANOS*

There are structural similarities between the organization of the gangs and those of the evangelical churches. The transnational gangs of Central America are franchise-like organizations of loosely knit *clicas* founded and organized by entrepreneurial young men, many of whom possess connections to the United States. Although they proliferated at least a decade earlier than the gangs, barrio evangelicals also display aspects of a franchise-like pattern of organization. Entrepreneurial pastors, usually from the local community, start congregations or rise through the ranks of already-established churches where they exercise a considerable amount of local control.[6] Like the gangs, many evangelical congregations, both historic evangelicals as well as Pentecostals, maintain loose ties with congregations and institutions from the same denomination in the United States. Finally, evangelical *hermanos*, like the homies of the gang, are a recognizable social group within the barrio. Boundaries are important to them as means of understanding who they are and who they are not. Their distinct practices and code of ethics set them apart from their neighbors and create a shared sense of identity as a social group.

But the contrasts between the gang and the church are as great as the similarities they share. While the evolution of the transnational gangs involved co-opting or eliminating all local street gangs, evangelicals have continued a pattern of denominational proliferation and now encompass literally hundreds of denominations. More important, the gang and the church promote starkly contrasting codes of ethics for their members. On the one hand the gang promotes risk taking and pleasure pursuits associated with *la vida loca*. Gang members and especially leaders prove their mettle by demonstrating their ability to *rifar* or "gamble" their personal security by engaging in crime and violence for the sake of the gang. On the other, evangelical *hermanos* value sobriety, modesty, and domesticity characterized by the traditional avoidance of "the Five P's." Avoiding alcohol and parties and wearing modest clothing are all strategies aimed at reducing the odds that an *hermano* might give in to the sexual temptation of "the flesh" thereby disrupting the home and spoiling one's "testimony" as an upright evangelical. In short, when it comes to pleasure pursuits, whereas the gang promotes indulgence, evangelicals espouse asceticism. Thus, despite some structural similarities, the gang cells and evangelical congregations represent two highly distinct social worlds that nevertheless occupy similar social space within the barrio. The social norms that guide life in the *maras* contrast significantly from those that guide the *hermanos*. This fact makes answering the question of why homies become *hermanos* all the more interesting from a sociological perspective. But before we address this question head on, we must explore the reasons why so many *muchachos* in the barrio choose to become homies in the first place.

3
Turning Shame into Violence

Shame and anger have a deep affinity.
—Helen B. Lewis, from Shame and Guilt in Neurosis

She told me that she was not my mother. At that moment a dog was passing by on the street and she said 'No. Look, there goes your mother.' Hearing her say that marked my life.
—Camilo, former M-18 cell leader

The truth is, man, I wanted to sow in other people what other people had sown in me since I was little. The only thing that mattered to me was hatred, you know? Vengeance.
—Pancho, former MS-13 cell leader

PANCHO'S STORY

Pancho is a twenty-three-year-old Honduran with a large frame and an energetic voice. A former leader of an MS-13 cell in San Pedro Sula, Pancho is now president of a group of thirty-eight former gang members, including many former rivals. The voluntary organization of ex-gang members calls itself aptly "Generation X." The challenges faced by Pancho and the other members of the group include finding employers who trust them, avoiding problems with former rivals still in the gang, and avoiding becoming a victim of "social cleansing" by off-duty police or local vigilantes. The day after I interviewed Pancho, another member of Generation X was killed.

Pancho had agreed to meet me after-hours in the back patio of a small home in San Pedro that houses the offices of Onward Youth, the organization that advises Generation X. Like any self-respecting sociologist, I try not to judge a book by its cover, but Pancho's physical appearance was hard to ignore. He is taller than average, well-built, and most of his body is covered with tattoos and the scars left by "erased" tattoos. When he removed a baseball cap worn low over his eyes I had to take care not to react visibly to the scar tissue that completely covered his face. Later in the interview Pancho told me that to remove the tattoos on his face as well as sixteen other tattoos on his body, he had simply applied acidic cream, the kind used for removing body hair, and then waited for ninety minutes (instead of the five to ten minutes recommended for hair removal) while the acid ate into his skin—a process he described as "excruciating" but necessary. "If I hadn't done it," he said, "I'd be dead by now."

Since this first interview was also our first meeting, Pancho wasted no time in sizing me up. Even after looking over the consent form and signing it, he pressed me to know why a gringo had asked to interview him and "what this study is all about and what is its motive?" I explained that my research was part of a dissertation, but that I hoped to publish a book that would increase people's awareness about the difficulties associated with leaving the gang. Once satisfied that the study was not meant to sensationalize the gang or demonize those who belonged to it, Pancho began to tell the story of his entrance in the gang, his rise within its ranks, and his eventual exit, after several years of prison. I spoke very little during the course of the interview, stopping him only momentarily in order to guide the direction of the interview and clarify certain details. His candor, evidenced by his unwillingness to hide his emotions, soon expelled my concerns about safety or forthrightness and we were able to establish a trust that allowed the interview to delve deeply into matters of family, the gang, and religion, in spite of the newness of our acquaintance. He delivered his personal story, punctuated by two or three moments of quiet weeping, much like a confession. The first half of his story helps to answer the question with which we began: What would possess anyone to join a society so dangerous and widely loathed as the gang and to inscribe its symbols on most of his body?

> The truth is that I never thought I would be a gang member, you know? I was raised with my grandmother. When I was five years old my mother became ashamed of me and left me to grow up with my grandmother. That's when I started to suffer because I didn't have a father or a mother. I was raised with my grandmother and an uncle of mine and some grandchildren of my grandmother. But this uncle was an alcoholic. He would get drunk every day and on account of the alcohol he would beat us and he would curse at us.

Pancho observed that this experience left him with *una estigma* (a stigma). What did he mean exactly by this word that would surface many times over the course of the interview?

> And so I grew up with this stigma of suffering without a family. I remember that when I was six my grandmother wanted to put me in school which, no, for me was something very difficult, you know? Mother's Day would come, Children's Day, Father's Day and I would see that all of the parents would visit their classes, eh, these important days for them—Mother's Day, Father's Day, their birthdays.

At this point Pancho began weeping silently. Apparently, the anguish of being a virtual orphan in a society that elevates family relations to near sacred status was still with him. Swallowing to regain composure he continued,

> I didn't have anyone to come for me because my grandmother suffered from a sickness in the brain and couldn't visit the school. And when I left classes the only thing waiting for me at home was a beating from this uncle who drank almost every day and would shout at us constantly.

Even more distant than his relationship with his mother was Pancho's relationship to his father, whom he met on a pair of occasions as a child:

> I hadn't known him at all before then. He would send me things but I never knew him because my mother must have told my grandmother not to let my father near me. That was the obstacle. But I didn't even have her close by because, I don't know—maybe I was the ugliest of my mother's

children. I don't know, but she was embarrassed by me and she went to Tegucigalpa. She is the director of a school in Tegucigalpa.

Pancho described the trauma of being singled out for abandonment by a mother whom he described as a capable professional. His father, on the other hand, was involved in one of the earliest Honduran gangs and was killed in a violent confrontation between two gangs when Pancho was only eight. The news devastated the boy who had only recently been allowed to meet his father. Again, Pancho became emotional as he related the experience of meeting his father as a six-year-old and the sheer joy of knowing that he mattered to someone:

> *¡Pucha!*[1] For me, that hit hard. For me to have met my father was, well, to be in contact with him was [trying not to weep], to be able to say that I had contact with him [pause], well, to be able to say that I had a father, you know? Because when I lost my father, when they told me that he had been killed, it was something painful. [pause] I said to myself, "Well, I'm going to start suffering again with this uncle of mine."

Pancho went on to tell about his move to the city. Worried about the way his uncle beat and mistreated her grandson, Pancho's grandmother took him to the city of San Pedro Sula to live with a different uncle who had several children of his own. "But things got even worse for me. He had is own wife and his own kids and for them I was always on the sidelines." Once again Pancho suffered the beatings and verbal abuse of an uncle who, doubtless, resented having to raise his sister's unwanted child. It was at this point, in the city of San Pedro Sula, that Pancho began to notice the gangs:

> When I was ten I learned about the famous gangs. In those times the gangs went around in their hobby—they would walk around *bien cholos* (in the baggy, Mexican style), with their money in their pockets, you know, getting the attention of the best girls of the neighborhood. I watched all of this, this hobby of theirs and I wanted to arrive to where they were but I didn't know how. I saw that they had it nice (*macizo*) compared to me, original you know. Well-dressed, on the corner, taking it easy. I saw that nobody messed with them. I said, "Why am I suffering

like this?" So at ten years old, almost eleven, I decided to seek these guys out . . .

I started to sneak out at night. I would escape at eleven or twelve and I would go to the disco at three in the morning and return to go back to sleep and no one in my family even noticed that I was leaving. All just to get closer to this group of guys. At eleven I remember I met a youth they called Wolf, and Wolf met another that they called Blackie, guys that were sympathizers with the gang. And of the sympathizers in those days there was only one that wore a tattoo and he was the one that told us what the MS was about. Because I had never seen a tattoo like this before, it hit me hard and I said to myself, "What is this about?" So this guy said, "If you want to know more about the gang, let's go to Medina." And we started to visit other places and we started to get involved with other youth. I remember when we had a fight in a disco and my family didn't even know that I was going out at night and hanging out with these guys. I remember a fight one time between the Dieciocho and the MS because in those days it wasn't like it is now. In the old days what happened was that if one gang member got a hold of another member of another gang they didn't kill each other. Maybe some blows but then they would let him go. Anyway, those guys told me, "You look like a guy that has something to offer the gang, so walk with us for awhile and then we'll see what you're made of." . . .

So I got to know more guys from the same gangs but [from] other sectors you know. By now the sympathizer who had introduced us to the gang was a [real] gang member. I started going around with these guys, started to get to know a little about the gang but not too deep you know? I wanted to get in but at the same time I was afraid. I wanted to get in because I came from a family with a stigma, with so many beatings, insults of different kinds and I wanted to meet that group of guys and find out what it was like to live like that. I remember that at the age of twelve the gang members told me, "We don't want you to go around like a sympathizer anymore. We want you to get jumped-in," they told me. They took me to a place here in Armentra. I didn't know what was going to happen to me. I remember that that day they took me there there were approximately eighty-five to ninety youth, gang members identified by their tattoos you know and they told me, "Do you want to be part of the gang?"

"Yes," I said. "I want to join this. I don't want to live with my family, I want to live with you all. I want to know what it's like to live what you live."

Pancho described his *bautizo* (baptism), the word the Central American gangs use for a jumping-in ceremony, as a memorable day in which he experienced a mixture of fear, curiosity, and excitement. The gang explained the ceremony to him, calling the beating he would receive from other gang members a "warm-up" (*calentón*). The ceremony also included a reading of the thirteen rules of the MS-13.

> Look man. I remember that that day they beat me—but I mean a REAL beating—afterward everybody was like, "Welcome to the barrio. Welcome to the barrio. Welcome to the barrio." You know, the beating didn't matter to me because now I could call myself a gang member. After being beaten and kicked like that, they tattooed me. I had them put one on my leg.

Pancho did not leave his home immediately after the baptism, but he kept his new identity a secret from his relatives. In any case, he reported that they showed little concern for his state even though he was so sore and bruised that he spent several days in bed recuperating from the beatings. Just to make sure, he told his relatives that thieves had assaulted him.

> But by now I felt a little better because I said to myself, "The blows are nothing—I'm a *pandillero* now!" So I started to hang out with those guys, to sneak out every night to go to the discos. I started consuming marijuana, the popular drug, and other drugs. For me when I smoked drugs it made me feel like a man. Like, "That little Pancho, the one that didn't matter to his family one bit?" Well, now I felt stronger. . . . So at the age of thirteen, with my blood brother *(mi carnal)* Javi,[2] the Fish, the two of us would always hang out. Together we met another guy named Bobi, his name was Daniel and he's dead now. The three of us made a pact to look out for each other. And we used to go around together, running the show (*corriendo el rollo*). And whenever anyone had anything to do with one of us, it was the business of all three. We started building the gang in that same sector where we hung out. I now felt like that other guy, the sympathizer who had introduced us to the

> gang. I'd wanted people to be afraid of me, for people to say, "There go those *brotheres* [*sic*]."[3]

Pancho's interview shows a homie identity that developed gradually. On the one hand he was proud of his new status as a gang member, but he worried about what would happen when his family and the neighbors found out. His first tattoos were on parts of the body that could be covered with everyday clothing. But secretly he wished that he could tattoo his face or arms "where people could see it and know that I was a gang member." He was, it seems, building up self-confidence for the day when he would "come out" with his new identity, angering, intimidating, and shaming his uncle and his relatives.

> The truth is, man, I wanted to sow in other people what other people had sown in me since I was little. The only thing that mattered to me was hatred, you know? Vengeance. When they killed my father I used to say, "When I grow up, as soon as I'm old enough, I'm going to avenge the death of my father." I carried around a stigma of that vengeance, you know, and hatred at the same time. We started hanging out, the three of us and one time I got a tattoo right here on my chest and I said to the others, "I'm the most tattooed homie of all, and what of it?!"

One day shortly thereafter, Pancho's uncle discovered the tattoo on his chest. A shouting match ensued in which the uncle cursed him and told him to choose the family or the gang. For Pancho, the choice could hardly have been easier: "I told him, 'You know what? Don't ever mess with me again because if you ever raise your hand against me, we're going to kill you.'" Pancho placed considerable emphasis on this crisis moment when his relatives discovered his homie identity. Important for Pancho was the fact that this time he was able to "stand up" to their verbal abuse rather than simply accept it and feel ashamed or bitter afterward. Like JJ, who recalled his abusive brother as a means to muster the courage to follow through with his assault, Pancho was learning to turn the shame of domestic abuse into a resource for anger, hatred, and later, violence. He continued:

> I felt like more—how can I tell you—like filled with more hatred, you know? I felt like I was a *pandiLLERO.* I felt like my family was that group

> of guys, you know? I left the house that day and I started doing the gig, you know. Already I was fourteen, and it wasn't the same gig anymore where you grab a guy and beat him up, give him a good working-over, and then let him go. By now we had the famous *chimbas*. So now if you ran across another [enemy] gang member, now the thing to do was to fire away with the chimba (*proporcionarle un chimabazo*) and if it killed him, good, and if it didn't kill him, you left him there with a hole in the back or wherever you'd hit him. So we started to hang out with the other guys, raising the gang to almost eighty youth in the sector of Lomas del Carmen. I felt like I had more respect, you know? More respect. I liked when people would say, "What's going on with that brother? He's a gang member you know."

Pancho's account bears so many of the common elements cited by former gang members as part of their experience of "becoming a homie." Like most of the sixty-three former gang members I interviewed for this study, Pancho remembered his experience in the gang with nostalgia at times but also with deep regret. He was not proud of his actions, but neither did he paint the story of a bloodthirsty villain, eager to take advantage of any and every innocent bystander as his victim. Just as important, the level of detail he provided in his account is exceptional. His story offers an excellent opportunity to explore why and how a youth becomes a member of a transnational gang and how belonging to the gang shapes actions and identity. Thus, I approach the issue of gang affiliation not as a one-time decision-event but, rather, as a process. In this process children and youth—mostly boys, but also girls—"try on" the gang identity by "walking with" the gang as sympathizers and learning about the rules, symbols, and rituals associated with the gang. After a time, these youth decide to join the gang or pursue other avenues. Even after joining the gang, youth follow different trajectories within the gang. Some become leaders while others keep a lower profile. In any case, if we wish to understand why some Central American gang members have chosen evangelical religion as a resource for escaping the gang, we must first understand the attraction of the gang to the tens of thousands of Central American youth who have joined them—and how that experience has shaped them.

LISTENING TO EX-GANG MEMBERS

A number of studies of gangs have sought clues for why Central American youth join the transnational gangs. Cruz and Portillo concluded from their study of gangs in greater San Salvador that only a multicausal approach could explain gang affiliation. Among other factors, they named social marginalization, family disintegration, few opportunities for work, educational exclusion, and the attraction of drugs as formative experiences (Cruz and Portillo 1998). While such observations are helpful and coincide with my findings, they do not go far enough in making clear how or why the experience of "social marginalization" or "educational exclusion" actually shape barrio youth toward seeing the gang as an opportunity or a goal. I hope to go beyond merely listing the social features named by gang youth as having contributed to their decision to join. What is it about growing up poor, or in a "broken" family or failing school that makes joining a gang an attractive option. To this end, I begin the next section by reviewing the common threads in ex-gang members' accounts of how they ended up in the gang. Incidentally, I did not ask these young men and women to tell me which "factors" were the most important in their decision to join the gang. Instead, I began the body of each interview with the question "Tell me how you came to belong to a gang." Since many of the youth interviewed had been involved in some form of "rehabilitation" or reeducation program, I wanted informants to avoid the temptation to provide stock answers to questions about what makes the gangs popular. I wanted them to describe their own experience even if that experience did not fit a standard narrative for why youth join gangs.

Of course, there are always liabilities when social scientists use open-ended interviews in order to gather our data. How do we know that informants are not "feeding us a line" rather than speaking honestly about their experience in the light of their best memory?[4] By quoting liberally from the stories of the former gang members I do not mean to imply that no former gang member would ever rearrange, omit, or amplify events in his or her personal story or that the memory of everyone interviewed is perfect and unencumbered by a desire to tell a compelling story (see Appendix A for more about my methods). When asked to recount the past, often several years' removed, I expect that my informants are elevating some moments in their accounts as especially important while ignoring other events that may have detracted from the arc of the story. We all do this when we are asked to summarize the events of multiple years in the space of a few minutes or hours. Nevertheless, my review of the narratives offered by these young men (and four women) led me to conclude that few, if any, ex-gang members were engaging in rampant self-deceit or fabrication, and my interaction with professionals, some of whom had intimate knowledge of the lives of the youth I interviewed, confirmed this conclusion. To the best of my knowledge, the interviews convey real-life events passed through the lens of personal experience.

For comparative purposes, I also interviewed twelve former gang "sympathizers," or youth who walked with the gang for a time, trying it out from the sidelines but never making a final commitment to join. Because these individuals can offer some insight into the reasons that otherwise "prime candidates" for the gang would choose not to join, I refer to their narratives occasionally. Such interviews are helpful in that they provide us with an idea of the alternative paths that lead otherwise typical gang recruits away from the gang and toward other outcomes. Since these interviews with sympathizers are few in number they cannot establish certainty, but they can offer clues as to why some youth find the gang attractive but not compelling enough to join.

A few studies have obtained much larger samples with large control groups. But some of these studies are weakened by other methodological problems such as the use of a written survey instrument among a population that is only marginally literate (Rubio 2007) or the selection effect at work when researchers interview only incarcerated gang members (Ranum 2007). In any case my goal is not the causal explanation or formal completeness of a positivistic approach but rather what sociologist Andrew Abbott has called the "semantic" mode of explanation (Abbott 2004). In the semantic mode often preferred by scholars of culture, theorists seek to understand social phenomena not by measuring or counting but by translating observations from one set of phenomena into the explanatory realm of another in such a way that they become more understandable and more concise. Thus, I relate Pancho's story and quote from many other former gang members, note patterns and exceptions in their narratives of joining the gang, and translate these narratives into the conceptual language of social theory in such a way that violent, self-destructive actions and life choices that appear shocking or outrageous on the surface become more comprehensible and "reasonable."[5]

Unfortunately, the question of why gangs emerge and why youth join them are not always treated separately. One result of this conceptual confusion is that many studies, especially in Central America, have concluded that youth join the gang due to macro-social ills such as poverty, unemployment, or "family breakdown." As the responses of ex-gang members in this study will show, it is certainly the case that many gang members come from impoverished families or have experienced domestic abuse or abandonment, and for this reason, I call these social characteristics "pre-disposing factors." But to simply assume that poverty, bad schools, or abuse "drive youth into the gang" is to adopt an oversocialized view of Central American gang members as wholly subject to the social forces that shape them. In other words, taking only the macro-perspective casts barrio youth in Central America as "social dupes" whose socioeconomic circumstances leave them with little choice but to join a gang. But in fact the majority of Central American youth, even in the "toughest" barrios, *do not* join a gang as there are many other ways to respond to poverty than by joining a violent gang. In fact, joining a gang is, in Central America, a giant step toward sabotaging your prospects for future employment. When Pancho took the step of placing a tattoo on his face, he severely undermined his prospects of ever finding a job and made himself an easy-to-spot target for the police and enemy gang members. There is a counterintuitive logic here that cries out for explanation. "Explaining" such self-inflicted violence as the work of "sociopaths," as some criminologists have done (Bruneau 2005), gets us nowhere.

Another approach to understanding gang affiliation is to look for psychological indicators, such as low self-esteem or a propensity to violent anger, that characterize gang members. I did not subject ex-gang members to psychological tests that could establish their own internal dynamics in the present much less at the time of joining, but their reports of entering the gang made clear that anger and low self-esteem were psychological traits common if not ubiquitous among joiners. But from a sociological perspective, this approach is even less helpful because it fails to acknowledge or investigate the social factors at the macro- and meso-levels that shape the psychological terrain of the Central American youth who join the gang. By itself, this perspective yields the impression that youth who join the gang do so because they possess a particular set of innate psychological characteristics conducive to gang life. What we need is a perspective that connects social contextual pressures with individual-level experiences and social psychological traits. Below I argue that the experience of shame is the key to understanding why Central American youth join the gang and why so many gang youth come to practice violence. Recent work in the sociology of emotions offers useful tools for exploring the connections between social structures that generate shame through endemic poverty, disrupted families, and weak schools, on the one hand, and the transnational gangs which provide alternative pathways to pride and *el respeto* (respect).

So what did the ex-gang members themselves have to say in response to my question, "Tell me how you came to belong to the gang," and what do their answers tell us about what makes gang life attractive? First, at least three negative social contextual themes surfaced: poverty, family problems, and difficulty in school. I call these "pre-disposing factors" since they do not, by themselves, or in concert, "guarantee" that a youth will join a gang. But the themes were so ubiquitous in the interviews that their inclusion was impossible to avoid. In each subsection that follows, I begin with Pancho's account of his own pathway into the gang and follow this with excerpts from interviews with other gang members.

POVERTY

While Pancho did not underscore or directly mention poverty as a direct contributor to his decision to join the gang, a close examination of his story shows that his upbringing was not one of privilege or even modest financial stability. He did not attend private schools and was shunted from one relative to another to be cared for. Furthermore, during early adolescence, Pancho reported being obliged to "water the street" every afternoon to keep the dust down. This detail indicates that Pancho's neighborhood did not have paved streets even though located in urban San Pedro. Though Pancho did not report ever going hungry, he spoke of admiring the gang members, who "went around with their money in their pockets." Testimonies from other former gang members show a much deeper resentment tied to growing up in poverty. For example, Leonardo, a Honduran who belonged to, and eventually led a *clica* of the "South 16" gang, remembered that after his parents separated when he was very young, his mother had difficulty finding work to support her four children. "My heart was full of hate," he recalled:

> I wanted to escape all of that poverty and I couldn't see any other way out. And I was young and had to watch my mother suffering like that . . . And sometimes I would watch other people that went around all well-dressed and everything and, well, I wanted to experience the same thing. . . . That's why I got involved in the gangs around the age of twelve, thirteen, fourteen.

Leonardo resented the "stain" of growing up poor in a deeply stratified society. He saw the gang as an opportunity to escape the grinding poverty in which he was raised and to experience a lifestyle with the means to purchase the accessories symbolic of full-fledged consumerism. For a few youth, however, joining the gang was simply a matter of survival. These youth lacked adult caretakers and needed a source of provision. Saúl described leaving an abusive home at age twelve to live on the streets of Guatemala City. Soon afterward he met members of the MS-13 gang. "They picked me up and helped me," he said. "They gave me a place to stay, clothing and shoes." Ernesto, who once belonged to the Dieciocho, remembered encountering a similar ethic of sharing when he joined the gang. Asked how he came to join the gang he reported:

> I started entering the gang (*fui entrando*) because I was looking—how do I say it—I was looking for what I couldn't find in my home. . . . [In the gang] they treated me well and whenever they got a hold of money, they would share it with me, half-and-half. So that's what I liked, that whole movement.

These testimonies suggest that poverty, both in absolute terms and as relative deprivation, is an important factor pre-disposing children and youth to consider the gang as a possible means to survive but also to achieve the consumer lifestyle important to so many urban Central Americans. Santos, who helps direct a youth program at a Jesuit "Fé y Alegría" (Faith and Joy) center in San Salvador observed that poverty pre-disposes barrio youth to joining a gang because it renders them "invisible."

> In our countries, youth are invisible. They don't count. And a child in one of these [impoverished urban] communities is stigmatized. Wherever he goes he is stigmatized as being poor and a gang member. So you have a kid like this with an inferiority complex and the gang is really enticing because he can be somebody. The gang makes the youth visible (*al jóven lo visibiliza*).

FAMILY PROBLEMS

By far the most common negative social contextual factor arising in the interviews was that of family problems. Time and again the young adults looked back with sadness and anger at a lost childhood filled with the pain of abuse, neglect, and abandonment. Pancho reported that his mother left him in the care of his grandmother and prohibited his father from visiting him until Pancho was six or seven. His voice cracked as he struggled to control his emotions when recalling the special days dedicated to the family at his school. In the traditionalist societies of Central America, such days carry enormous symbolic weight. Children receive gifts on Día del Niño, parents who have jobs in the formal economy are given the day off on Día del Padre and Día de la Madre. Thus children receive visits on Father's Day and Mother's Day as well as the Day of the Child and these visits carry enormous importance in the life of a young child. Whatever its complex status in everyday reality, the *idea* of the family continues to be held aloft as a sacred institution and blood relations are deeply revered. Thus, the absence of a mother or a father, or the marginal presence of an uncaring one in these family-oriented societies, is especially devastating to children who feel the absence of being deprived of something so universally validated. It is "relative deprivation" of a cultural nature. Furthermore, when the veracity of taken-for-granted blood relations is thrown into question, the results can be devastating. Camilo, a former member of the M-18 in Honduras, was raised by his grandparents. When his grandfather died, he went to live with his parents—or so he thought. As his sixth-grade graduation approached, he asked his mother for money to buy graduation pictures, but she refused to give him any:

> She told me that she was not my mother. At that moment a dog was passing by on the street and she said, "No. Look, there goes your mother." That word marked my life.
>
> [*What word?*]
>
> Saying that she was not my mother, that my mother was a dog. [She said] they weren't my parents and I should stop bothering them . . . That left a mark on my heart because afterward I went to my dad to ask for money and he told me to work for it myself. All this affected my life. I remember that a week later I left for San Pedro.

A few months later, Camilo, at thirteen years of age, was living on the streets of San Pedro, owned a pistol, and belonged to the M-18. But he still felt the pangs of being deprived of a family, even as his life became more and more violent:

> I remember moments when I would watch parents with their children, and it was difficult for me to see them there while I couldn't have that (begins to weep). When you can't have that opportunity. You can't even laugh. Everything was bitterness and hatred for me. I considered myself the worst of this world. I was nothing.

A disproportionate number of gang members grew up removed from both parents. Part of the reason for such parental absence can only be attributed to the increase in migration among the urban poor, including women and young mothers. Not surprisingly, many of the youth left behind in the care of grandparents, aunts, uncles, or even siblings have difficulty coming to grips with their parents' decision to migrate. Lacho, fifteen years old and already struggling with alcohol and drugs in the Guatemalan barrio, remembered the day he learned of his mother's departure:

> I was in early high school and I was having problems getting through it. I had a problem. My mother, well, she left for the United States and that

> affected me greatly. She didn't tell us anything. She just left a piece of paper, a letter with a neighbor and she left for the U.S. and that affected me greatly. The fact that she would leave, that she would just take off. After that there was no one to tell me anything.

Lacho reported that his criminal career took off after this experience. Tomás, a Salvadoran member of the M-18, reported that his mother had left for Los Angeles in the mid-1980s when he was two months old. "I lived with my uncle and aunt in El Salvador. The home was a crazy place. There was no such thing as mutual respect." Where was his father, I wondered? His answer was curt. "I don't like to talk about my father," he said. "I've seen him twice in my whole life." Leti, a Honduran, was more understanding of her mother's decision to leave.

> My mom went undocumented (*de mojada*) to the United States but what she wanted was for us to live better. We were very poor but I was very young. I was six. When she left, she left us in the care of my brother. He was barely thirteen or fourteen. We stayed in the house. We went about raising ourselves with his help. Later an aunt took us in, my sister, and brother and me, the youngest. And then we started to feel afraid because the husband of my aunt wanted to abuse us, my sister and me. He was always harassing us in those days. Time went by but we looked out for each other, always. Later, the gangs hit and we started to feel their presence.

Leti left her aunt's home at fifteen to live with an abusive boyfriend, but shortly thereafter, a friend invited her to join her in a gang cell called *Torres 13*, a decision she made gladly in order to escape the abuse of her boyfriend.

The role of mother carries deep and reverent meaning in macho Central America (Giralt and Cruz 2001; Martin-Barò 1996). In the accounts of Lacho, Tomás, and Leti we find evidence of the added social strain placed on families in which a parent, especially a mother, sets out for *el Norte*. Of course, not all children of migrating mothers join gangs or experience tragedy as a result of their mother's absence. Some are fortunate enough to experience strong support from an extended family network and perhaps benefit as well from the financial boost provided by their parents' remittances. But the stories of children feeling abandoned and of experiencing abuse at the hands of family members or stepparents make the impact of migration impossible to ignore. For in Central America, where the family has for generations provided the most important, and sometimes the *only*, social safety net for children living in impoverished conditions at the urban margins, the absence of one or both parents is an important social factor pre-disposing the already disadvantaged children of the barrio to seek safety, provision, and belonging on the street.

In addition to suffering from parental absence, many of the youth recalled experiencing abuse at the hands of parents, grandparents, and relatives. Pancho recalled receiving both verbal and physical abuse from two different uncles, one at his grandmother's home and another at the home of his aunt in San Pedro. Ester, an attractive young Guatemalan who spent several years in the late 1990s as a member of *Las Calacas* ("The Skeletons") in Guatemala City's rough neighborhood of El Milagro, reported that poverty had nothing to do with her decision to join the gang. Despite growing up in a marginal neighborhood, her father, now deceased, had owned a store and a pick-up truck and the family lived in a decent home. When I asked her why so many youth continue to join gangs based on her experience, she reported that neglect and abuse were instrumental in convincing her to leave home and join the gang. Tired of being locked inside her home every day while her mother and father worked from dawn to dusk, Ester escaped by a window and was sitting on the curb when her father returned from work.

> I had long hair at the time. He grabbed my hair, wrapped his hand in it, dragged me into the house and there gave me a kick so hard in my midsection that I doubled over and fell on my knees. So it's the beatings that you get that oblige you to leave your home. Because if I'm going to suffer here, I might as well suffer in the street. On the street I don't have to let them and I have friends who can defend me.

Ester also reported that her father had tried to sexually abuse her. But not all gang joiners seek out the gang as an escape. Others saw in the gang an opportunity to seek vengeance for violence experienced in the home. Ismael, a Guatemalan who formerly belonged to a local street gang, stated: "I remember when I was seven I would watch my father arrive in a drunken state to beat my mother. That was very sad and painful for me. I didn't have any way to defend her and I started to feel the need to belong to a gang in order to get help from my companions in the gang in order to kill my father." Although Ismael never followed through with his plan, he stole a pistol shortly after joining the gang and felt better at least for having the *power* to kill his father if he so chose.

Emerson's memory of anger at spousal abuse was similar. The former member of an Eighteenth Street-affiliated *clica* in Guatemala City's Mezquital barrio remembered trying to protect his mother from his father:

> When I was fifteen or sixteen I was still calm (*tranquilo*) you know. I did my studies and all. But you know in my case there was a lot of alcoholism and the truth is my dad drank. Not every day but when he would drink he would arrive home to do things to my mom, to hit her and to hit us and everything. I suppose that sounds like an excuse that somebody clings to you know? Like, "It's just that my dad drank!" or this or that. But something always stays with you, a scar you know, in your mind and all. I didn't like to see my dad hit my mom. I had to hold him back so that he wouldn't do anything while my mom would escape running and soon enough he would turn and take it out on me for getting in the way, you know?

Emerson's observation that witnessing abuse leaves "a scar that stays with you" is especially evident in the account of Isaac, who also belonged to a cell of the Eighteenth Street gang in another part of Guatemala City. Isaac's mother died when he was very young and his father was an alcoholic, whose occasional presence only brought jeers from friends who teased Isaac for having a *charamilero* (homeless man) for a father. Following his mother's death, Isaac and his brother moved in with their grandparents, who had arrived to the city from the rural countryside some years earlier.

> I was five years old and my brother was six when we used to play soccer with a plastic ball [in the yard]. Sometimes the ball would break a leaf off my grandfather's corn stalks and my grandfather would get so mad that he would take a belt, grab us by the arm and beat and beat and beat us over the back until he'd left our backs laced with marks that wouldn't go

> away for days. For a while he preferred using a [leather] machete case. . . . My grandmother, his wife, would get in the way to try to defend us because we were just children but still he would say, "Don't get involved, old lady. This doesn't concern you. Don't be such a softie," and then he'd start to beat her too. So my brother and I would be left hugging each other in the corner and I would say to my brother, "Just wait. Some day we're going to grow up, and he's going to be a *viejito* (little old man). When he's a *viejito*, it will be easier for us to kill him because he won't be able to defend himself." And so all of this anger kept building until one day we got tired of it and my brother went and joined the gang. He was one of the first.

Isaac would follow his brother's footsteps shortly thereafter. By the time I interviewed Isaac at the age of nineteen, bullet marks in his scalp and his leg revealed the places he had been shot several times at close range. His older brother had been dead for years.

SCHOOL PROBLEMS

Pancho's account of his gang entrance reveals one more important predisposing factor present in many of the lives of those joining the gang—difficulty in school. Like many of the other ex-gang members I interviewed, Pancho reported never fitting in quite right in his school. Ashamed by the lack of visitors on special days, he decided early on that school was not for him and thus never finished his primary education. Similarly, Ricardo, a Honduran former gang leader, recalled that his difficulties in the school system began early. "I was in first grade when they expelled me for being violent," he said. "A boy was hitting me, picking on me, and I went and grabbed a broom stick and broke it over his arm, his left arm. So in first grade they expelled me for being violent."

Ricardo, who grew up in a traditional, two-parent home, blamed his violent tendencies as a child on the neighborhood where he lived, claiming that the abundance of market vendors created an atmosphere of hectic distrust among neighbors. Whatever the reason, his propensity to fight was soon catalyzed by the traditionalist authoritarian approach to discipline he encountered in the public school classroom.

> Once [in the third grade] I threw a piece of paper on the floor in the hallway and [the teacher] came up and said, "Ricardo, come here and pick up that piece of paper. Open your mouth." I opened my mouth but when I looked I realized she was going to stick the paper in my mouth, the one I'd dropped. So I pushed her hand away like this [makes a motion] and I went running out the door. After that, I never went back.

In the overcrowded and underfunded public schools of Central America, teachers have difficulty maintaining an educational atmosphere, and many resort to strict control measures including corporal punishment. Even in this context, protecting the most vulnerable children can be nearly impossible. Roberto, a Guatemalan ex-member of the Eighteenth Street from Amatitlán, dropped out of school shortly after a classmate tried to rape him. But dropping out of school compounds the problems of poverty and elevates the attraction of the gang because it provides children and adolescents with a surplus of unsupervised free time and virtually eliminates the already meager possibility of obtaining work in the formal sector. Furthermore, dropping out of school greatly enhances the possibility that a child will build friendships with older adolescents who have already abandoned traditional pathways to adulthood and employment. Children who drop out of school early—that is, prior to junior high—make prime recruiting targets for gang leaders seeking to enlarge the ranks of their cell.

Pancho's account of "becoming a gang member" as well as excerpts from many others, reveals the commonality among ex-gang members of a variety of negative social experiences early in life. Poverty, family problems, and problems in school can be conceptualized as "predisposing factors" causing children in the barrio to be especially at risk for joining the gang. Of course, the short list of factors provided here is hardly exhaustive. Combing through the dozens of accounts of joining the gang would generate other commonalities less prominent but still shared across numerous stories of entrance. But the factors reviewed here were by far the most frequently cited in the narratives of joining the gang. Still, we are left with the question of how it is that such experiences actually "pre-dispose" youth toward joining the gang. To answer this question, I turn now to social theory and the sociology of emotions.

SHAME AND THE SOCIOLOGY OF EMOTIONS

The emotional character of many of the interviews I conducted with ex-gang members took me by surprise. Whereas I had spent considerable time preparing myself for how to handle evasive answers or how to ensure my safety as a gringo researcher, I was not ready for the long pauses and quiet weeping of these so-called hardened criminals. But it did not take long to conclude that many of the events the young men and women recounted to me were inseparable from deep and enduring emotions of shame, anger, and regret. Indeed, I sometimes found myself navigating my own emotional reactions during the interviews. By the time I sat down to analyze the transcripts—sometimes accompanied by new waves of disgust or sadness as I reencountered the tragedies of so many broken lives—I knew I needed to pay careful attention to the role of emotion in the lives of these youth. The sociology of emotions offered a toolkit for making sense of these emotions.

Most sociologists have paid scant attention to the role of emotion in their research, perhaps in part because human emotions were too closely identified with the individual and the body (Turner and Stets 2005), and sociology sought to avoid these topics as terrain more appropriate to psychology or biology (Turner 1997). As a result of this avoidance, social theory took for granted the shaping influence of sociocultural forces without specifying how or why individuals might be subject to such forces. This was especially true in the case of cultural theory, where many sociologists assumed that "cultural norms" shaped individual action without offering an explanation for why individuals might obey such norms. An individual's actual motivation, either to follow a norm or to violate it, was a kind of "black box," the contents of which social theorists had agreed not to examine. The result was a two-tracked sociology. On the one hand macro-theories of social structural change and stasis argued the importance of the social context (culture and power) in shaping human behavior at the individual level. On the other, symbolic interactionists such as Herbert Blumer (1967) and Howard Becker (1963), insisted on recognizing individuals as active agents capable of defining and redefining situations to deviate from or subvert cultural norms. But in neither case did the theorists attempt to specify how it happens that society and culture actually exert influence on the actor,

nor why some actors deviate from such norms. Thus the sociology of emotions emerged as an attempt to address this weakness by conceptualizing both the experience and expression of human emotions as central to the shaping and motivating of human action in society. Sociologists of emotions approach their topic from a variety of angles. Most borrow in some way from Emile Durkheim, the French theorist who helped found sociology as a discipline. In *The Elementary Forms of Religion* (1995 [1903]) Durkheim highlights the capacity of social rituals to generate emotion, which he terms "collective effervescence," that can be harnessed by communities and individuals for action and to create solidarity. For example, by participating in rituals such as the singing of a national anthem or a sacred hymn, individuals build upon their emotional attachment to the community that celebrates these symbols as sacred. They also further sacralize the symbols in the process. Erving Goffman, though not himself a theorist of emotion, developed Durkheim's observations into a dramaturgical approach using the metaphor of a theatrical stage and script to suggest that all human interaction, including everyday encounters, is guided by ritual and shaped by cultural rules for interaction. Following these rules leads to "successful" interaction and a positive emotional payoff for participants in the ritual (Goffman 1959). Just as important, Goffman states that "failed" interaction leads to the negative emotion of embarrassment. In most everyday interaction, participants go to considerable lengths to repair the social fabric and save "face," thus avoiding or minimizing the experience of embarrassment and protecting the solidarity of the group. Though Goffman rarely made open reference to them, the *emotions* of embarrassment and pride, and the attempt to avoid the former and access the latter, are key elements in his theory of interaction ritual.

Contemporary social theorist Randall Collins places emotions at the center of his theory of "interaction ritual chains" (Collins 2004). His ambitious theory draws heavily from Durkheim's observation that participation in rituals provides "emotional energy" which he describes as

"a feeling of confidence, the courage to take action" (2004:39). Collins expands on Goffman's concept of "encounters" noting that the rituals associated with everyday encounters such as smiling or shaking hands are "chained" across time. An individual who plays a key role in a successful ritual carries the emotional energy gained from that experience

into future encounters. Furthermore, she seeks out similar encounters in order to capitalize on her ability to meet or exceed others' expectations in these settings and gain more emotional energy. When interaction rituals fail, the result saps the energy (or solidarity) of the group and erodes individual emotional energy leading participants to try to avoid similar encounters in the future. Nor does participation in a ritual benefit all participants equally. "Energy stars" is the term Collins gives to individuals with a high reserve of emotional energy who carry their confidence with them into interaction rituals and tend to benefit disproportionately by virtue of their ability to capture the attention of others and facilitate a positive encounter. Those with little emotional energy, on the other hand, tend to gain little from their participation and therefore seek to avoid most encounters. For Collins, emotional energy can be represented as a single dimension ranging from high energy experienced as happiness or joy to low energy experienced as sadness or depression. Although much of life takes place between these two ends of the spectrum at mid-level emotion, experiences of joy or deep sadness punctuate these underlying states and, in the right context, can give rise to significant shifts in personality or lines of action. Finally, Collins describes the characteristics of ritual encounters that "work." The most successful rituals, says Collins, are those that incorporate (1) bodily copresence, (2) high barriers to outsiders, (3) mutual focus of attention, and (4) a shared mood. When a ritual contains all of these ingredients, it tends to produce a high payoff in terms of solidarity, enhanced emotional energy for participants, and a sacralizing of symbols associated with the group. Successful rituals create a "feedback loop" raising the expectations for exciting encounters and thereby making future rituals even more successful. Collins's theory is impressive in its breadth, and time does not permit a full examination of its most sweeping claims. But his larger goal is a worthy one. Collins is trying to explain how emotion works to motivate and guide human interaction. He does this by revealing the social conditions under which emotional resources are "heated up" or "cooled down." His approach to ritual helps make sense of the violent initiation rites described by many of the former gang members. But his emphasis on "pride" or its absence is less helpful for understanding the criminal violence so prevalent among the personal accounts of gang life.

Social psychologist Thomas Scheff helps fill the gap. His theory of "the social bond" shares much with Collins's approach in that it pays special attention to the emotional impact of participation in interaction rituals. But rather than focusing primarily on "high" versus "low" energy, Scheff centers his theory on a discussion of pride and, especially, shame (Scheff 1988, 1991, 1997). At the center of Scheff's theory is Charles Horton Cooley's observation that the self is a product of social interaction in which the individual judges himself in the "looking glass" of others' assessments of him. But for Cooley, those judgments are not purely cognitive but involve emotion. When a person imagines how others think and feel about him, the result is "some sort of self-feeling, such as pride or mortification. . . . The thing that moves us to pride or shame is not the mere mechanical reflection of ourselves, but an imputed *sentiment*, the imagined effect of this reflection upon another's mind" (1902:184 [emphasis added]). It is the experience of these feelings of pride or shame, or the avoidance of them, that Scheff insists guide human interaction and shape the formation of the self. Put simply, as humans we seek to maximize our experience of pride and minimize our exposure to shame.

SHAME: THE SCAR THAT STAYS WITH YOU

Understanding shame as a debilitating emotion that all humans seek to escape sheds important light on the question of how poverty, abuse, and school problems pre-dispose many barrio youth toward seeing the gang as an attractive option. After all, it is not enough to point out, as some Central American gang analysts do, that youth who are poor and have little formal education are attracted to the offer of economic support via non-legal means (Sibaja et al. 2006). That purely Marxian, essentially rationalistic explanation seems too simplistic after listening to Pancho's firsthand account. Although Pancho certainly noticed that gang members "went around with money in their pockets," he seemed more interested in the prestige (and access to girls) afforded by such money than by its potential for providing survival or economic stability. Nor is it enough to point out that Central American youth who experience severe abuse or abandonment at home seek an alternative family in the gang experience. The observation is certainly true, but it only gets us so far. It fails to adequately address the root cause of this search for solidarity—one so desperate that it can bring youth to both commit and undergo extreme acts of violence on the way to becoming a "respected" homie.

Beyond a mere quest for survival and community, the reports from ex-gang members share a common element—the profound experience of shame. Pancho begins his account of entrance into the gang by making it clear that he never "intended" to be a gang member, at least not as a young child. From there he immediately recounts being abandoned by his mother who "became ashamed of me and left me by myself." Although Pancho uses the term "suffering" to describe his early experiences of abandonment and abuse and the loss of his father, it is clear that shame is at the heart of this suffering. He uses the term "stigma" three times during the course of the interview in order to describe the experience of abandonment by his mother, abuse from other relatives, and the desire to avenge the death of his father. That Pancho is in fact describing a first-hand experience of shame seems clear among other things from the fact that at multiple points in the interview, always when describing his family experience, he finds himself weeping or pausing in order to control his emotion. Even today Pancho has trouble coming to grips with the pain of being singled out for abandonment by his mother. After all, his siblings were not similarly abandoned: "Maybe I was the ugliest of my mother's children, I don't know, but she was embarrassed by me," he recalled.

Pancho's experience of shame at being abandoned or abused is hardly unique in the interviews. Camilo's experience of being disowned by his mother—of being called, quite literally, a son of a bitch, in his own words, "marked my life." Similarly, Antonio, a Guatemalan whose father died when he was young and who later joined the Eighteenth Street, remembered feeling ashamed of his alcoholic mother:

> When I was nine or ten years old I remember how it stung so much to see my mother completely drunk and have to help her home. I mean, for me it was something that made me so ashamed (*me daba tanta verguenza*). I realized how other parents of my friends I went to school with—I saw them, you know, taking their kids to school, going over their homework in the evening, right? . . . It wasn't like that for me.

Antonio's experience of shame stemmed, among other things, from being deprived of a cultural good—a loving, moral mother. This experience caused him to experience profound, inescapable shame throughout his childhood and beyond.

The experience of poverty also generated a feeling of shame in the lives of many other youth who later joined the gang. It was not so much the experience of physical want that was prominent in the interviews. After all, actual malnourishment among children is relatively rare in urban Central America. Instead, it was the feeling of belonging to an invisible underclass that characterized the frustration of growing up poor. "I was young and had to watch my mother suffering [in poverty]," remembered Leonardo. Even difficulties in school are expressed as experiences of shame as in Ricardo's story of the teacher attempting to stuff a wad of paper into his mouth. The experience of being shamed in public was enough to drive Ricardo from school for good. Once outside the school system, he experienced further shaming from his father who put him to work in view of his "incorrigible" character.

By pointing to the role of shame in the lives of gang members prior to affiliation, I am not attempting to exonerate the youth who participated in gang violence by painting them as innocent victims of psychosocial trauma. Rather, I am trying to identify what it is about early experiences of poverty, familial discord or abandonment, and school problems that allows or prepares these youth to see the gang as a viable option. That is, I am trying to go one step further in revealing the actual links between micro-behavior and macro-structures. The payoff for doing so will be clearer later in the book when I examine the process of "un-becoming" a gang member and how evangelical religion contributes to that process. Scheff's work is instructive here. For Scheff, mild shame is a normal part of human interaction and plays a necessary role in conscience, modesty, and remorse. In a relationship between relative equals with regard to power or status, shame can be brought to the attention of the other and dealt with or "discharged" and the sense of pride restored. But when the damaged social bond is not addressed, for example when one member is at a severe power disadvantage, the person experiencing shame may attempt to "bypass" or "mask" shame often through acts of conjured bravado or violence. The result is what Scheff calls a "spiral of shame" in which the individual (or group) experiencing shame develops a chronic sense of shame and attempts to hide or "mask" this shame by attempting to shame others. This shame spiral describes well the process set off by the experience of domestic abuse and especially abandonment. But it also extends to experiences of public shaming by a person of authority such as a teacher. In relationships in which one member holds considerable power, as in the case of a parent over her child, or a teacher over his student, an abused or abandoned child has little recourse for confronting the other. Scheff argues that persons suffering from what psychologists call "low self-esteem" are those who have experienced shame and are unable to effectively manage or discharge it by bringing it to the attention of others. These individuals therefore suffer from chronic or "pathological" shame. Such persons are unable to access the energy necessary for expressive action and thus they "will do anything to avoid pain" (Scheff 1991). In the next section I propose that what makes the gang most attractive to youth who experience pathological shame is its offer of a set of strategies for masking shame and accessing pride, albeit temporarily, through rituals of solidarity, violence, and sex.

FINDING RESPECT IN THE GANG

So far I have examined those negative contextual factors in Pancho's life and many other pre-gang youth that "push" them toward the gang, and I have used the sociology of emotions to explain why such experiences might pre-dispose youth to seek to escape shame by joining a gang. But what is it about the gang specifically that makes it so attractive to these barrio youth? After all, Pancho's account makes it clear that he was not obliged to join the gang against his will. Nor did he simply weigh the costs and benefits of joining versus not joining and then proceed rationally. Rather, he began learning about the gang and "walking with" gang members because it "felt good." Although a few ex-gang members emphasized the gang as a mode of survival, most, like Pancho, spoke of the allure presented by the gang with its symbols, its rituals, its camaraderie, and its pastimes. Any examination of gang entrance then, needs to take into account not only the "push" of pre-disposing factors creating a situation of uncertainty and suffering in the lives of the gang joiners but also the "pull" factors that make the gang such an attractive option for the same youth. For example, Pancho remembered that at the age of ten or eleven, by which time he had already dropped out of school, he began to notice the gangs and their "hobby":

> They would walk around *bien cholos* [in the baggy Mexican style] with their money in their pockets, getting the attention of the best girls of the neighborhood. I watched all of this, this hobby of theirs you know. I wanted to arrive where they were but I didn't know how. I saw that they had it nice compared to me. Original you know?

Pancho watched as the young boys and men flaunted their freedom, making their presence known through "original" clothing, tattoos, speech, and violence even as they engaged in "adult" pastimes such as drinking, taking drugs, and engaging in frequent sex. To young boys experiencing chronic shame, the opportunity to be part of a group that inspired awe and "respect"—at least among youth in the barrio—must seem like a dream come true. The quotations in the following section focus on three of the features of attraction mentioned most frequently in my interviews. I categorize them broadly as solidarity, violence, and "adult" pastimes.

SOLIDARITY

Many youth spoke of the sense of solidarity experienced within the gang—at least in the early stages. Some used the term "solidarity" to describe life in the gang while others simply spoke of the family-like atmosphere of support and camaraderie. In either case, ex-gang members spoke of a Robin Hood-like band of brothers whose "outlaw" reputation only added to their sense of unity. Indeed, in some cases, the gang acted like the famous band from Nottingham by providing impoverished, abandoned children with a means of survival. Saúl, a Guatemalan, remembered how the *Mara Salvatrucha* provided him with clothing and shoes in his early days after he had abandoned an abusive household for the street. Joining the gang seemed like the natural response afterward. For his part, Pancho spoke of the gang as the family he never new: "I felt like my [real] family was that group of guys, you know?"

Pablo, a Guatemalan who joined the M-18 while living in Los Angeles, remembered how his mother fled with her children to the United States after learning from her son that her children's father had tried to rape Pablo's sister. After describing the pain of living in a family fraught with fear and distrust, Pablo described the attraction of gaining a surrogate family by joining the gang.

> It was like—it wasn't that they forced you [to join]. They would talk to you and you felt supported. "*¡Vamos!* (Let's go!) We're a family! We're a family!" And that's when I felt love among them and support. And that's when I joined the gang.

The experience of solidarity from belonging to a group produces a *feeling* that in everyday language we call "pride." Durkheim called it "emotional effervescence" and regarded it as stemming directly from one's participation in a group and the rituals associated with that group. Randall Collins renamed it "emotional energy" and described how individuals come away from successful interaction rituals with a "feeling of confidence" and "the courage to take action" (2004:39). Melchor, a Honduran who had belonged to the Wonder-13, remembered how being a part of the gang made him *feel strong:*

> What gets your attention most is the idea of the companionship of everyone. If one [person] has a problem—maybe you have some enemies in another area and you can't go there—just being with the gang makes you feel stronger. So you lose your fear and you feel like you've got others around. You go out stronger, ready to fight with everybody else.

While just being together with other peers who seek companionship makes the gang attractive, the gang offers more than this friendship based on spending time together. Gang cells build strong identities through interaction with neighboring cells. Nestor, a former member of the Guatemalan White Fence remembered:

> [The gang] offered to bring me in, to integrate me into the gang so that whatever problem I might have, they would help me. They offered to help, you know, whenever I might have a problem.

> [*What kind of help and what kind of problems?*]
>
> Help in the sense that—help with problems that I might have with other guys that might do something, beat me up or threaten me. So the help they offered was to help me defend myself or to go do something to [the other guys].

As Nestor's comments illustrate, gangs enhance in-group solidarity through conflict with rivals. Georg Simmel noted more than a century ago (Simmel 1955) that conflict has the social function of uniting allies into a single group with a shared identity when faced with a common enemy. In effect, while there is a sense of camaraderie built around simply spending time together, the excitement and mutual focus generated by the experience of confrontation with the opposing gang or with non-gang members adds an even greater emotional thrill. Indeed, Nestor's description of the gang's "offer" of membership sounds like a petition for enemies. "Join us!" the gang seems to say, "and bring your list of enemies." For when each new gang member brings a set of enemies, additional opportunities emerge for confrontation and the building of in-group solidarity.

Another key aspect of the experience of solidarity is the cultivation of symbols via embodied identity markers including clothing and tattoos. Pancho reported that seeing the tattoo of the young sympathizer was an important component of his early curiosity with the gang. The "original" baggy clothing of the *cholo* style also attracted him. Many local gangs have their own clothing and hairstyle parameters although these often overlap. For example, members of cells belonging to the M-18 tend to keep their hair very short and prefer baggy clothing representative of the Mexican-American oppositional subculture that emerged in the mid-twentieth century in the U.S. Southwest. Rosaries and the Virgin of Guadalupe appear in many M-18 murals and tattoos, sometimes right next to images of sexually objectified women. Such markers set off members and provide youth with a strengthened sense of self through identification with a recognizable local group. Oscar, a former leader in the Honduran M-18 attributed his own entrance to the gang to the arrival of an uncle, an ex-gang member who was deported from Los Angeles. Although Oscar's parents sent generous remittances to pay for his private schooling, he hated school and remembered watching his uncle with fascination. He used the present tense when describing the experience of observing his uncle's body and his way of carrying himself. "I start to watch him, tattooed and with a great muscle-bound body. I start to admire the way he walks, his way of changing clothes, his manner of speech." Soon afterward, members of the rival MS-13 killed Oscar's uncle. Angry and in search of revenge, Oscar joined the M-18 gang to which his uncle had formerly belonged. Although Oscar emphasized the death of his uncle as instrumental in his decision to join the gang, his account revealed the extent to which the gang *manner*—a way of dressing, walking, and talking built on the self-confidence of strength-in-numbers—attracts the attention of youth who feel isolated and ashamed. Several ex-gang members remembered being attracted by the possibility of learning the insider vocabulary employed by gang members, a selection of which is included in Appendix C. Gang members have a name for this set of unique symbols, vocabulary, and mode of action—*la clecha*. Learning how to navigate and display *la clecha* provides gang members with a pathway to respect and a chance to move up in rank. JJ described it like this:

> Clecha is something secret—like something that you have to learn for an exam in school. It's a secret, a key, right? . . . Knowing what the barrio is all about is clecha. I got it. I got it. I picked it up quickly . . . My *ranflero* used to tell me "You're going to be somebody. You're going to take my place and be in charge of the *clica*. You're going to be a *ranflero*."

Thus, not only belonging to the gang but the possibility of rising in its ranks by demonstrating a thorough grasp of clecha holds out for youth experiencing shame, an alternative pathway to pride and "respect."

VIOLENCE

In addition to learning to practice clecha, the price of respect in the gang is violence. On the one hand, a good deal of gang violence is strategic and economically motivated. Selling drugs, robbing residents of neighboring communities, and extorting business owners and bus drivers are all violent activities that provide the gang with resources for buying "original" clothing such as Domba athletic shoes and gold chains. Gang violence is also defensive. Most gang members see themselves as protecting their communities from thieves and assailants including other gang members from other communities. In at least some cases, they do provide local protection although they also increase the need for protection elsewhere by bringing violence to neighboring communities. Beto described the growth of his local Eighteenth Street cell in Honduras:

> We used to go everywhere to rob, but never permitting it in our own barrio.
>
> [*So others came here to rob?*]
>
> No. We didn't allow stealing. If we found someone stealing we would tie them up and put a sign on them so that everyone knew they were a thief. Every day we would [take turns] patrolling until the wee hours of the morning.

Violence, as a means of defense and as a strategy for acquiring resources, provides impoverished youth with access to money as well as a heightened sense of belonging. Like a police squad or military unit, the young men feel the "call of duty" and see their participation in defensive gang violence as an act of masculine sacrifice on behalf of their community. In the act of violence, gang members deepen their shared identity as a "band of brothers" and prove their worth and belonging individually. The *brinco* or "jumping-in" ceremony, also called a *bautismo* (baptism), is one of the most important moments in the life of the individual gang member and an exciting ritual for the group as a whole. "Baptisms" provide adolescents with the opportunity to prove their loyalty to the gang by demonstrating their willingness to sacrifice their physical integrity on its behalf. Having already undergone a months-long process of chequeo as a sympathizer, Pancho was given his opportunity to demonstrate his ultimate loyalty to the gang by undergoing violence in the midst of a group of dozens of peers. Pancho's description of his own baptism gives a sense of the excitement and energy produced by the event. Although he, like many others, described the beating as physically agonizing, the payoff in emotional energy is clear. "The beating didn't matter to me [because] I could call myself a gang member . . . I said to myself, 'The blows are nothing—I'm a *pandillero* now!'"

It would be difficult to think of a more fitting illustration of Collins's theory of interaction ritual chains. For in undergoing the baptism, Pancho received a clear "payoff" in terms of emotional energy—one that he carried with him into future interactions both within the gang and within the context of his abusive family. In a sense, Pancho sacrificed his physical well-being in order to experience the solidarity and excitement of belonging to an identifiable group with a clear set of sacred symbols and behavioral norms. The gang cell in turn benefited by the emotional energy generated when dozens of members observed an act of violence. That such rituals imbue the symbols of the gang with meaning seems clear given that the event concluded with the application of a gang tattoo. All of the elements of a "successful" interaction ritual are here: bodily co-presence, high barriers to outsiders (since non-gang members are not allowed to participate or observe the baptism), a mutual focus of attention, and a shared mood. If Collins is correct in his contention that chronic shame represents an enduring shortage of emotional energy, we can safely conclude that the gang baptism addresses this shortage both for the newly inducted and for the "baptized" faithful who witness and perform the ritual.

Although almost all of those interviewed reported having undergone a baptism, only a few described the event with as much detail as Pancho. Even so, there was little agreement as to the specific parameters of the ritual. Most informants reported that the baptism lasted thirteen or eighteen "seconds" counted out slowly by the leader. A few, like Pancho, reported that the rules are recited during the ceremony. One gang member even reported that the baptism lasts thirteen or eighteen *minutes* for the MS-13 and M-18 gangs, respectively. Such discrepancies illustrate a high level of variation in rules and practice from one cell to the next.

Not only the violence of baptism but crime itself is a means of escaping shame and accessing emotional energy. The opportunity to witness and participate in criminal violence further enhances the attractive nature of the gang for barrio youth experiencing shame. Other research has acknowledged the attraction of crime and violence to youth but usually without addressing the language of emotions as such. In his book, *Seductions of Crime* Jack Katz noted that crime can be attractive because it provides people with a sense of "thrill" and agency (Katz 1988). Breaking the law allows delinquent youth to feel powerful (Matza 1964).

Here the resemblance to Collins's "emotional energy" is clear. For youth frustrated by situations of vulnerability and impotence, the emotional high of committing a crime, especially a violent one that abruptly subjects another to one's own whim, is all the more enticing. Pancho's description of the "hit" preceding the tattooing of his face is a good example of violence as a means of "making something happen."

> I didn't want to have just the tattoo on my chest anymore. I wanted to tattoo my whole body, you know, to identify me as a respected gang member among the other youth. So we decided to carry out a mission, and whoever participated in that mission that day would tattoo his face. The mission was to go assault an enemy gang, and then get tattoos. Well, we went, man, we hit them, and the three of us together went and tattooed our faces. We had more respect with the gang. We were now leaders in the sector.

Although he does not detail the specific nature or impact of the "mission," that it involved violence is clear. Committing a violent act toward the enemy gang rewarded the perpetrators with emotional energy that could be "stored" in the facial tattoos, reminding the wearer and his friends of his risky sacrifices for the barrio. "We had more respect with the gang you know. We were now leaders in the sector. . . ." Violent crime offers a temporary escape from chronic shame in part because it is an interactive encounter that humiliates the other.[6] JJ "dedicated himself" to carjacking even though he couldn't drive and had to enlist the help of a nephew to drive the stolen vehicles. "I liked to take people's cars because I liked to watch their faces fill with fear," he recalled. "I liked to humiliate people because people had humiliated me so much. I was trying to avenge all that (*desquitar toda esa*)."[7] JJ was trying desperately to discharge his own shame and he found in violence a means of experiencing the "thrill" of emotional energy.

James Gilligan, a psychoanalyst and clinical psychiatrist who spent decades evaluating the most violent offenders in the Massachusetts prison system, concluded from his work that most criminal violence committed by men can be understood effectively as a desperate attempt to ward off shame. In his book *Violence: Reflections on a National Epidemic*, the clinical professor of psychiatry at Harvard's School of

Medicine wrote that criminal violence is, in effect, the outworking of the "logic of shame" (1996:64). For Gilligan, violence is a destructive vernacular that says, "I cannot be shamed by others. I will shame them instead" (1996:120). In this sense, Gilligan's work shares much with Scheff's most recent writings on masculinity and violence. Scheff describes violence as a form of "bypassing" shame, especially among males who, in most cultures, are taught to avoid affective attachment: "One ingredient of violence, its incredible energy, is produced by masking shame with blankness or anger" (2004:120). In short, the perspective that shame provides an engine for violence helps us make sense of gang violence that seems "irrational," "over the top," or gratuitous. If it is indeed the case, as I have argued, that the experience of chronic shame plays an important role in pre-disposing Central American youth to join a gang, we should not be surprised to find that violence—even "excessive" violence—abounds within the gangs. And so it does. One Guatemalan female ex-gang member described witnessing the decapitation of a (female) friend by her own gang. The young woman had been accused of fraternizing with the enemy. Another ex-gang member described witnessing a similar scene, with the exception that in this case the victim was a (female) neighbor who had reported gang members to the police. Many of the men described their own participation in acts of murder, usually carried out against other men. Though I did not probe for more information, over the course of the interviews more than a dozen men reported having directly participated in at least one homicide.[8] In short, it is incorrect to argue that the Central American gangs are merely innocent victims of poverty who engage in mild delinquency. What is needed instead is an approach that helps us make sense of the very real and often-horrific violence committed by gang youth. Understanding gang violence as an answer to chronic shame provides just this lens.

Lest I be accused of promoting an individualistic, psychological account of gang violence, it is worth pointing out that pride and shame accrue to groups, not just individuals. In an innovative article on gang murders in Chicago, Andrew Papachristos demonstrates the cyclical nature of gang violence through what he calls "murderous networks." He argues that gang murders are best understood not as individual acts of pre-meditated crime or personal score-settling but rather as patterned instances of "paybacks" aimed at maintaining respect and dominance *for the gang*. Put differently, gang murders are interactive rituals providing valuable currency in an urban economy of honor and social status. Gangs serve as "conduits" of violence, directing who is to be killed by whom (Papachristos 2009). This network-level approach to gang violence is important in that it makes sense of the tit-for-tat, reciprocal nature of gang violence. A "successful" murder bestows respect (pride) on the gang that carried it out, while shaming the gang that lost a member. The side that succumbed then seeks to reassert itself through a violent counterattack and the process goes on. Unfortunately, in his zeal to demonstrate the contextual nature of "murder by structure," Papachristos ignores the stakes for individual members who carry out the murders. Gang members who take the initiative to commit murder for the gang gain respect and rank within their own gang, while also acquiring notoriety—with a price on their heads—in the opposing gang. Nevertheless, the larger point is an important one. Gang members who shame others with violence on behalf of the gang win respect for their own gang but also for themselves.

Not just overt violence but weapons themselves provide access to emotional energy. When small arms began to circulate more freely in the 1990s, gangs with access to these weapons became even more attractive to youth experiencing the powerlessness of shame. Where formal firearms were not available, homemade pistols called *chimbas* or *hechizas* (home-made's) were crafted out of steel tubing in local weld shops. I asked Emerson, formerly of the Guatemalan cell "SPL-18," an M-18 cell whose initials stand for "Only for the Crazy," what it felt like when his all-male gang was presented with a.38 Special (also known as a ".38 Spl") and three *hechizas* courtesy of their Eighteenth Street liaison. "Aaaaay!" he exclaimed recalling the feeling. "When we had the.38 we felt like we were the greatest in the neighborhood."

Similarly, Calín's description of life after his initiation reveals the connection between carrying weapons and an invincible feeling of masculine power.

> Being in the gang I felt was a man's thing (*cosa de hombres*). I started to feel untouchable, like I believed I was bigger than God already. I used to say that being in the gang, nobody could touch me, nobody had the right

> to tell me anything. I remember that many times I carried automatic weapons, aka's [AK-47's], mini-Uzzi's, M-16's, M-14's, 9 mm's,.38's—all kinds of weapons the majority at the age of 14. And on January 5th or 6th of 2000, I tattooed the number [18] on my chest.

Although it is doubtful that Calín, at fourteen, actually owned the semiautomatic weapons he describes, it is not uncommon for the younger members of the gang to carry major weapons. In fact, some gang leaders capitalize on the fascination with guns among young males in the barrio by using the weapons as recruiting devices. Gustavo, a Guatemalan youth who had belonged to the M-18, remembered:

> I started junior high at the public school in the neighborhood of Belen. That's when I started to meet members from the other side and hang out with them. I even got to meet the leader of that gang. Then they started lending me their weapons. First a 12-gauge, then a.22, then a.38. This started to make me curious so I asked them to show me how to use them and they took me to a firing range.

Gustavo did not fire the weapons at first. But merely handling them was an incentive for becoming more involved in the gang. Cell leaders, mindful that they are under scrutiny by local police, are often glad to dole out the responsibility to carry weapons and to use them, to the youngest recruits, who see in the guns an opportunity to prove their mettle and earn more "respect." Such was the case with JJ, who "proved" himself as a nine-year-old by robbing a store with a handgun lent to him by the gang. Later on in the interview, JJ described experiencing an emotional high from a particular instance in which he fired the gun to commit a crime in another city:

> I went to my mother's house, washed my face, changed clothes and went racing back to the capital and I told the homies, "Now I'm a real man. I just [describes the crime] with *this* [referring to gun]. And anyone who gets mixed up with me is going to meet with *this mother*. That weapon had been my, like my God.

The excitement provided by weapons is not unique to young men in the Central American barrio. Forty years ago John Lennon sang of weapons as the young man's security blanket: "Happiness is a warm gun, Momma." Social psychologists have proven the song to be more than witty satire. A 2006 study of college males used a controlled experiment to test the impact of handling a handgun (versus handling a toy) on testosterone levels among thirty college males. Using pre- and post-tests of saliva samples, the researchers found a measurable increase in testosterone levels among the young men who had handled a weapon as well as higher levels of subsequent aggression (Klinesmith, Kasser, and McAndrew 2006). No wonder JJ felt like "a real man" when he showed the "warm" gun to his friends. For young men of the barrio, many of whom have been made to feel invisible by poverty, school problems, and wrecked home lives, carrying a weapon bestows a sudden, unquestionable "visibility" in the street. For nothing makes neighbors, pedestrians, or even middle-class professionals pay attention like carrying a loaded weapon under your belt.

"ADULT" PASTIMES

In addition to violent initiation rites, crime, and the aura of weapons, "adult" pastimes such as drug and alcohol abuse and sex also make the gang lifestyle attractive to many. Many ex-gang members spoke of drugs as a key feature of gang life that garners both the curiosity and the loyalty of barrio youth. A simple word search on *drogas* (drugs) among the interview transcripts produced 492 hits. Melchor described it this way, "What [kids] like the most [about the gang] is to be crazy, to get high, to do what you want." On the one hand, the attraction of youth to drugs and alcohol requires little explanation. Drugs and alcohol have the ability to make people feel good, and youth of all social classes worldwide seek opportunities to experiment with substances that offer a burst of endorphins, regardless of the physical, psychological, or social consequences that may follow. Central American youth from the barrio are no different in this regard. But other social factors enhance the attraction to drugs and alcohol even more for marginalized youth. Sustained use and abuse of alcohol and drugs offers an easy escape in the form of a high that dulls the pain of having been shamed and marginalized. Several youth reported using drugs, especially chemical glue in order to escape the grief of an abusive home. Furthermore, drug and alcohol abuse, which are typically understood as "grown-up behavior," give adolescents and pre-adolescents a way to feel like adults. Pancho remembered that smoking dope made him "feel like a man." Also, drinking and taking illegal drugs allow gang members to assert their independence by breaking cultural taboos. In addition to the "chemical" high produced by the narcotic itself, barrio youth experience an emotional high from asserting their independence through risky "adult" behavior while building solidarity through participating in a corporate ritual.

Solidarity and violence, including substance abuse, important though they are as "pull" factors making the gang attractive, do not tell the whole story. A third factor attracts especially young boys—sex. The Colombian scholar Mauricio Rubio observes that access to sex and girls is an often-overlooked feature of gang life perhaps because it does not fit the Marxian paradigm interpreting the gang as a means of economic survival (2007). Gang interventionists like Santos at the Salvadoran Fe y Alegría youth center agree: "First and foremost is [a factor] that nobody seems to mention—sex. Adolescent boys join because they can get sex there." Pancho remembered watching with awe as the gang members attracted the attention of the "best girls" of his neighborhood. The same impression was shared widely among the youth who cited sex as instrumental in their early fascination with the gang. Osvaldo, a former Honduran leader of the MS-13, remembered his own experience:

> The truth is, when you enter the gang you're young, a kid, you don't reason well . . . It's a flock, a hobby right? At first it's all, "Look at all the nice women!" you know, ". . . drugs, alcohol." . . . There are times when women [have sex with] three, four, five six, even sometimes the whole gang. That was their thing. So when I joined the gang I saw all of this as really nice.

Osvaldo reported that gang leaders often "used" girls as a recruiting tool in order to attract young boys to their cell before the opposition could reach them. As a reward for joining the gang, new members were allowed to "choose" among three or four "available" female partners. Gangs refer to young women, especially those who consort with the gang, as *jainas*, generally associating them with loose sexuality and opportunities for exploitation.[9]

Like drugs and alcohol, the "attractiveness" of early and abundant sex for young males requires little explanation. After all, what could possibly be more alluring to adolescent and pre-adolescent boys than sex? But simply addressing this feature of the gang as a biological desire would be to miss an important point. Part of what makes sex attractive to young males is its symbolic association with power and manhood (Connell 2005). Sex is, after all, an interactive ritual, not merely a biological act (Collins 2004). In the context of the machista barrio, sex represents to young boys a combination of adult independence and self-assertion. Ronaldo's description of "access" to girls makes clear this symbolic attraction of sex:

> First when I was small, when I was like nine, it started when we would go down to swim in the river, since the river was close and maybe we used to look at the guys that had tattoos and they would tell us how great (*macizo*) the gang was, that it was nice, that they had lots of *jainas*, lots of women. They used to talk a lot about the chicks. "The girls pay attention to you!" they would say. When you're just a kid, that's what you want, girls. You want to be the Daddy of all of the girls right? The Rich Daddy (*Papi Rico*) of all of the girls. That's what it was like when we'd go swimming.

More than simply a means of meeting a biological desire or of experiencing recreation, Ronaldo's account illustrates how sex for the male gang members provides a means of accessing and communicating power. Nor was his account exceptional. I asked many former gang members what they liked best about life in the gang and although many spoke of camaraderie, weapons, and drugs, sex was usually near the top for the men. Enrique, the Salvadoran former MS member who joined in the early 1990s, answered my inquiry about the "best part" of being a gang member matter-of-factly: "To fuck," he said. "To have the best chicks."

Sometimes sex is forced. Many news stories report rape on the part of gang members, who threaten to eliminate family members who press charges. Two of the ex-gang members I interviewed recalled having participated in instances of gang rape and others acknowledged its prevalence. Such mixing of violence and sexuality was sometimes described as having been aimed at shaming a rival gang leader by attacking his partner or his sister or by simply spreading fear and insecurity in the territory of a rival gang. But in most cases, interviewees reported that young girls who participated were willing sex partners, perhaps enamored themselves of the power, money, and manner of the gang members. Although my data do not allow for a thorough comparison of perspectives from a sizable sample of female gang members, it should surprise no one that none of the four women I interviewed named sex as an attractive aspect of gang life. While one young woman did mention having taken part in the practice of sharing partners, two others named female companionship and solidarity as key in their decision to join. They reported having to "look out for each other" in view of the male gang members' well-known intentions toward them. Doubtless, such rituals are rarely mutually satisfying given the power differential involved, and it may be the case that the young women who provide sex for the male youth are obtaining other goods while allowing the male gang members to build a macho persona as, in the words of Ronaldo, "Papi Rico." Furthermore, as is the case with drug and alcohol use, having sex is associated with manhood. The pre-adolescent who visits a prostitute or "chooses" his partner feels as though he has come of age. Thus abundant sex, more than just a biological attraction, provides a means for male barrio youth to assert their own efficacy, accessing emotional energy, often by humiliating young women, and escaping, for a time at least, the shame spiral.

THE SOCIAL SOURCES OF SHAME

Although the experience of shame is a universal aspect of being human, the experience of chronic shame is not evenly or randomly distributed throughout societies (Gilligan 1996). The reason for this skewed distribution has much to do with the structural exclusion of stratified societies in which whole sectors of the population have relatively few opportunities to access the cultural goods that reflect positively on them, garnering the respect or "recognition" of others (Honneth 1995). Poverty in Central America is widespread, but it also exists alongside great concentrations of wealth. The result magnifies the shame of the poor due to relative deprivation (i.e., the sense of being deprived of resources that others take for granted). In Table 3.1, statistics from the United Nations' most recent development reports show that both poverty and stark inequality characterize all three countries of the Northern Triangle.

On the one hand, low levels of income per capita and a high percentage of the population living on less than $2/day mean that thousands of Central American youth grow up in grinding poverty. But the pyramid-like nature of wealth distribution is even more pronounced in these countries. According to both the Gini index, which measures the overall variation in income levels within a country, and the ratio of the income of the richest to the poorest 20 percent within a country, the countries of El Salvador, Guatemala, and Honduras all show higher levels of income inequality than do their neighbors to the north (Mexico) and to the south (Costa Rica and Nicaragua) making them the most economically stratified societies in the region. Thus, a youth living in a poor neighborhood of San Pedro Sula or San Salvador grows up in the midst of a society deeply divided by class. In this context, barrio youth, who tend to have darker skin and less obvious European facial features,

TABLE 3.1. Select Economic Indicators for Mesoamerica

	Human development rank (2009)	*Per capita GDP (PPP)**	*Population living below $2/day (%)*	*Gini Index***	*Ratio of richest 20% to poorest 20%*
Mexico	53	14,104	4.8	48.1	12.8
Costa Rica	54	10,842	8.6	47.2	15.6
El Salvador	106	5,804	37.2	49.7	20.9
Honduras	112	3,796	50.7	55.3	17.2
Guatemala	122	4,562	56.2	53.7	20.3
Nicaragua	124	2,570	47.9***	42.3	8.8

*Adjusted for purchasing power parity.
**The Gini index lies between 0 and 100 with 100 representing absolute inequality.
***This statistic refers to data from a year prior to 2000.
(*Source*: United Nations Human Development Programme 2009a.)

find themselves under extraordinary pressure to consume, since it is by wearing brand-name clothing, carrying a late-model cell phone, or shopping in an American-style mall that a youth "proves" that he or she is not poor.

In addition to the shame due to relative deprivation in societies with steep economic pyramids, a weak and underfunded public schooling system reduces the odds that youth from poor families will be able to "study their way out" of poverty. In the early 2000s El Salvador's spending on education was equivalent to 2.8 percent of its overall GDP (gross domestic product) compared with 4.9 percent spending in Costa Rica and 5.4 percent in Mexico. Nicaragua, with a lower overall income, spent 3.1 percent of its GDP on education. Although recent figures are not available for Honduras and Guatemala, in the early 1990s these countries spent relatively little on education. Honduras, at 3.8 percent, spent more as a percentage of its GDP than did El Salvador or Nicaragua, but far less than Cost Rica or Mexico as a proportion of its meager income. Meanwhile Guatemala, at 1.3 percent virtually ignored education preferring instead to spend its resources on a military sector. While spending on education has increased in Guatemala and El Salvador since the war years of the 1980s and 1990s, neoliberal economic policies aimed at reducing the size of government and privatizing social services have kept these nations from investing sufficient resources in public education. These statistics help to illustrate why public schools in northern Central America face an uphill battle to provide youth with hope and the means to achieve prestige by way of academic performance (United Nations Development Programme 2009b). Indeed, in major cities where gangs are prevalent, attending a public school is itself a sign of poverty since even working-class parents with meager resources seek to help their children succeed by enrolling them in one of thousands of private "bilingual" schools.

Finally, the experiences of child abuse and absentee parenting—which generated deeply emotional responses among many of the ex-gang members—also have roots in the economic structures and labor markets of northern Central America. Increases in migration, especially to the United States, have disrupted many family networks and placed emotional strain on parent-child relations. Although exact numbers reporting the increase in emigration of Central Americans are difficult to find since many if not most Central Americans emigrants to the United States are undocumented, data from the Pew Hispanic Center and the latest UN Report suggest a general increase in the rate of migratory flows northward in the 1990s and the early 2000s (Passel 2004; UNDP 2009b). Table 3.2 shows the staggering rate of emigration among Salvadorans, who migrate almost exclusively to the United States.[10]

Perhaps even more important than the overall increase in migration is a trend that a number of scholars have called the "feminization of migration" (Ehrenreich and Hochschild 2003). Globalization patterns have eroded the traditional industrial and agricultural employment opportunities in the "middle countries" of the developing world, such as Mexico and Central America, while a new class of global financiers has emerged in "global cities" of the North. More and more upper-middle-class women have entered the professional workplace and few men have altered their work or career patterns to compensate. This trend has created a "care deficit" in the private realm that has increasingly been addressed through the influx of "global women" who migrate in order to send remittances to address the increasingly precarious finances of their own homes. The care deficit has generated increasing demand for domestic and cleaning work in homes, day-care centers,

TABLE 3.2. Select Emigration Indicators for Mesoamerica

Country	*Emigration rate (%) 2000–2002**	*Remittance inflow as a percent of GDP (2007)*	*U.S. residency requests (in thousands) by country of origin: 1990s*
Mexico	9	3	2757
El Salvador	14.5	18.4	273
Guatemala	4.9	10.6	126
Honduras	4.3	24.5	72
Nicaragua	9.1	12.1	80
Costa Rica	2.6	2.3	17

*The number of emigrants of a country as a percentage of the total of its residents. (Source: United Nations Human Development Programme 2009a.)

and elder homes of the industrialized world (Sassen 2003).[11] Central American immigrant mothers, like millions of their counterparts around the world, find themselves saddled with the Herculean task of providing parenting and income from afar. Not surprisingly, many of the children and youth left behind in the care of grandparents, aunts, uncles, or even siblings have difficulty coming to grips with their parents' decision to migrate. Many feel the absence as one more contributor to the shame of being culturally and socially deprived.

In sum, although the experience of shame is a deeply personal experience, the sources of shame can be traced to the institutions and policies that perpetuate endemic poverty, weak schools, and precarious family systems in the barrios of northern Central America. In effect, the concept of shame represents the intervening variable between these negative social phenomena and a small army of youth who have chosen to abandon traditional pathways to economic stability and respect in favor of the dangerous and frequently violent shortcuts offered by the gang. My explanatory framework is not entirely unique. In some respects, the approach I have taken resembles Elijah Anderson's description of youth violence in his book titled *Code of the Street: Decency, Violence, and the Moral Life of the Inner City* (1999). In his widely read ethnography of life on the precarious inner-city streets of Philadelphia, Anderson describes the "code of the street" as a "set of prescriptions and proscriptions, or informal rules of behavior organized around a *desperate search for respect* that governs public relations" in the ghetto (1999:10 [emphasis added]). Although Anderson's work examines life on the streets of the inner city, not just gang life, he sees the dealers in the drug gangs as most clearly embodying the code. These men are on a continual quest for respect (which Anderson also describes as "juice," "personal power," and "credibility") and thus must be constantly on the lookout for any hint of disrespect since "dissing" erodes one's credibility.[12] The result is an inner city rife with violence, much of which is aimed at preempting disrespect from others by humiliating them first. Of course, as Anderson makes clear, the root of the problem lies not in corrupt or neurotic individuals but in social structures that have generated hopelessness and alienation through a combination of disappearing jobs, underfunded schools, an eroded family structure, and racist or

ineffective law enforcement. Having experienced racism as part of mainstream society and its institutions, these youth give up on the "decent" lifestyle, with its trust in the future and its belief in personal responsibility, and adopt instead a disposition projecting individual dominance, implying "If you mess with me, there will be consequences" (Anderson 1999:313).

By highlighting the role of emotions, my approach reveals that the quest for respect, far from a neurotic obsession, is rooted in a thoroughly human desire to escape shame and access pride. In the barrios of Central America that quest for pride/respect has been institutionalized by the gangs in the form of clecha—a system of symbols, rules, and status codes built on the attempt to ward off shame by adopting a coherent identity, sharing rituals and symbols, and humiliating others. Whether through its offer of drugs, alcohol, and abundant sex; its recognizable identity; or its participation in violence, the gang offers barrio youth an escape route from shame via a shortcut to respect. As Pancho put it, after joining the gang, "I felt like I had more respect, you know. More respect."

PATHWAYS: WHY SOME YOUTH DO NOT JOIN

Not everyone who grows up in an impoverished Central American barrio, or who experiences a chaotic home or school, joins a gang. In fact, many urban youth "walk" with the gang for a time, some becoming sympathizers, but ultimately choose not to join for one reason or another. Although many of these youth also experience the disenfranchisement of poverty and family or school problems, they never formally join the gang. Though my research design was not created in order to establish causal certainty regarding a bounded set of factors for joining the gang, I did interview a dozen Central American youth who had been gang sympathizers but had eventually chosen not to be jumped-in. In addition, some of the men who currently work with gang members to try to help them escape and establish alternative lifestyles were themselves natives of the same communities in which they worked. In a few cases, these young men had grown up alongside the young men they were now assisting in leaving the gang, but the facilitators themselves had never joined the gang.

The reasons for not joining varied widely. Not surprisingly, some youth cited strong family ties as factors that caused them to second-guess their decision to become sympathizers, and to ultimately reject the gang lifestyle. Thus, parents who provide a stable, or even semistable, home can play a key role in helping adolescent sympathizers break ties with gang members. In some cases these parents could, by sending their child to another region, help him or her to break ties with the local gang cell. On the other hand, the interviews made it clear that some parents' best efforts were thwarted by youth who seemed determined to join the gang. Other youth reported success in school as key to helping them decide to keep studying and move away from the gang. During the "chequeo" stage in which sympathizers are "checked-out" for their gang promise—and are themselves evaluating at some level the costs and benefits of actually joining—some youth discovered, often because of an encouraging teacher, that they showed academic promise. One such Honduran youth, Aldo, decided to stay in school rather than join the Wonder 13 gang as most of his friends were doing. He was proud to report that he was nearing his high school graduation and planning already to attend the university. His was a rare story of success for a youth in his neighborhood. In other cases, the reasons for not joining the gang seemed more random. Nathán, the eldest sibling of Leti, never became a gang member *or* a sympathizer even though his sister and many of his friends did so. When their mother left for Los Angeles, Nathán was already thirteen years old and for a time the responsibility of looking after his three younger siblings fell on him. Nathán became a father at fifteen, shortly after his siblings were taken in by an aunt and her abusive husband. Although the relationship with the mother of his eldest child did not last, Nathán soon became involved with another woman whom he later married and with whom he had four more children. Thus, while many of his friends were founding the local Vatos Locos *clica*, Nathán became "sidetracked" by family responsibilities—both to his siblings and to his children. Nor was early fatherhood the only factor distracting Nathán from *la vida loca* enjoyed by his friends in the gang. Soon after uniting, Nathán and his fourteen-year-old partner began attending the local Mennonite church, and, at the behest of the pastor, were later married.

Thus, it appears that in Nathán's case, early fatherhood may have been instrumental in causing him to seek stability in the church, rather than the risk-prone lifestyle offered by the gang. Affiliating with the church took him even further in the direction of a domestic lifestyle and made gang life seem alien, even though Nathán continued to live in poverty and had long since abandoned school.

How then do we make sense of these diverging pathways? If joining the gang is indeed a *process* that only some youth complete, what theoretical tools might help us make sense of the divergence? One way to do so is to borrow theoretical insights from another, related subfield of sociology, that of social movements. Doing so involves changing the question from, "Why do some youth 'end up' in the gang while others 'escape' it?" to "Why are some youth successfully *mobilized* into the gang while others are not?" Viewed from this angle, joining the gang involves a process of "weeding out" or "winnowing down" a large population of youth into a small group of gang joiners. In an important paper published in the 1980s, Dutch sociologists Bert Klandermans and Dirk Oegema developed a four-stage model for determining why some people join a social movement while others do not (Klandermans and Oegema 1987). In their model, protest participants were made up of a select group of individuals who (1) believed in the cause, (2) met requirements that made them targets for mobilization, (3) were motivated to participate, and (4) did not face competing time commitments. Although the resemblance is far from perfect, when we compare joining a gang to joining a movement, we can see similar stages of mobilization at work. Figure 3.1 provides a graphic illustration of the adaptation of Klandermans and Oegema's four-stage model to the phenomenon of the gangs.

Stage 1 illustrates the stratification and urbanization involved in the first step of mobilizing gang youth. Almost all Central American gang members come from impoverished urban neighborhoods. Very few middle-class youth or youth from agricultural communities join gangs. Middle-class youth, nearly all of whom attend private schools, and many of whom are involved in extracurricular activities or simply not allowed to spend time in unstructured activity *en la calle* (on the street), are both protected from the gang environment and encouraged to develop concrete life plans and trajectories. By contrast, gangs have an audience in

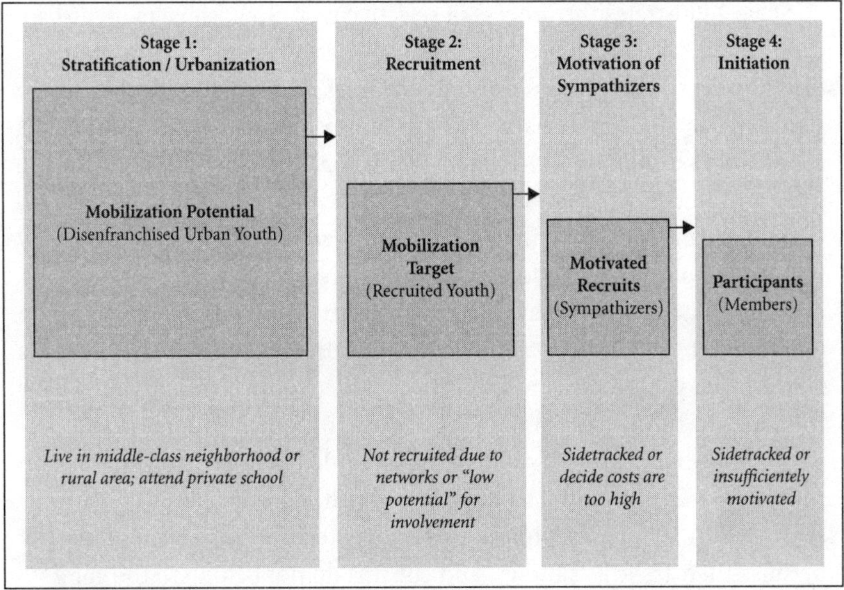

FIGURE 3.1. provides a visual illustration of a four-stage model for understanding how Central American youth are successfully mobilized to join the gang. The dark gray area represents the minority of youth actually selected at each stage. The light gray area represents those "weeded out" at each stage of mobilization.

the marginal barrio since most children in these dense neighborhoods walk to school and run errands to the corner store or *tortillería* every day. For all of these reasons gang leaders and members spend little time or energy recruiting sympathizers in middle-class gated communities, at exclusive private schools, or in very rural areas. Among Central American youth, the mobilization potential is made up of children and adolescents from the impoverished, densely populated, urban barrio. According to the UN's most recent estimates, just over half of the population in northern Central America lives in urban areas (the percentage is somewhat higher in El Salvador) and about half again live under the poverty line (37 percent in El Salvador) (UNDP 2009a). Since the poverty rate is lower in urban areas than in the countryside, it is safe to assume that considerably less than a quarter of Central American youth are ever even at risk of joining a gang.

Stage 2 illustrates the process of selective recruiting, since many urban, disenfranchised youth are never actively recruited by a gang member. Gang leaders, who possess limited resources and social networks, know that even in the urban barrio where family resources are limited and schools weak, many children and youth make poor candidates for the gang and thus make poor candidates for recruitment. Thus, gang members are far more likely to invest their mobilization efforts strategically by targeting children and adolescents from precarious or violent families or by approaching children who have already demonstrated an ability to use "street logic" in petty crime or violence. In fact, journalistic accounts suggest that gang members specifically target youth whose parents have migrated to the United States (Preston 2010). Furthermore, social networks, especially those of siblings and extended family, provide common means of "reaching out" to mobilize youth. Children and teens from strong families are less likely to be targeted for recruitment simply because their friends, siblings, and cousins do not belong to the gang.

Stage 3 illustrates the fact that many urban, disenfranchised youth who are actively recruited by the gang resist these attempts by choosing not to become "sympathizers." They may share the gang's oppositional subculture and admire its symbols and pastimes, but these youth do not decide to enter the three- to six-month-long period of chequeo and therefore never become "sympathizers" in any formal sense.[13] Instead, they become "sidetracked" by other activities and life plans. Nathán was far too busy taking care of siblings and, soon afterward, with finding a steady income to support his own family to be interested in the gang. Joining a local congregation, with its high demands on personal lifestyle issues and its many evening services, further helped to restrict his time and energies to the domestic sphere.

Youth who do become sympathizers and enter chequeo do so because they are highly motivated. Their motivation stems from a combination of both the "push" factors of having experienced shame as a result of poverty, abuse, and school problems and the "pull" factors of attraction to the gang's offer of solidarity, violence, and sex. It is the job of the jumped-in gang members and the leaders to present these attractions without making them entirely accessible, since doing so would eliminate the need to actually join the gang. In other words, an "at-risk" youth targeted for recruitment (mobilization) into the gang may be more or less motivated to join based not only on the gang's ability to promote its ideology, symbols, and lifestyle benefits but also on a youth's own prior experiences of abandonment and rejection. Scheff's "shame spiral" helps to explain the intense motivation of youth attracted to the gang's high-risk offer of escape through exciting, solidarity-inducing rituals of crime and violence. Youth caught in a "shame spiral" are especially susceptible to viewing the gang's offer of solidarity, sex, and violence as a highly attractive means of escaping shame and accessing pride.

Nevertheless, not all sympathizers decide to become formally jumped-in members. In the final stage of mobilization, one which Klandermans and Oegema label the "removal of barriers," only a fraction of sympathizers undergo baptism and formally join the gang. Of course, in the gang, as distinct from a social movement, nonparticipants' reasons for not joining have little to do with busy schedules or conflicting time commitments but rather to serious doubts about the relationship of costs and benefits to becoming a full-fledged gang member. For some sympathizers the time of chequeo proves ultimately unconvincing or too risky. A police crackdown or a spate of gang killings in the neighborhood may cause them to second-guess their earlier decision before it's "too late"—that is, before their own baptism makes them permanent members. Such events, whether local or national, can sometimes serve to remind sympathizers of the high costs associated with being a gang member. A few former sympathizers in Honduras who came of age in the early 2000s mentioned the "hunt-down" of gang members unleashed by the Maduro administration in 2002–2006 as a factor causing them to reevaluate their intentions to join the gang. The fear of being killed or arrested presented a psycho-social "barrier" to joining the gang. Just as important as "barriers" though, are the distractions, which can ultimately sidetrack sympathizers. Aldo, a Honduran sympathizer, cited success in school as well as increasing gang violence as factors leading him to abandon his friends and avoid following through with a baptism.

In the end, such barriers or distractions are not enough to sidetrack highly motivated youth. Beto became more active in the gang *after* the birth of his daughter despite the potential such an event held for distracting him by shifting his attention to a different moment in the life course. Nor were increases in gang killings or mass arrests and incarcerations of gang members enough to stop Central American youth from joining the gang. For youth experiencing a spiral of shame, "rational" evaluations of long-term costs (incarceration or death) versus short-term benefits (access to respect) may be difficult if not impossible. Similarly, Klandermans and Oegema note that in the final stage, overcoming "barriers" to participation may have more to do with a sympathizer's level of motivation than the movements' supposed ability to "remove" such barriers (1987:529).

My point here is not to try to bestow legitimacy on a violent organization by comparing it with a social movement as some scholars have done with less violent gangs in the United States (Barrios 2007; Brotherton 2007). Rather, viewing gang affiliation as a "weeding out" process reminds us of the processual nature of joining the gang and highlights the impact of social structures on the interactive experience. Social structural factors such as poverty, migration, and meager social spending expand the population of disenfranchised barrio youth, making them more susceptible to being targeted for gang recruitment than rural or middle-class youth even while micro-contextual factors such as abuse, abandonment, and school problems contribute to the likelihood that youths will be motivated to join the gang by laying the psychosocial groundwork for the experience of chronic shame. In this environment, the gang markets its symbols, values, and pastimes to frustrated youth as attractive and "worth the risk." They accomplish this by allowing children and youth a "taste" of the gang life in recruitment and chequeo. Sympathizers are then encouraged and further "motivated" to join the gang during the time of chequeo through increased interaction and new access to weapons, drugs, and sex. Eventually, some youth decide that the benefits do not outweigh the risks of joining. Others choose to go through with baptism. By the time these youth have received their first tattoo, they have passed through several stages of selection and view themselves as an elite few, ready to experience the benefits and take on the risks of the gang lifestyle—permanently.

CONCLUSION

Most studies of Central American gangs tend toward either an individualistic explanation or an oversocialized account of why Central American youth join gangs. For some, Central American youth join a gang because they have an innate psychological tendency toward violence (Bruneau 2005) or because poverty or social exclusion literally drives them into the gang (Foro Ecuménico por la Paz y la Reconciliación 2006). But examining gang entry through the lens of the sociology of emotions makes the decision to join a gang more comprehensible while rendering the risky, violent-prone nature of life in the gang more intelligible. Furthermore, the approach allows us to specify how social forces actually shape youth toward joining the gang and which features of gang life make the gang attractive for precisely these youth. In short, the experience of poverty, family problems, and educational difficulties contribute to a spiral of shame among some barrio youth. This experience of "chronic shame" gives rise to a desperate search for pride and self-confidence. The gang, with its symbolic rituals of baptism, tattooing, violence and access to drugs and weapons, and macho sexuality looms large as a potential source of the seemingly elusive pride known as *el respeto*. Barrio youth in search of *respeto* can "try out" the gang lifestyle as a sympathizer, learning of its symbols and structure, and tasting the thrill of emotional energy. When cell leaders deem a youth ready for entrance, he can choose, like Pancho, to take the final step of ritual solidarity and prove his loyalty in an act of symbolic sacrifice that provides the gang with excitement and enhanced solidarity. And while many sympathizers choose not to join the gang, perhaps because they have other more promising pathways to emotional energy available to them, those who do decide to join, have, by the time of the baptism, already been thoroughly groomed toward the chaotic world of *la vida loca*. In short, the gang provides youth like Pancho a means of escaping the shame spiral, at least for a time, by providing them with a cohesive family-like social network and by showing them how to transform shame into anger and vengeance. The result is an exhilarating—and dangerous—sense of personal potency. "Now" said Pancho, "I felt stronger."

4
Dodging the Morgue Rule

Leaving the gang is like losing your identity. It is worse than being assassinated. It is a social death.
—Ricardo Falla, S.J., Guatemalan sociologist

The gang commits, obliges, formats, and marks for life—like a tattoo.
—Mauricio Rubio, Colombian gang scholar

Getting in is easy. The hard part is getting out.
—Camilo, Honduran former M-18 leader

The gang keeps its eye on you at all times. The gang knows what I do, where I live, and what I think. And sometimes I think they even know what I eat.
—Pancho, Honduran former MS-13 member

On September 18, 2007, twenty-three-year-old Antonio was walking with his wife[1] on a sidewalk near the Market Terminal in Zone 9 of Guatemala City. Antonio, who had left the M-18 three years earlier, was shopping for supplies for his shoe shine and repair business, when two armed youth grabbed him from behind and shoved his wife to the ground. Just before the young men opened fire, Antonio shouted to his wife to run away. Moments later, Antonio, who had spent his teenage years in the gang and was one of the most articulate subjects interviewed for this study, was dead from gunshots to the head. His wife, also a former member of the gang and still grieving a second miscarriage that would have been their first child, was left to pick up the pieces of a second chance cut short. As is typically the case with murders of youth suspected of having ties (past or present) to the gang, the police did not open a formal investigation and no criminal charges were ever filed.

Antonio's life in the gang, which he described to me in an interview two months earlier, bore many similarities with the experience of other gang members in the region. He had joined the gang at age thirteen, frustrated by his family's poverty, ashamed of an alcoholic mother, and angered by a stepfather who showed favoritism toward Antonio's step-siblings. As a fifteen-year-old he learned accidentally of the source of his mother's lifelong struggle with alcoholism—she had been raped by her own father. Incest had resulted in the birth of Antonio's older brother. Antonio, ashamed and angry, decided to channel his shame-filled rage into a budding career as a gang member. Describing the process of learning about the incest of his mother, Antonio's voice trembled and grew barely audible: "I said to myself, 'Now I see the problem.' I started to understand my Mom and her alcoholism, and all that she had done for us in spite of this. [pause, voice returning to normal] So I went deeper into the gang. . . . I started spreading havoc." In place of a dysfunctional family that brought shame, dead-end poverty, and favoritism, Antonio found in the gang a family that, at least in the beginning, offered mutuality, opportunity, and a road to "respect."

> I fought for my barrio. When I entered, I found there what I'd never experienced in my house—acceptance and support. Maybe not support of the kind like, [in a grandmother-like a tone of mockery] "Oh come here, you!" No. Support in the sense of understanding. "Want a cigarette? Here, have one of mine. Want a drink? Here have one of ours." That was what made me feel good. Meanwhile in my house my Mom drank all the time but wouldn't let me near the stuff.

Antonio began smoking marijuana and crack, and at sixteen, soon after he learned of his family's traumatic secret, he began selling drugs as well. About the same time, the gang cell to which Antonio belonged began to, in his words, "evolve." Violence became more commonplace. Drive-by shootings, called a *draiver* in the anglicized lingo of the gang, had earlier been prohibited in the M-18 *clica* to which Antonio belonged, but now drive-by's were being ordered with great frequency. Violence and murder were increasingly directed not simply at members of the opposing gangs but at non-gang members including neighbors and business owners. In addition to selling drugs, Antonio began collecting extortion fees called *la renta* (rent). His tattoos, including the digits "1–8" on opposite temples of his face, made him an easy-to-spot target for police. At the age of nineteen he was arrested and incarcerated for the twelfth time, but this time he was charged as an adult and sent to prison. While there, he witnessed the killing of two friends from his own *clica*, killed by the gang itself for "misconduct." Although leaving the gang had become increasingly difficult, Antonio wanted out.

> At that point I thought to myself, "I'm nineteen years old. ¡*Puchica!*[2] I've been in jail twelve times. I've been shot [in the back] once. Brought right to the point of death. And I've been shot at many times. . . ." I said to myself, "Is this really what I want for my life?"

One component of the "evolution" of the gang involved the tightening of restrictions prohibiting desertion. Antonio and other ex-gang members reported that earlier in the life of the gang, leaders granted permission to leave for gang members who had "done their part" for the gang. But increasingly, gang members were being denied a safe exit. By 2004, when Antonio decided he had had enough, he knew better than to ask for his "squares." "I knew that if I asked permission, they weren't going to give it to me anyway. Five, six years ago maybe they would have. Not anymore." So Antonio did what many other experienced gang members have done. He fled to another region of the city. Distance, he hoped, and the "file" that the gang keeps of its members' record of participation during gang life, would offer him at least a modicum of safety since gang leaders could look back and remember his contributions to the barrio. Safety from his former fellows, it turned out, was only one of many obstacles he had yet to overcome. At the advice of a friend, Antonio had the tattooed numbers "1" and "8" "erased" from his temples using a painful infrared method involving multiple treatments, and he began wearing band-aids over the smaller tattoos on his neck. Like many former gang members, he worried that the visible scars left from "erased" tattoos could earn him more problems from his former gang mates than the original tattoos themselves had brought from police. But the growing demonization of the gang meant that police were now arresting tattooed youth with little regard for their actual behavior or current membership status. And Antonio had no intention of returning to prison.

Only a year after seeking anonymity in the home of his grandmother, he was shot once again, this time while visiting his mother in his former neighborhood. The assailants were two adolescent recruits "probably in *chequeo*" he guessed, and thus hoping to gain a quick entrance into the gang by demonstrating their willingness to kill a deserter. Antonio managed to escape this incident with "merely" a few bullet wounds—one in his hand and one in each leg. But by this time, Antonio realized that he was a marked man, living, perhaps, on borrowed time. He managed to land a job washing cars for US$20 a week and moved to yet another area of Guatemala City, this time with his girlfriend who was also escaping the gang. After learning the skill of bread baking at a government-sponsored project for reforming gang members, he began teaching bakery workshops at the rehab center, earning him his post-gang moniker *el Panadero*, "the Bread Maker." Later, he would participate in a special reality TV show aired nationally called "Challenge 10." The show, a creative take on "The Apprentice," brought ten ex-gang members to live together in a house while trying to make a new start as entrepreneurs. A well-known Guatemalan entrepreneur offered "life lessons" to the youth, divided into two business teams. Most of the gang members wore masks during taping to avoid being identified but by the end of the two weeks of filming, several of the youth, including Antonio, had concluded that it was safe enough to stop wearing them. Five youth worked at a car wash while the other five worked at a shoe shine and repair shop. The "challenge" was to see which group could produce the more effective business model.

When I met Antonio, some six months after the airing of the show, he was the only former participant in the reality show who continued to be employed at the shoe shine and repair shop, essentially taking it over as his own when the others left to find better-paying work.[3] The shop, located in a sleek high-rise complex called "Europlaza," could not support multiple employees although Antonio paid a younger brother to help him on occasion. He still wore the band-aids on either side of his neck, removing them only when we arrived at a secluded outdoor park where we conducted the first interview. At the time, Antonio was still grieving the death of his elder brother, also a former M-18 member, killed just two months earlier by the rival MS-13. And although Antonio himself had been shot twice, once during his gang tenure and once afterward, he spoke with a remarkable mix of realism and optimism:

> Right now I need to move [again] because there are a lot of guys in the area I live that are getting out of prison and they know me so I'll have to leave because to tell the truth, I still have problems with the gang. I have a green light [death warrant] for years now and if they haven't killed me yet it's because God is great and who knows what purpose he has for my life. I'm not a Christian and I don't go to church—why should I lie and say otherwise—but I know that when I stop to really think about it, it's God that has helped me and if it weren't for him who else would have stuck up for me?

That was in early July. By late September, Antonio, the Bread Maker and shoe shiner, at twenty-three years of age, was dead.

¡ME VOY! WHY GANG MEMBERS LEAVE

Why do some gang members try to leave the gang, and what are the challenges to doing so? The story of Antonio reveals some of the reasons gang youth grow weary of the gang lifestyle and illustrates the difficulty of abandoning the gang, made especially clear by the most intimidating barrier of all—the morgue rule. When a Central American youth joins a local cell of a transnational gang, he takes on what is supposed to be, and quite often *is in fact,* a lifelong commitment. Abandoning the gang at any age, he is told, is not in the cards. But the morgue rule is not absolute. Gang leaders make exceptions under certain circumstances, and gang cells are not always sufficiently competent or motivated to find and eliminate deserters. Still, in the minds of thousands of current gang members, exceptions to the morgue rule do not outweigh the utter finality of the cases in which the rule was applied to other homies. Whatever the actual reasons for Antonio's death, the message it sent was unmistakable: ex-homies beware!

Joining the gang provides access to pride—*respeto*—and an exhilarating escape from the shame spiral by way of experiences of violence, sex, and solidarity. But emphasizing the attractiveness of the gang life raises the question of why anyone would wish to leave in the first place. If the experience is so exhilarating, so "liberating" from shame, why should any youth reconsider his decision? Why not remain in the gang indefinitely? The ex-gang members I interviewed cited a wide variety of factors, including the desire to start a family, disillusionment upon learning the "reality" of gang life, and the fear of death. Interviews with gang experts and rehab workers echoed these claims. Sometimes the participants reported that the gang itself had begun to "wear them out" while at other times they spoke of having been inspired to leave by external relationships and experiences that "pulled" them toward establishing a new life outside the gang.

I did not conduct interviews with *active* members. Although such testimonies may well have contributed detail and an element of methodological rigor, I chose, principally for reasons of safety, not to make serious efforts to track down *current* gang members (see Appendix A for more about this methodological choice). Furthermore, as some gang experts in the United States have pointed out, testimonies of committed gang members are often aimed at impressing a listener or improving a negative image of a particular gang in society. Active gang youth committed to the barrio have been known to "feed outsiders and themselves a set of standardized answers" to inquiries about gang life and gang values (Spergel 1992). Instead of comparing the accounts of deserters to those of current gang members, my tools for measuring reliability involved comparing ex-gang members' accounts of their own reasons for leaving with factors cited by other former members as well as interviewing and spending time with many gang experts possessing years of experience in gang intervention.

WORN OUT AND FED UP

One of the most common complaints cited by the ex-gang members was that the gang lifestyle eventually became difficult or impossible to sustain. Many ex-gang members summed up their decision to leave the gang, whether made in a particular moment or over period of time, with the phrase, *"Me aburrí,"* or *"Me cansé"* (I got tired). Although a literal rendering of the phrase *"Me aburrí"* would be "I got bored," when used in Central America, the Spanish phrase does not imply a simple *ennui* such as that of an American teenager "bored" of playing a video game. A better translation might be "I got fed up with the gang" or "I became sick and tired of the gang" or simply, "The gang wore me out." Ivan, a former member of the MS-13 who joined the gang while living with his mother in New York City, put it simply, *"Me aburrí de esa vida"* (That life wore me out). What exactly wore him out? "Stealing cars, taking people's things, shouting at people that their stuff belonged to me." A Salvadoran, and former member of the M-18 said, "I was fed up (*aburrido*) with killing. Tired of bothering people." In effect, what begins as a thrilling game of daring, of showing off one's ability to take risks and intimidate others, can become, over time, a kind of duty or drudgery. Winning "respect" through violence and intimidation becomes more and more difficult to sustain as the stakes get higher. Ivan described the growing feeling of weariness brought on by the constant need to intimidate others and project strength:

> Every gang member pretends to be somebody but really when we do all of those things we have these moments when we get tired of being that person. I would lock myself in a room and cry to myself. I didn't want to be like that anymore and I would regret all the things I'd done. And after those moments when I would say, "That's it. No more. No more!" That's when I would get even worse and go out and do even worse things. But there comes a moment when you get tired (*cansado*) of hearing everyone say, "These guys are good for nothing."

In short, the gang's proposed "escape" from the shame spiral—violence and confrontation—offers only a fleeting respite and can become the source itself of further shame. This practice of suppressing or hiding shame, what Scheff calls "bypassing shame," has been theorized as a common source of violence among males (Gilligan 1996; Scheff 2004) since it leads to a vicious shame-rage spiral in which males, "ashamed of being ashamed" commit further violence in an unsuccessful attempt to deal with their shame (Retzinger and Scheff 1991). Similarly, Antonio "went deeper" into the gang after learning of his mother's incest. Feeling himself unable to *do* anything to address his family's secret shame, he became even more violent in the gang. But violence only postpones the experience of shame and, as Ivan's comment shows, committing violence provides new grounds for shame. After the congratulations, celebrations, and emotional thrill of the violent act wears off, the gang member remains a resident of a community and connected, even if only marginally, to family and neighbors who view such acts as "shameful." Committing violence and intimidating others with weapons "feels good" as long as one is surrounded and, to an extent, isolated by the gang, but the gang member cannot live completely isolated forever. Few youth sever family ties completely and most continue to live in the neighborhood of their childhood after joining the gang. Thus, they are not immune to the negative comments and the criticisms of those who see them as "good for nothing." Asked why he made the decision to try to leave the gang, Nelson, a former Vato Loco from Honduras said, "I did it for my family, and because people look down on you. Lots of people look down on you. They know that you're involved in making a ruckus and they call you a thief or worse. That's why I felt the need to leave." Nelson's comment illustrates that as the gangs became involved in more serious and violent forms of delinquent activity, belonging to a gang became, in itself, a source of shame for many gang youth.

Female ex-gang members also reported growing worn out with gang life. Olivia, who participated in the M-18 with her two older brothers, remembered feeling ashamed not of being looked down upon by family members—indeed, her own father was a professional thief who taught her how to steal. She complained instead of the feeling of being *feared* by her own family.

> While you're in the gang, it's true, you start to earn respect little by little but also . . . you get sick of it (*se aburre*). Sometimes I just wanted to be like the other girls that lived in tranquility and had their parents and their brothers and sisters, but my brothers and I, we learned so much while in the gang—and because of course they don't teach you anything good—that my mother came to fear us. She was afraid of all three of us. And what a terrible feeling when your own mother is afraid of you!

If Olivia's account is any indication, it may be that female gang members tend to feel ashamed of their violent behavior but for slightly different reasons. In traditionalist societies, such as Central America, that socialize young women to be nurturers and caregivers, especially toward relatives and immediate family, the prospect of being the daughter, sister, or friend who must be "feared" wears out quickly. In contrast, JJ did not report feeling ashamed or being concerned by his mother's fear of him. Instead, by his own testimony it seemed that he was pleased that "She would just give me whatever I asked for and then some."

Another reason that participating in violence and intimidation "wears out" as a means of bypassing shame is the "boomerang effect" of reciprocal violence. As Papachristos (2009) has argued concerning the gangs of Chicago, murder is a constant in the barrio. The gang helps direct murders and keeps the cycle going by ensuring that a gang murder will be felt as an assault not just on an individual but on the entire gang of the victim, warranting—demanding—a response in kind. The "boomerang effect" refers to fact that the longer a youth stays within the gang and the more authority he acquires, the more enemies he makes, and thus, his chances of falling victim to gang violence heighten. Increased notoriety comes with a price. Asked how he came to leave the gang, Ernesto, a Honduran who once led an M-18 cell, described his motivation this way:

> The problem was when my name started to circulate. My tattoo (*mi placa*), my nickname started growing. Now more gang members from the other gangs were starting to realize who I was and that I was a member of the M-18. That's when they started looking for me to kill me. So I decided to move away from the gang. I was tired of running.

Ernesto's account echoes JJ's recollection of sleeping with multiple weapons at his side as his growing *fama* as a White Fence cell leader resulted in an increasingly long list of enemies. Camilo, another Honduran who led a different M-18 cell, recounted similar pressures.

> After two years [as a gang member] they promoted me to gang leader and there I was apparently better off. But it was worse because then people were looking for me—members of opposing gangs and relatives of dead victims, the police and others.

But gang veterans have more to fear than those outside the gang. Death can also come at the hands of your own homies. Intra-gang violence escalated especially as drugs and weapons became increasingly available, raising the economic stakes both between and within gangs in the late 1990s and early 2000s. As the gang "evolved," the "band of brothers" often became a "band of rivals" since leadership came with economic, not just social, privileges. Antonio described the experience of watching the gang kill two friends from his own clique for "misconduct," and witnessing this was enough to start him rethinking his future and asking himself if the gang life was really worth it.

Nevertheless, leaving the gang is by no means a sure escape route from danger. Indeed, as Antonio's case and others illustrate, ex-gang members are often killed *after* leaving. Still, many gang members come to see their profile in the gang as the greatest threat to their own immediate security. Meme, a former member of the MS-13 in Honduras, recalled making the decision to leave the gang while still in prison:

> I spent six years in prison. At one point there were three hundred forty of us gang members in one module. Things happen there that if you don't have your mind clear, your own homies can betray you. They'll hang you because that's the way things work in prison. Things happened there while I was still active, that, well, that affected me directly. So one night a voice said to me, "Get out of this module. Leave because your own homies are going to kill you." So I listened to the voice. And that voice was God and he's the reason I'm here right now.

Meme's was not a generalized fear of risking death but a more concrete one, based, no doubt, on a no-nonsense assessment of his prospects if he continued in the presence of so many gang members. And although Meme himself admitted that leaving the module where the gang members were incarcerated was only the beginning of his journey out of the gang, it was clearly his fear of death—made plainer by what he experienced as the voice of God—that brought his situation into focus and compelled him to leave. Enrique, an early member of the Salvadoran MS-13 in San Salvador, decided to leave after he began to receive death threats. Raymundo, a Honduran former member of the Vatos Locos, came to fear the death squads that had begun eliminating members of the gang in his own neighborhood. Sometimes the death of a relative or companion made the threats of the gang seem more real and immanent. Three interviewees reported that the death of a biological brother who had been active in the gang was instrumental in their decision to leave. Rina fled to Mexico after her partner, also a gang member, was shot and killed by rival gang members. Several others, like Antonio, were wounded in gang shootings, and that experience helped kick-start their own reevaluation process. In other cases, nearly fatal shootings can force a member to seek a new start. Two Honduran interviewees, Ramón and Chuz, saw their gang careers come to an abrupt end when they were permanently disabled in gang shootings. Both men lost the use of their legs and are now confined to wheelchairs. Nevertheless, disablement aside, the fear of an early death while in the gang is neither a necessary nor a sufficient cause for leaving the gang. Several gang members, such as Antonio, who was hospitalized for months after receiving the first of multiple bullet injuries, actually responded to these brushes with death by deepening their involvement in the gang. Regardless, the experience stuck with them and many cited the memory of it as a motivator in their decision to leave months or even years later.

Other factors cited by ex-gang members as contributing to their growing unease with the gang, their "wearing out," were growing concerns about their own drug addiction and the fear of prison and the police. Sometimes substance abuse went hand in hand with the fear of death, such as in the case of JJ, whose lungs began to fail because of the combined maladies of a collapsed and dysfunctional lung from a shooting and the overuse of marijuana. Although JJ initially resolved to take the doctor's advice and leave the gang, he changed his mind after regaining his health and returning to his neighborhood. Still, the hospital visit was the first of several experiences causing him to reevaluate his future in the gang, where drugs and bullets were plentiful.

One less frequently cited feature of gang life leading some gang members to question their commitment is the failure of the gang to live up to its own ideals. Oscar, a Honduran who joined the M-18 after watching his deported uncle fall prey to opposition MS-13 members, found in the M-18 both a close-knit family and a means of earning respect. After "demonstrating" his ability to work for the gang both by eliminating enemies and by organizing drug sales, his crimes landed him in prison—an event he likened to "winning a Nobel prize" for the amount of respect it earned him within the gang. In prison he was

given the task of monitoring discipline for all M-18 members in the unit. Here, he oversaw early morning exercises, convinced sympathetic (some would say naïve) evangelical groups to donate weights and benches, and made sure all M-18 homies dressed and acted in a way that projected discipline and respect. However, his authority soon became a burden as he learned of the reality of decision making at the top:

> I was tough. But I believed in solidarity with our own. But these leaders were so tough that they started to forget about the gang itself and lost their sense of solidarity. I started to see how the leaders themselves would give orders to liquidate others on the outside, people that I knew, just for some little mistake. Sometimes I would even say, "No. No, don't do that." And they would say, "What are you saying? The majority rules." There were eight of us [leaders] and I knew that if you go against six or seven, they're going to ask you what you have against the barrio anyway. I did this once or twice but then the third time I didn't want to anymore. So they sent out to execute a member that I knew and had walked with and who, I knew, had done a lot for the barrio. He had killed who knows how many enemies of the MS and had lots of power on the outside and these guys by simply raising their hands were going to liquidate him. So I said, "This doesn't make any sense. If that's the way things work when I commit a little mistake, it means they're going to raise their hands and I'll be liquidated too. This is no family at all."

There are echoes in Oscar's account of "wearing out" given the imminence of death, but Oscar insisted that what caused him to tire most of the gang was his increasing sense that the gang had lost its way and no longer stood for mutuality and respect, at least among its own. Part of Oscar's idealism had been inspired by El Charo, a deported M-18 member whom Oscar met while in prison. El Charo claimed that the "original" vision of the M-18 gang in the United States had been one of solidarity and mutual aid in the face of a hostile society. "If one of our members didn't have shoes and we have three pairs, we would give him one. That was the ideology of El Charo, and mine too," said Oscar. In the prison meetings El Charo began to argue against selling drugs to children, saying that doing so violated the laws of the "original" M-18 code.

Shortly thereafter a vote was taken and El Charo was found dead of poisoning. That experience helped make up Oscar's mind. "I said to myself, 'I'm an M-18 for now, but when I get out of prison I'm getting out of the gang too.'"

I do not have sufficient evidence to establish as fact a widespread "loss of principles" within the transnational gangs of Central America. Still, Antonio's account of the "evolution" of the M-18 in Guatemala coincides with Oscar's report of increasing violence and chaos in the Honduran M-18 about the same time. Meanwhile, members of other gang members told similar accounts with similar timelines. Oscar, as well as others, attributed the change to increasing greed among the leaders of the gang as the drug trade opened new opportunities for income. Some ex-gang members and experts attributed increasing gang violence to the breaking of the *Pacto Sur* or "Southern Pact" which held that all Latino gangs were in fact part of the same "Southern race" and ought to, at the very least, keep their wars from spilling into public places.[4] The breaking of the Southern Pact, whether brought on by a specific altercation at a party in Los Angeles, as one gang expert reported, or simply because of the increasing availability of drugs and weapons, ultimately meant the escalation of open warfare between rival cliques. The ensuing chaos in the early 2000s changed the nature of gang affiliation, increasing criminality and causing more than one gang member involved in this study to conclude that if the barrio once stood for solidarity and respect, it now promoted only greed and violence.

FAMILY TIES

Not all factors contributing to a desire to leave the gang are internal to the gang itself. One topic that surfaced repeatedly in reports of gang exit was the influence of family. Edgar, a former Vato Loco, began to look for a way out when his mother became ill, soon after the death of his brother in a gang shooting. Wilmer, also a Vato Loco, began to rethink his future in the gang at the urging of his mother after his brother also died. He recalled his mother's words when she would visit him in prison: "'Son, get out of the gang. Get out!' She would say. 'Look at your brother.' So I began to think hard about this." Indeed, active mothers often played a key role in stimulating a process of introspection on the part of the gang member regarding the possibilities for exit. Many ex-gang members recalled particular encounters with their mother that spurred in them both a regard for the future and a sense of shame for their gang lifestyle at the time. Leonardo, who led a Honduran *clica* called "Sur-16," remembered returning to his home late one night after a shooting to find his mother in a feverish trance, literally "worried sick" about the safety of her son in the gang. Although he did not leave the gang immediately afterward, he felt ashamed for causing his mother such anguish and considered this a key moment in his reconsideration of the gang life. However, it was not only mothers who were responsible for instigating shame. After years of complete isolation from family, Pancho first began to consider the prospect of leaving when his grandmother, who had helped raise him as a child, visited him in prison. He recalled how she could not even recognize his tattoo-covered face and entreated the guard, "Please won't you bring me my grandson. This isn't him." Although he did not leave the gang then, Pancho recalled feeling deeply ashamed by the encounter. He missed and felt sorry for "this dear little old lady" who could not believe that the tattooed youth in front of her was her own grandson. Similarly, Leti never knew her father, and her mother lived in far-away Los Angeles, but her siblings played a key role in motivating her to leave.

> Once when I stopped in to the house my brother and two sisters were there and they were crying because they hadn't seen me in a long time. When I arrived Nathán just stared at me with this look of happiness and he said, "Sis!" And I, well, I turned around and put my head down. I was ashamed. And he got up, gave me a hug, and then started to cry. He said, "You're going to change, aren't you?" And I said, "Yes, I will." But then, I just waited for them to go back to what they were doing and I went right back to the streets.

As Leti's story makes clear, family ties merely provide an incentive for leaving. These ties alone were usually not enough by themselves to motivate, much less facilitate, a successful gang exit. Still, among the several factors consistently raised in interviews with ex-gang members, one's ties to family and the stress placed on them by gang membership were common elements in the motivation for rethinking the gang life. Even in the absence of real or strong family ties, the dream of starting one's own family motivated some youth to consider leaving. While few disenfranchised youth experience anything remotely akin to the tranquil scenes of the Holy Family pictured in the cathedrals and at Christmas, they are not immune to such ideals. Some respondents reported that as they grew older, they began to think about their own prospects for starting or having a family. Even though the gang itself initially played the role of surrogate family for such youth, as they approached adulthood and learned of the more brutal realities of the gang's "family values," the prospect of beginning a more traditional family gained attraction. Armando, a Honduran and former cell leader, had joined the gang after living the life of a street orphan for several years. Even before he met the woman he eventually married, he remembered beginning to wish for a more "normal life" despite never having experienced such a thing himself.

In other cases, the birth of a son or daughter caused a gang member to reflect on his or her future and motivated the gang member to desire to leave the gang in order to "formalize" and begin a family. The onset of parenthood is in fact a common theme in the literature on gangs in the United States going back as far as Thrasher's study of Chicago youth gangs in the early part of the twentieth century (Thrasher 1927). Evidence at the time indicated that as gang youth approached adult life, getting a job and starting a family became more attractive than gang life or street delinquency, and, thus, youths tended to leave the gang. Most gang members "aged out" of the gang. This pathway appears to hold true for gang youth in the United States (Klein 1995) where the prospects for earning an income in the formal economy, though far from certain, are more realistic than in the Central American barrio. Nevertheless, I was surprised to find many Central American youth had continued within the gang for years even after the birth of one or more children. Rina was in fact brought into the gang by her partner and continued her activity there after the birth of their child. Osvaldo, who formerly led a Honduran MS-13 *clica*, recalled that it was the presence of his four-year-old daughter that prompted him to make the decision to leave. Obviously, the mere arrival of parenthood was not enough to tip the scales toward leaving. Pablo, who joined the M-18 in Los Angeles, began to seriously reflect on the desire to settle down after being imprisoned in Guatemala, and then only when his two daughters began to grow older and he thought of the life he would miss if when he left prison he were to continue in the gang. Thus, it was not so much the onset of parenthood that prompted in gang members a desire to "settle down" but rather the culmination of a variety of factors among which the desire to live a more "normal" or domestic life played an important but not exclusive role.

Finally, in a number of cases that we examine later, evangelical religious experiences played a key role in creating or enhancing a desire to leave the gang. Although churches, pastors, and religious gang ministries did more to *facilitate* exit than to prompt a desire to leave, in several cases the church, a pastor, or a religious neighbor or relative provided an additional force of attraction toward life outside the gang.

So far I have tried to separate the internal factors that make life in the gang lose its luster from the external factors attracting them outward. But few interviewees actually separated these motives. Many spoke of the desire to "have a future" and followed up the expression with recollections about fearing an early death and wanting to have a family. Thus, the "internal" and "external" often worked in tandem. As life in the gang became more risky and precarious for leaders, non-gang family members began to exert pressure on them to leave the gang and settle down to a more domestic existence. Nor was the decision to leave a simple matter of rationally calculating changes in the costs and benefits of belonging to the gang. Rather, as life in the gang became increasingly oppressive, gang youth began considering the prospects of life beyond the gang for the first time and often this led them to begin seeking out contexts that would allow them to cultivate an identity not related to the gang.

BARRIERS TO LEAVING THE GANG

If social networks and cultural forces such as the desire to live a "normal" life and start a family entice gang members to leave, other social forces stand as barriers to leaving. Most gang members probably question their original decision to join at some point, but a great many of these youth, probably the majority, never manage to completely extricate themselves from the gang. In the United States, gang affiliation was traditionally seen as merely a "stage" of adolescence—albeit one often associated with street crime and delinquency. Even today most gang members in the United States are expected to eventually "mature out" of the gang (Boueke 2007b; Vigil 1988). A few highly involved leaders may stay on and remain active, but most will find a job or begin a family. In the Central American transnational gangs, however, all indications point to a much smaller percentage of youth who actually leave. Why is this the case? In the following section I describe three key barriers to leaving the gang mentioned by multiple ex-gang members in each country. These factors can be summed up in the parlance of the gang as *la morgue* (the possibility of being killed for leaving), *la vida loca* (a taste for risky, debilitating addictions), and *el chance* (the possibility of finding a job).

THE MORGUE RULE

There is a very simple reason why a great many gang members in Central America never leave the gang—they simply do not live long enough to get out. Their involvement with drug dealing and gun wielding eventually catches up with them in the form of the "boomerang effect" of homicides that ricochet around the barrio, ending the lives of teenage gang members long before they can "age out" of the gang. In other cases, "social cleansing" at the hands of police or local vigilantes ends gang members' lives before they can leave. I asked former gang members from each country and a variety of cliques to recall as best they could, the number of gang members formerly belonging to their own clique who were still alive. In nearly every case, the ex-gang members claimed that *a minority* of the original clique were still alive.[5] Following is an excerpt of a conversation I had with Emerson, an evangelical convert who left the M-18 following a dramatic conversion event in 2006:

> [*What about your former gang mates? Where are they now? The one's that didn't leave the gang?*]

> Hmm. Of the thirty-five of us in the clique, give or take a few, three or four are in prison, one serving a sentence of 106 years. Four others are Christians, of these only two are, you might say, doing well, and the other two have their ups and downs. The rest, maybe twenty, are no more. "They've taken up mining" as we used to say in the gang.

I expressed dismay at the high mortality rate of his estimate—over half of his *clica* of thirty-five had been killed. Were these vengeance killings I wanted to know? Emerson did not think so. Rather, he believed that the majority of these youth were killed by non-gang members, usually the police. "What they do is they'll pick someone up, take them away and kill them and dump the body in another place." As an example, Emerson cited the story of one member of his own clique who was overweight—so much so that the gang nicknamed him "Fat" (using the English word instead of the very common and generally inoffensive "Gordo").

> Fat always used to have problems with the police and they always gave him a hard time. One day the police arrived in a box truck. They grabbed him, threw him inside and took him somewhere else, tortured him and threw his body in a ravine. His face and arms were all scraped like they had dragged him from the back of a pickup or something.

Emerson, who had himself been beaten by police behind closed doors, expressed anger at the police for killing his former gang mate in such fashion. "There's no need for that kind of torture. If you're going to kill someone, just put a couple of bullets in his head. Instead they just, from all appearances, killed Fat by mutilation. The police hate gang members." Police killings of gang members and other forms of "social cleansing" have indeed been documented (McKinley 2007; Moser and Winton 2002; Payne 1999). Even high-ranking officers of the Guatemalan National Police have admitted that some members of the police take part in such extrajudicial killings although the officers argue that institutional and governmental authorities do not approve of their actions (Hurtado, Méndez and Valdés 2007; Ranum 2007). However, a lack of formal investigations means that there is no way to be certain just how many of the bodies of gang members turning up daily on the streets of Guatemala City, Honduras, and San Pedro are victims of rival wars, police, or armed vigilante groups. Roberto, a Guatemalan who spent a decade in the M-18, reported that of twenty-two former members, only four were alive at the time of his interview in 2007.

> Only four of us are still alive and of these, one is completely overwhelmed by alcoholism, one is an entrepreneur who owns two bakeries and takes care of his family, one more is a pastor and myself. Only four. The rest—all, all, all, all—were assassinated. The last one died this year. He was the youngest. Only nineteen.

Roberto went on to describe the circumstances of several of the deaths, most of which he attributed to gang paybacks or drug wars. Antonio reported that of the twenty-five members belonging to the clique he founded, three were still alive when he left the gang at nineteen. At the time of the interview, he knew of only one other member who was still living.

Although I know no means of establishing with certainty the actual proportion of gang youth who are killed while still in the gang, evidence exists to support the very high mortality rate reported by the ex-gang members interviewed for this study. For example, in Honduras, from 1998 to 2002, *before* the government crackdown on gangs, the nonpartisan youth rights organization Casa Alianza documented the violent deaths of 1,250 Honduran minors and youth twenty-two years old and younger (Bardales 2007). During a similar four-year span from 2001 to 2005, the number of violent deaths of minors jumped to 2,825 (Sibaja et al. 2006). We have no way of knowing how many of these youth had ever belonged to a gang. Only in prison are formal records of gang deaths kept since gang members there are kept in separate cell blocks or units. Not included in the figures cited above were 235 gang members killed while serving time in a Honduran prison during the early 2000s. Nearly 200 of these died in two separate incidents involving prison fires of suspicious origin. Meanwhile, the Ombudsman of Human Rights in Guatemala documented 358 incidences of youth homicide during a thirteen-month period from 2002 to 2003 in that country and found evidence of "social cleansing" in 16.5 percent of all cases (Ranum 2007). More than one-half of all of the deaths were classified as gang-related.[6]

Thus, even allowing for considerable error in the reports of ex-gang members, it is clear that many gang youth live a very short life, often not long enough to make a formal break with the gang. Furthermore, the above statements and statistics lend evidence to one of the most widely publicized features of the Central American gangs—the morgue rule. When youth join the Central American gang, most are told over and over again that a commitment to the gang is a commitment "all the way to the morgue." This rule is expressed in a variety of forms. In murals and tattoos, some variation of the phrase *¡Vivo por mi madre, muero por mi barrio!* ("I live for my mother, I die for my barrio!") drives home the point. Symbols such as skulls and graves represent the imminence of death while the spider's web, pictured in Figure 4.1, is said to symbolize the lifelong hold of the gang on its members.

In this sense, the statement *¡Hasta la morgue!* which can be translated as "All the way to the morgue!" or "See you at the morgue!" is an affirmation, a slogan meant to underscore gang members' lifelong identification with the gang. Isaac, a Guatemalan who had belonged to the M-18, remembered being warned by a neighbor not to leave his neighborhood since several members of the MS-13 were armed and waiting near the bus stop. Having already survived a gunshot wound to the head from the rival gang only one year earlier, the seventeen-year-old told his

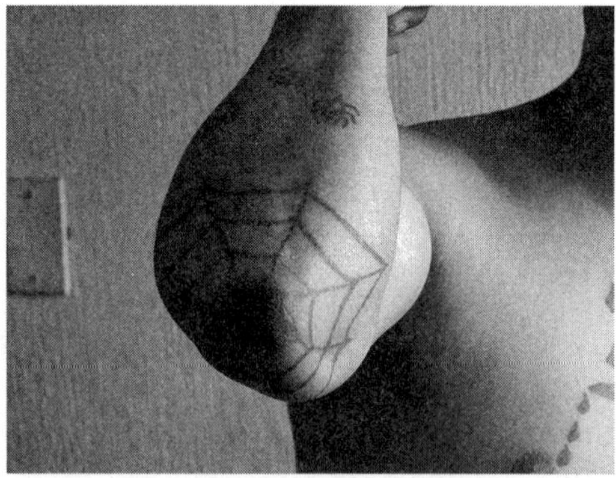

FIGURE 4.1. shows a spider web tattoo belonging to a former member of the MS-13. The young man, who asked not to be identified, wears long sleeves whenever he leaves his home.
Photo Credit: Robert Brenneman

neighbor, "I don't care. I'm not afraid of them. I'm in this *hasta la morgue*. I'm going to die for my barrio." A short while later, after a chase on foot, Isaac suffered two more gunshots, one in his leg and another in his chest, puncturing a lung.

While the phrase was used as a rallying cry for some, in other contexts it carried the connotation of a warning. In multiple interviews, ex-gang members told of being reminded by their leaders and gang mates that once in the gang, reconsidering the commitment was not an option. Neftalí, formerly of the White Fence, remembered it this way: "As our leader, a ranflero named Angel, used to say, 'Here there is only one way to get out and that's by way of your pine-box suit.' 'Your pine-box suit?' I said. 'What's that?' 'Your coffin,' he said. 'Ahh,' I said." Enrique, the Salvadoran former MS-13 member, reported: "Nowadays the gang has undergone an evolution and has lost its concept of living the gang life. It's not the same anymore. You used to be able to leave the gang. Now, once you're in, the only way out is via the cemetery."

On the surface, the morgue rule seems counterproductive. What could possibly be accomplished through the application of such a brutal and inhumane code? After all, as some youth remembered wondering, "Wasn't this supposed to be my new family?" Several youth described the logic of the morgue rule in their interview. Olivia's experience in a Guatemalan cell of the M-18 taught her that:

> If you want to go straight (*cuadrar*) you have to do something big like make a hit (*hacer algún jale*). You have to kill someone. But nowadays they're not giving out squares anymore. Nowadays because so many people left, because they left and they kept on robbing and smoking up, the homies had to put a stop to giving out squares. Now the homies that want to leave, they just kill them right off the bat. Imagine how many guys would love to leave if they could because they get tired of it, especially now the way things are.

In Olivia's view, the morgue rule was the gang's response to an earlier wave of attrition. It was a pragmatic move aimed at discouraging gang members from disaffiliating. But there are other "rational" motives behind the rule. Oscar, the former M-18 cell leader, described the logic of the morgue rule as an attempt to stop information leakage:

> Remember that [when you leave the gang] you're taking information with you, their contacts. So in that sense they liquidate you not because the gang would be weaker if you're not there because the same day you leave, three or four more will enter. No, it's the information, and it's the means of repressing the rest, to make sure they don't leave. It's a control mechanism. . . . If there weren't any rules, there would be no more gangs.

In short, the morgue rule helps underscore the seriousness of the enterprise for all members. By punishing deserters with the most severe form of punishment possible—the death penalty—gang leaders demonstrate to the rest that joining a gang is not to be confused with an everyday commitment like joining a club or a team. The morgue rule illustrates classical sociologist Emile Durkheim's observation that punishment builds group solidarity because it provides a ritual means of making group values sacred (Durkheim 1982 [1895]). Gang members who withdraw, especially those who do so without the permission of the gang leader, violate the solidarity of the group. In Honduras, gang deserters are given a special name, *pesetas*. To *pesetear* is to back out of the gang and is usually considered a capital offense. Beto, the Honduran former M-18 leader, recounted in chilling detail his participation in the application of the morgue rule on a former M-18 gang-mate who had tattoo-ed an "X" over his gang tattoos in attempt to "prove" his disassociation from the gang:

> One of them (*pesetas*) left the gang after awhile and was going around with his tattoos crossed out. And we would roast anyone who crossed off his tattoos. So somebody told us that he was around. We caught him and took off his shirt and all of us gave him a good kicking. Then we took him to the river and the other ranking member decided that a gun would make too much noise. "We'd better kill him with a machete," he said. "But I want to test you (*probarlos*)." "Let's see what you're made of." And of the four of us that were there that day, I'm the only one still alive—and anyway he told me, "Okay man, (*orale buey*) you first." So I grabbed the machete . . .

Beto's description of the killing illustrates with chilling clarity the extent to which the application of the morgue rule can take on a ritual character with obvious symbolic meaning for the group. All four members present were obliged to play a role in the act, thereby solidifying their own commitment to the gang, its principles, and its symbols. The sacredness of the tattoo, violated by this unfortunate youth, was to be protected with jealous and brutal zeal.

EXCEPTIONS TO THE MORGUE RULE

Despite constant warnings and affirmations, the morgue rule is *not* absolute. It is clearly *not* the case that every gang member remains active in the gang until death. In fact, most of the data for this book come from sixty-two interviews with youth who joined the gang, left, and, as far as I am aware, continue living. To my knowledge, only Antonio has been killed in the three years since I first began interviewing ex-gang members.[7] So, how have these former gang members, some of whom still bear tattoos in prominent places, managed to dodge the wrath of their former homies? A number of alternatives exist in order to escape or assuage the wrath of the barrio. First, the gang is not always *capable* of enforcing the morgue rule. In some cases the death of a leader can lead to a chaotic and violent power struggle that eliminates or forces into seclusion the most active members of the clique, providing a window of opportunity for lower-level members to disaffiliate. If a neighboring gang is also struggling and fails to immediately annex the territory of its rival, especially younger members of the gang may seize the opportunity to abandon the gang completely, erasing tattoos, changing their manner of dress, and going back to school or looking for work. Although several of the ex-gang members interviewed reported this pathway of escaping a wounded or destroyed local clique, such moments appear to be somewhat rare.

A second, more common strategy for gang members who become "worn out" with gang life involves becoming a *pandillero calmado,* or "settled-down gang member."[8] Gang members who have reached adulthood, generally around the mid- to late twenties, and desire to "settle down" are occasionally allowed the option of retaining their affiliation but lowering their profile and level of activity in the gang. Among the typical reasons given for wanting to *calmarse* are the birth of a child or cohabitation with the intent to start a family. A settled-down member does not typically remove tattoos, and although he or she may modify his or her mode of dress, the *calmado* must continue to respect the gang mystique and hate the rival gang. Some authors suggest that what sets calmados apart from currently-active, full-fledged members is that the former do not participate in violence or consume illegal drugs (Cruz and Portillo 1998). However, several participants in this study suggested that calmados are often expected to "help out" in the event of a major gang war or a significant criminal venture. Others reported that calmados must continue paying gang dues in order to keep the gang supplied with weapons. In fact, one former calmado reported that he himself "wore out" after living as a calmado for a time due to the constant expectation to contribute and attend meetings. Similarly, Neftalí achieved a kind calmado status after announcing to the gang that he would be moving in with his girlfriend. Nevertheless, he was told by the ranflero (gang lord), "It's true, things will be different now, but we'll still expect to see you at three meetings (*mítins*) a week. None of this, 'Congratulations-now-be-sure-and-send-us-a-postcard!' business." Asked if he had been hoping to be allowed complete freedom from the gang after announcing his intention to begin a family, Neftalí responded, "I was hoping, in my heart, that this would be my second chance." In fact, Neftalí continued attending meetings and "going after enemies" until, at a later date, a religious experience would lead him to make his break with the gang formal and permanent.

One way to think of the option to *calmarse* is to compare it with the status of a reservist in the armed forces. *Pandilleros calmados* vary considerably in their level of ongoing commitment to the gang, and it is likely that those who continue long enough will, because of their diminishing network ties with new leaders and younger members, retire from the gang for all intents and purposes. On the other hand, some calmados find their status changed from reservist back to active duty precipitously and against their will when a gang war is initiated, be it by the local or the rival ranflero. Thus, in a sense, the calmado option is often viewed as less than ideal and scarcely an improvement over regular membership, especially since calmados rarely receive financial compensation as reservists. Still, in light of the spike in gang violence and the fear of the morgue rule, the option to calmarse is one of the most common means of dealing with a limited array of exit options.

One reason gang leaders have reportedly downplayed or eliminated the reservist option is that some ex-gang members reported that the calmado option sometimes becomes a smokescreen for criminal "freelancing" in the drugs and organized crime sector or for becoming a professional hit man. After all, once a youth has learned to navigate life on the street—accessing and using firearms and learning the "tricks" of the drug trade—why should he have to use his skills in the exclusive service of the gang? If by diminishing his formal ties with the gang, he is able to find a modicum of safety as a calmado reservist, the lucrative nature of criminal street work is no less attractive than before. This perspective helps to explain the reports of Olivia, Enrique, and others who testified to the gang's increasing reticence to give calmados a "pass." To the extent that some calmados continued in trades the gang wished to monopolize, gang leaders began to view them as unwanted competitors for business.

Since calmados never truly *leave* the gang, one relatively common strategy of exit is to migrate. Leaving one's community or city to pursue a life either permanently or semipermanently elsewhere is one of the most common escape routes for youth *aburridos* of the gang lifestyle. Not surprisingly, the United States is one of the most popular destinations for migrating gang members. In fact, some gang members who migrate to the United States are in fact "returning" to their gang home after having been deported by U.S. authorities (Quirk 2008) while others are seeking refuge from the violence of their gang home. Sometimes, fleeing to the United States leads to a truly "settled-down" lifestyle in *el Norte,* as in the case of Lorenzo, a Honduran ex-member of the Vatos Locos who is well-known to several interviewees. Lorenzo has even helped other ex-gang members from his former clique by occasionally sending money when they are unable to find work. In other cases, the trip to *el Norte* does not go as planned or ends in deportation. For instance, Beto set out for the United States from northern Honduras only to lose the use of his foot in an accident while trying to board a moving train in Saltillo near Monterrey, Mexico. Sergio, a Honduran former Vato Loco, had been deported from Miami just a few days prior to our interview. Since leaving the gang several years earlier he had spent over two years in the United States. Not that escaping the gang is always the sole incentive. The motives for migrating to the

United States probably involve a mixture of a search for opportunities as well as an escape from the gang and the morgue rule.

Instead of heading northward for the United States, many gang members move "horizontally" across Central American borders or between major cities in order to escape their ties to the gang. Miguel, a Guatemalan who had belonged to the MS-13, reported having left Guatemala City and moved to San Marcos, a mostly rural province bordering Mexico. He made his decision to migrate when he learned of his girlfriend's pregnancy and decided it was time to settle down, but the move itself was *facilitated* by the death of the local leader, which left the local *clica* too weak to track down deserters. Other gang leavers used family networks to move back and forth across Central American borders in order to acquire anonymity. Oliver returned to Honduras from Guatemala after several relatives died in a drug-related killing. Andres left San Salvador to move with his partner to Guatemala, where his grandmother lived. After two years of struggling to find work, he returned to his home in San Salvador where the original cell had lost most of the members who could identify him. Among female gang members, the pathways to leaving appear to be more numerous and accessible. Recent survey and interview research affirms the view among male and female gang members interviewed for this study that women are more commonly allowed to disaffiliate than men (Medina and Mateu-Gelabert 2009). Olivia reported that, although most cells have stopped granting permission to leave, a female gang member who has "done her part" for the gang has at least a chance of receiving her "squares" if she reports that she is pregnant.[9] Male gang members are not necessarily granted permission to leave when they become fathers.

Finally, in addition to migrating or becoming a calmado, gang members seeking a viable means of dodging the morgue rule have one other alternative—they can become an evangelical Christian. In dozens of interviews with both religious and nonreligious ex-gang members, and with Catholic, evangelical, and nonreligious rehab coordinators, participants told me of a religious exception allowed by almost all gang leaders in the application of the morgue rule. In fact, so many informants spoke of this exception that I eventually came to call it "the evangelical exemption." Perhaps in part because of a latent religiosity of their own, many gang cell leaders are fearful of applying the morgue rule to a deserter who has reported having undergone a religious transformation. Thus, "converted" gang members are typically given time and space to "prove" the authenticity of their transformation by adopting and maintaining the strict, pietistic morality of their new evangelical fraternity. No more smoking pot, crack, or cigarettes; no more hanging out at the bar or going to the discotheque; and no more selling drugs or carrying weapons. Oscar, one of a handful of ex-gang members interviewed who managed to leave *without* converting or leaving his country, nevertheless confirmed the existence of the evangelical exemption:

> If you become a Christian the gang leaves you alone and doesn't bother you. But they're still watching you, following you to see if it's for real or if it's just an excuse you're using. They find you drinking some place and, oops, you've been lying to them. Maybe they'll let you have a good time for the night but pretty soon they find you and liquidate you. That's the way it works.

Clearly, both the escape and the need for "proof" sought by gang leaders have motives and consequences that cry out for a deeper sociological analysis. I examine the exemption in more detail later on. For the moment, my point is merely that the pathway exists and that, like migrating or becoming a calmado, leaving via religious conversion carries requirements and risks of its own. In short, despite the various alternatives and exceptions to the morgue rule, the fear of falling victim to it nevertheless remains an enormous disincentive to leaving the gang even among older gang members who no longer wish to continue. Gang members must weigh the dangers of continuing in the gang and falling victim to the "boomerang effect" on the one hand, with the possibility on the other that the gang may punish them with the morgue rule if they try to desert. In either case, there are no guarantees.

EL CHANCE

The morgue rule is not the only obstacle to leaving. Finding a job with a steady income to replace the revenue provided by gang work is a second major barrier. In the popular vernacular of northern Central America, work and a steady job are often referred to as *chance*, and individuals, especially men, who have put in a long day may say that they have been *chanceando*. Foremost in the minds of gang members seeking to "settle down" is the matter of finding *un chance*.[10] The term is a curious Anglicism, the English roots of which highlight the precarious nature of employment in Central America. Finding a steady job for young men in the barrio is similarly a game of chance requiring among other things a mixture of perseverance, trusting friends and family, and a good deal of luck. For young men who are known by family, friends, and local authorities for having belonged to a gang, the possibility of finding un chance is especially remote. Very few gang members hold a high school diploma. In fact, the decision to join the gang usually coincides with abandoning formal education in junior high school if not earlier. Thus, most gang members lack the formal requirements for any jobs except the lowest-paying blue-collar or *maquiladora* (clothing assembly plant) jobs, salaries of which pale in comparison to a single afternoon's work selling drugs.

Furthermore the vast majority of gang members who have been active in the gang for any considerable amount of time have acquired during those years a criminal record. When employers require that job applicants present *antecedentes penales* (an official record showing any prior penal record)—and many if not most employers seeking to hire for the formal economy make this requirement—gang members find that their chances become even slimmer. Many of the ex-gang members I interviewed had spent time in prison. In the especially tight job market of Central America, few employers are willing to take a chance on hiring someone with a criminal record. Like the African-American men in Devah Pager's study of job seekers with a felony record (Pager 2009), Central American gang youth are "marked" by their criminal record and few have skin light enough to "override" their criminal past.[11]

The presence of tattoos is a further hindrance to acquiring formal employment. Wilmer, a former member of the Vatos Locos, spent two years looking unsuccessfully for work following his release from prison for participating in a homicide. But his tattoos, compounded by his reputation and his criminal record, have so far kept him from acquiring even the low-paying maquiladora jobs:

> The truth is, with these tattoos it's really hard to find a job. You can go out looking for work. I'm a painter and an artist. I'll do any design or mural for you, and I've done several projects for Brother Nathán [the local gang ministry promoter] with lettering and everything. I'm very good at this stuff so I do little odd jobs (*chambitas*) that come up but right now that's what I live on, little odd jobs.

Wilmer's income from *chambitas* was stretched even thinner by his responsibility not only for his own daughter but for the three children of his brother, killed several years earlier in a gang war.

In order to remove the visible stigma carried by tattoos, tattoo removal has become an increasingly common clinical procedure for job-seeking youth and adults, many of whom may never have belonged to a gang at all. At *Adios Tatuajes*, a Catholic-sponsored tattoo-removal clinic on the outskirts of Guatemala City, the staff estimated that about one-half of the youth seeking the inexpensive but painful infrared treatments, have current or former ties to the gang. Many private security firms and maquiladoras, which provide the most likely job opportunities for Central American males without a diploma, now require a strip search of all job applicants prior to serious consideration for employment. In fact, the fear of the gangs is so great, that some current employees are now being required to remove tattoos, even after years of problem-free work, in order to "prove" their gang-free status. Obviously, given the gang's jealousy of its status and symbols, gang members seeking to remove a tattoo in the process of leaving the gang must also consider the possibility of repercussions from former homies. For this reason, some ex-gang members who are able to find work via family or social networks choose not to remove some or all of their tattoos. Antonio removed only those on his face, leaving others on his neck and body, but he still found himself the target of his former gang. In the second unsuccessful attempt on his life, the two youth who shot at him at close range referred to his erased tattoos shortly before they opened fire. Another reason for delaying removal is that the infrared method, the only safe technique economically within reach for most Central Americans, does not always produce a desirable result. Scarring or "staining" is common, and provides erstwhile homies with an easy means of identifying an ex-gang member.

Even youth who do not have prominent or visible tattoos or who take the risky step of removing them nevertheless find themselves at a disadvantage when seeking a job. Social ties, perhaps even more than in the United States, represent a key currency when looking for work and joining the gang typically involves some degree of bridge-burning with family, friends, and especially neighbors. Gang members seeking to leave the gang and settle down to a "work-a-day" lifestyle find that outside the gang, few hold them in any regard other than that of fear or loathing. Nor are such fears completely without basis. Many stories circulate of mom-and-pop corner stores or other small businesses who hired youth to work the counter or the back room only to find themselves robbed or extorted by these youth or their gang friends. Thus, even the former gang member who has promised to leave behind all former ties to the gang faces an audience of skeptics among would-be employers including, and even especially, those who know him and watched him grow up.

GIVING UP *LA VIDA LOCA*

Asked what was the hardest part about learning to live outside the gang, JJ, the Guatemalan former White Fence leader, responded, "Respect, homies, and cocaine—in that order." A third barrier to leaving the gang involves the third aspect in JJ's list—the addictions associated with what gang members refer to as *la vida loca*. This "crazy lifestyle" goes far beyond Ricky Martin's innocuous song about a girl who makes men crazy to the point of "dancing naked in the rain." For the gang member, la vida loca represents all manner of macho risk taking including violence, drugs, weapons, and unprotected sex. Leonardo found that giving up carrying a gun was one of the most difficult aspects of leaving the gang. Tomás, one of two gang members interviewed in prison, felt that giving up womanizing and drugs was the hardest.

> Here in prison it's harder to be an ex-gang member. Doesn't matter which side you're on. For an ex-gang member, what's hardest to give up are women and drugs. I never had a problem with the drugs. For me the hardest thing to give up is the women.[12]

Many interviewees spoke openly about the drug and alcohol addictions that dogged their attempts to be free of the gang. Substance abuse, especially the consumption of illegal substances, requires considerable investments of time and money, and both of these resources are in short supply for the ex-gang member. Clearly, a few of the former gang members I interviewed in Honduras still had problems with substance abuse—as many as five years after their gang had disbanded. Ovidio, a former Vato Loco, complained of his miserable *maquila* salary of US$45 per week and dreamed of going to the United States where he could make real money. The same youth also confessed that he liked to smoke weed and that his girlfriend kept "nagging" him for money for taking care of their baby daughter. However, abusing alcohol and drugs produces more than chemical dependency. The ritual of getting wasted *together* is one that both produces solidarity and builds the gang member's macho, devil-may-care image. Thus, swearing off drugs and alcohol can undermine his status and erode his "respect." Since the gang provides plentiful access to recreational drugs, leaving means giving up easy access to drugs and the recreational rituals associated with them. When Beto spoke of obstacles he faced when contemplating a decision to leave the gang, he said that relinquishing drugs was one of the greatest obstacles. "First, drugs. Drugs and respect. In the gang you have to act furious. No one can tell you anything and anyone that talks back to you, you give them a fist or worse. I said to myself, 'If I leave, then people are going to go around humiliating me.'" Beto's statement underscores the extent to which gang members become attached not merely to drugs and violence but to the practice of using the gang lifestyle of using chemicals, anger, and violence as a means to escape chronic shame. To leave the gang is to risk returning to the humiliation of chronic shame. And, indeed, many gang members did speak of entering a deep depression when they migrated or went into hiding to escape the gang. Antonio found himself in depression when he couldn't find a job after moving to a different area of the city. Smoking pot provided a temporary means of escape but further drained his resources and kept him from continuing his job search. "Shut in, running from the gang, without work or money. I thank God that my Mom helped me out. If not, I would have starved, you know? Or I would have had to go back to robbing people."

THE HAVEN THAT BECAME A HELL

Many of the "barriers" to leaving the gang cited by the ex-gang members were the same phenomena that prompted them to consider leaving in the first place. The young men and women who reported wanting to leave the gang "before it's too late" also worried that by leaving, they would forfeit protection from their enemies as well as earn a "green light" or death warrant from those who remained in the gang and sought to uphold the morgue rule. Similarly, the same drug habits that caused the youth to wish to be free of the gang lifestyle also proved very difficult habits to break, even though many gang leaders expected calmados or deserters to rid themselves of their former habits. While many gang youth dreamed at first of "settling down" to a work-a-day lifestyle with a steady job and a family, actually finding a job proved extremely difficult because affiliation with the gang, past or present, had come to hold a loathsome status in many local neighborhoods and the national media. Furthermore, many aspects of gang life that prompted youth to leave the gang were in fact the very same features that brought them into the gang in the first place. The two-sided nature of gang experience struck me as I listened to ex-gang members describe life in the gang as both exciting and comforting—a *haven* where disenfranchised youth could express themselves, find belonging and experience pride. But alongside that description of gang life as family—the "haven in a heartless world"—was a very different description of the gang. Often the very same participants, who described gang life as exhilarating on the one hand, also described it as frustrating, fear-inducing hardship—a hell-on-earth that prompted them to take great risks and undergo real hardship in an attempt to be "free." Which is the real nature of the gang? Is it heaven or hell—an oasis of solidarity or an island of nightmarish torment? In fact it is both. Most ex-gang members remembered their earliest experiences with the gang with a mixture of nostalgia and excitement. Taking part in violence and crime was exciting at first. Drugs, alcohol, and la vida loca provided a shortcut to adulthood and a sense of power and personal efficacy. The gang cell was a haven of fraternity and solidarity. Taken together, these experiences led to a new sense of pride and an escape from chronic shame. However, in the lives of the young men I interviewed, what felt at first like a social escape eventually turned into a solitary prison. Participating in violence brought with it consequences such as escalating barrio wars and the acquisition of more enemies from rival gang members. "Success" in carrying out strikes on enemy territory brought increased privileges for the perpetrators. It also brought increased notoriety among enemy cells. Police began to arrest and torture gang members, often simply giving them a "working over" rather than going through the paperwork and court hearings necessary to prosecute a minor. Furthermore, friends and families of gang members' victims, frustrated by the inability or unwillingness of the police to properly punish suspects, often took it upon themselves to identify and "punish" those they believe to be responsible for their loved one's death. All these factors led to the boomerang effect that brought a brutal element of realism to a violence that seemed at first like entertainment. Similarly, what began as an affirmative rallying cry, the slogan *¡Hasta la morgue!* eventually morphed into an ominous warning. Gang members who were thought to be considering abandoning the gang were reminded of their commitment and the motto soon became a curse.

Just as important, even as the subjective experience of individual gang members changed from one of euphoria to one of fear given their own changing position within the gang structure, the nature and structure of gangs in the region as a whole "evolved" as well. What several ex-gang members described as an "evolution" of the gang has been described as the larger shift from the pandilla street gangs of the 1970s and '80s to the violent, organized mara of the late 1990s and 2000s (Rubio 2007). The testimonies of the ex-gang members in this study provide further evidence of a transformation in gang structure and tactics due in large part to the increasing availability of illegal drugs and weapons. Although the pandillas of the past no doubt engaged in a certain level of drug consumption, violence, and crime, an emerging "small arms race" in the hemisphere (Moser and Winton 2002) and around the globe (Fleshman 2001) meant that the gangs suddenly found themselves equipped to "protect the barrio" and its enterprises in a far more brutal fashion than ever before. What had begun as a game of identity-enhancing skirmishes over disputed territory and symbols soon appeared more like a large-scale street war. And as in any war, mutiny lurks among the rank and file whenever the chances of survival become increasingly uncertain.

CONCLUSION

For many youth who have spent years in the gang, the thought of leaving is at once enticing and intimidating. The fear of being killed by the "boomerang effect" of payback violence or by jealous gang mates while still in the gang, a weariness from having constantly to project intimidation, the pull of non-gang friends and family, and a desire to start one's own family all affect aging gang members at some point, prompting them to at least consider the possibility of leaving. But leaving carries its own hazards. The morgue rule and the constant fear of being killed as a deserter or *peseta*, the pull of addictions related to la vida loca, and skepticism about the possibility of ever being able to find un chance (a steady job) all provide disincentives to leaving the gang, and taken together these obstacles keep many gang members from ever severing ties with the gang. Even those gang members who do decide to make a definitive break with the gang find themselves hemmed in by a variety of personal and social barriers that make learning to live "on the outside" a major challenge. After four years of rebuilding his life after the gang, JJ, the former Guatemalan White Fence cell leader, summed up the challenges of learning to live without the gang in this way: "When you leave the gang, it's like you've just been born." The image of rebirth captures the sense in which ex-gang members are in an especially precarious position of vulnerability and innocence when they abandon the gang. "Marked" in both a literal and a figurative sense, many find starting over without the gang to be a difficult if not impossible task to accomplish by themselves. No wonder Rudolfo Kepfer, a clinical psychiatrist who treats gang minors in detention, when asked how gang members might be helped to leave the gang, shook his head and offered, "Take them to another planet." He was emphasizing the sheer difficulty of succeeding in life after the gang by highlighting the need for a wholesale change of social context when starting over. Extraterrestrial migrations are out of the question, at least in a literal sense.

Yet there is a cultural voyage that, in some respects, comes close to planetary relocation. The gang member seeking to completely sever his ties to the gang and publicly renounce his former affiliation can "emigrate" to a social planet with a vastly different cultural landscape—he can join an evangelical congregation.

5

¡A-Dios, homies!

Every gang member knows perfectly well that the only known escape from the gangs is by death. But the evangelical Christian, those of us that do the work of God, we know that Jesus Christ is the other escape.
—Danilo, Honduran ex-member of MS-13

If you want to leave to seek out God's paths, fine. We will support you. But if you're messing with the barrio and with God, we will cut off both your hands and both feet . . .
—Pipa, Honduran gang member (quoted in Castro and Carranza 2005)

The pastor said to me, "Do you want to be a Christian?"
"No!" I said. "I'm a pandillero. I live for my barrio and kill for it too. . . ." And I said to myself, "If you do this, you'll be a fag. You'll be a homosexual. Don't be stupid. [Think about] the money, the women. You're going to have to quit smoking. No, no, no!"
—Calín, Honduran ex-member of MS-13

On the day Ricardo, alias "El Pescado" (Fish), found himself weeping at the foot of the altar at the Prince of Peace Pentecostal church across the street from his home, the news spread so rapidly through the neighborhood that the half-empty church quickly filled with curious onlookers. "When they heard that El Pescado of the Vatos Locos was accepting Christ crying, people gathered around the church building," Ricardo remembered.

> They were jumping above the wall just to get a look and see if it was true that I was really accepting Christ. I mean, it was really a special moment,

> not just a regular old service but a service where the people realized that I was really accepting Christ. Afterward I went straight to my stash and grabbed my three cartons of marijuana and dumped it in the toilet. A few days later I took my chimbas (homemade firearms) and gave them to Brother Ricardo [the local Mennonite peace promoter]. That's when I started preaching and declaring, as the Bible text says, "Therefore if anyone be in Christ, [they] are a new creature."[1]

Ricardo, former leader and founding member of the local Honduran cell of the Vatos Locos, tells his story of a sinner-to-saint transformation of the kind heralded in religious magazines and evangelistic sermons. When I met Ricardo in 2007 it was hard to imagine him as a homie, much less a gang leader. The twenty-five-year-old had a paunch, no visible tattoos, parted his hair on the side, and kept a perennially upbeat demeanor. He used the evangelical insider greeting of *hermano* or *hermana* (brother or sister in the Lord) when addressing other evangelicals on the street and he spoke often and with excitement about evangelization opportunities in this neighborhood and others. Ricardo pastors a new church in another community, and soon after we met he told me excitedly that his congregation had been upgraded from *campo blanco* or "white field"—evangelical-speak for a church plant in the early stages—to a full-fledged congregation by the denomination. In addition to pastoring, Ricardo works part time as a peace promoter for the Honduran Mennonite Peace and Justice Commission and has taken several classes toward a certificate in conflict transformation. He is also in charge of planning and coordinating occasional tattoo-removal campaigns, a trade he learned from the *¡Adiós Tatuajes!* clinic sponsored by the Catholic Maryknoll community. If that were not enough, Ricardo is studying to finish his high school diploma and looks forward to beginning studies at the university. He is a busy man.

Ricardo's charisma spills over into his everyday interaction, so much so, that when interviewing Ricardo I had trouble getting a word in. Glad to have the opportunity to tell his story, Ricardo spoke quickly and at length, describing his entrance into the gang and the part he played in its transformation from a mildly delinquent local street gang to a well-organized criminal organization involved in the drug trade and violent crime. He used the sing-song cadence of an evangelical preacher, emphasizing words at the end of a line or in a thematic climax. Despite his troubled past, or maybe because of it, Ricardo is proud of his status as an evangelical *hermano*.

Was Ricardo's transformation from pistol-packing homie to Bible-quoting hermano a miracle from God? Surely it appeared as such to those neighbors who had grown weary of fearing him. But as a sociologist my interest lies not in categorizing social phenomena as miraculous or mundane but in understanding the social dynamics at work in the course of the transformation. What is it about evangelical conversion that allows the evangelical hermano to succeed in the extremely difficult and dangerous task of un-becoming a homie? Furthermore, what are the benefits and the drawbacks to former gang members who convert and just how common does evangelical conversion appear to be among homies seeking to leave.

STAYIN' ALIVE

Although "deserting" the gang is in many cases, a capital offense, many gang cells—perhaps even a majority—allow a special pass for gang members who report having experienced an evangelical conversion. In a journalistic account of the MS-13 in Mexico, the authors reported:

> Nobody gets out of the Mara Salvatrucha alive, they say. The only door that opens to them is that of the evangelical religious groups. . . . Many ex-gang members have found a place in churches and evangelical movements. In the mythology of the *mareros* (gang members) you don't touch those that have found God and his pardon (Fernàndez and Ronquillo 2006).

Likewise the former gang members interviewed in my study agreed that the evangelical exemption provided the safest, surest means to escape the gang without being targeted as a deserter. Some youth mentioned other means of exit such as migrating to another country or another city or simply waiting for one or more gang leaders to be killed leading to the opening of a "window of opportunity" for the rest of the members. A few ex-gang members reported paying a hefty fine in exchange for their freedom from the gang, but only members who had been out of the gang for several years cited this action. Nevertheless, none of these exit strategies was mentioned as often or explained as explicitly as that of the conversion pathway. Ester, an ex-gang member interviewed at the Catholic tattoo-removal clinic responded to my question about how an ex-gang member might get out of the gang today saying, "Really, the only way to get out is to get involved in the church one hundred percent. But the gang keeps watch over you day and night to see if you're actually completing it." Ester herself was not religious. She had managed to escape the gang several years earlier when her father sent her to a special home for recovering gang youth. During her second stay—she escaped and returned to the gang on the first visit—the leader of her cell was killed and many of the other members fled. Thus, she herself had decided to leave during a "window of opportunity" that allowed her to abandon the gang without leaving the community or joining the church. But she was convinced that leaving the gang now was a very different enterprise than when she left several years earlier. "Right now, leaving the gangs is hard," she said.

Ester's comment reveals more than the difficulty of leaving or the popularity of conversion as an escape hatch. Indeed, if claiming the evangelical exemption were as simple as merely going forward to "accept Jesus" during an evangelistic event, or attending worship every now and again, many more exiting gang members would, no doubt, claim to be converts. But claiming to be a *cristiano*—regenerate, saved, and transformed as evangelical pastors believe a true convert must be—involves agreeing to a strict moralistic program that is starkly opposite to the lifestyle of the gang. Ester and many other informants reported that gangs "monitor" ex-gang members who claim to convert in order to make sure that their conversion is in fact genuine. Uriel, a Guatemalan former member of the M-18, explained it this way:

> You know there are many that have been given permission to leave the gang but what they tell you is . . . "Well, we're going to give you your squares—squares means that they're going to take you out of the gang without problems . . . [but] you have to attend a church. You can't smoke anymore, you can't drink anymore. If we see that you're not attending

> church, that you're drinking, you're smoking, then [we] will kill you because if you left it was [supposedly] because you were going to change, to follow the paths of God." But if you left to take it easy, to be free of the gang, that's when they'll kill you.

I found the claim that gang members "watch over" professed converts difficult to believe at first. The report that a former gang member can actually be killed for "falsifying" a conversion was even more difficult to believe. But over and over and in each country, I was told a version of the same rule: false converts are treated as the worst kind of deserters and are therefore subject to the same "green light" death warrant issued to those who leave without permission. I began asking converts if they knew personally of individuals who had converted but had not been able to keep up the strict moral demands of evangelical faith. What happened to them, I inquired? At least three gang members knew personally of homies who, after reporting a religious conversion, were killed for not giving up the gang lifestyle completely. One converted ex-gang member reported that a good friend of his had become an itinerant evangelist after a long career in the MS-13. This same friend was later killed after having been found by the gang to be involved in extortion. The informant reported having disbelieved the rumor of his deceased friend's ongoing criminality at first, since his friend had also been a spiritual mentor. But later evidence led him to accept as true the accusation of his friend's extortion. Gustavo, a Guatemalan ex-gang member I met at the tattoo-removal clinic, had converted after attending a Pentecostal congregation in his neighborhood. During the course of his decision to convert, he informed his gang leader, *El Gato* (The Cat) of his intention to leave the gang and join a church:

> When I went to El Gato, he told me, "Here, whoever enters only leaves dead." But I wanted to leave and I wanted a peaceful life. So he said, "Okay. You leave and you have to go straight (*cuadrar*). If not, I will personally kill you." The gang told me that I had to change my vocabulary, my way of dressing, and no more tattoos, no weapons, and no keeping watch for anybody (*ni esquinas ni chequeo*). Then they still charged me three thousand quetzales [US$420] . . .
>
> [*Do you know of anyone who was ever caught breaking the rules after joining the church?*]

> (Pause.) Yes. Owl (*El Buho*). He went to church and kept the rules, dressed right and everything except he liked to smoke marijuana. He used to go with his girlfriend to the Assembly of God church. One night the gang pulled him out of church and shot him outside.
>
> [*You mean they pulled him out right in the middle of the service?*]
>
> Yes. They saw him. He smoked a joint right outside before going into the church. Look, the gang takes religion very seriously and they don't it like when people mix the church and the gang.

The gang, it seems, views religious conversion and the barrio as two separate, very distinct, but equally serious endeavors. Gustavo's account implies that while the gang respects religion, gang members are not to be caught "mixing" church and barrio. Thus, a gang member who professes a conversion must abandon the gang lifestyle completely, including the abuse of drugs and alcohol and even the cholo style of dress. Both Gustavo, who was an active convert, and Ester, who had not converted, asserted that behind the warning to would-be converts to "walk the talk" is the gang's high regard for religion itself. Such "respect" for religion probably has something to do with the widespread nature of popular religion in Central American culture and heritage. Although many Central Americans are not active members of a religious congregation, the vast majority describe themselves as Catholic or Protestant Christians and professed atheism or agnosticism are extremely rare in the barrio. In many Guatemalan homes, for example, children are taught the oft-quoted phrase: *No escupís al cielo o te cae encima*—that is, "Don't spit at the sky or it may fall on you." In the deeply religious social fabric of Central America, including the homes and schools in which many of the gang leaders themselves were socialized, "spitting at the sky" with open sacrilege invites a violent response from an angry God. Thus, Fernandez and Ronquillo (2006), quoted above, claim that part of the gang "mystique" itself involves a high regard for strict religion. In other words, in addition to the desire to make sure that leaving the gang is hard by promoting strict, moralistic religious commitment as "the only way out," gang leaders themselves do not wish to kill ex-gang members who have genuinely made a commitment to God. Beto, a Honduran former member and cell leader who abandoned the M-18 in 2006, put it this way:

> Around here there is permission to leave but always and only when you become a Christian. If you leave just to get away, Oof! Barbecue! And you have to talk to them too before you leave. And so [I went to see] a leader up the way in another neighborhood . . . who asked me, "Is it true that you're going to church?"
>
> "Yes," I told him.
>
> "So, what's up? Are you going to change?" he said.
>
> "Truth is, yes," I said.
>
> "Okay. You know that nobody messes with Curly (*el Colocho*). Not with Curly, not with the barrio. If you're going to change, you'd better do it once and for all."

Not sure to whom or what Beto's "Curly" referred, I stopped him to ask for clarification:

> [*Don't mess with what?*]
>
> With Curly. That's how they call God, Curly.
>
> [*Oh, I get it. So you don't mess with*]—
>
> Curly.
>
> [*Yes but you said*—]
>
> Not with Curly, not with the barrio.

In the street vernacular of the gang, "Curly," or *el Colocho*,[2] represents God, and for gang bosses like Beto's, neither Curly nor the gang ought to be "messed with."[3] Nor was Beto the only gang member to warn of the dangers of "messing" or "playing around" with God. Participants from all backgrounds in this study mentioned one version or another of the phrase "You don't mess with God" on many occasions. The same phrase is found on the lips of gang members interviewed in other studies. For example, in a study of gangs carried out by the Honduran Jesuit think tank, ERIC, "Pipa," a *current* gang member in Honduras, reported: "If you want to leave to seek out God's paths, fine. We will support you. But if you're messing with the barrio and with God, we will cut off both your hands and both feet so that you're maimed for the rest of your life" (Castro and Carranza 2005). During an interview in El Salvador, Lucas, a former member of the M-18, agreed saying,

> If you can leave, you'd better do it by accepting God and living up to it (*ser cabal*). You have to live up to it. You can't mess with Him. Because if you mess with Him, it's like you're messing with the Eighteen at the same time. And then, and then, well . . .

Lucas did not finish the sentence, but the meaning was clear. Gang members who convert and then renege on their commitment flout the seriousness of both gang and church and are thus subject to serious punishment, possibly even death. In fact, some ex-gang members even described the gang's practice of policing conversions and punishing "halfhearted" conversions as a kind of just reward to those who would "mess with God" by simply using a conversion as cover for a quick and easy exit or for transferring their allegiance to another gang. Camilo, a Honduran convert, went so far as to say that the gang's practice of policing conversions to verify their authenticity is in fact a good thing.

> If somebody is in the gang and he decides to serve God and to serve God clearly—there are moments when they'll screw you, when they'll look for ways [to trip you up]—but over time they'll say, 'Okay, we're going to give you a pass. But if you fail, *¡Ah, hombre muerto!*' And in some ways it's good, in some ways because if you fail God then that means others will lose the opportunity.

For Lucas, Beto, and Pipa, "messing with God" is just as serious as "messing with the gang." Both God and the gang represent symbols and values of a sacred nature and ought to be respected. In fact, while "messing with God" was usually voiced in reference to playing false with a religious conversion, the gang itself, some participants reported, must be careful not to "mess with God" by killing a convert who is in fact genuine. Neftalí, a former White Fence member from Guatemala, recalled that his ranflero admonished members not to punish a deserter: "We're not going to kill him because he's a Christian." Asked to explain this comment further, Neftalí reported, "It's well known that if you mess with somebody who is up to God's work (*anda en las cosas de Dios*) it's going to go badly for you. That's why they say, 'He's a Christian. Let's leave him alone.'" In short, the gang "respects" gang exit by way of a conversion because to eliminate an ex-gang member who has honestly committed himself to "Curly" is just as dangerous as faking a conversion since this too is "messing with Curly."

Anthropologist Jon Wolseth (2008) reported similar findings after conducting ethnographic research for his dissertation on youth violence in a Honduran barrio. Noting that Pentecostal conversion provides refuge and "sanctuary" from street violence for barrio youth who "claim exemption" from the gang because of their Pentecostal identity, he observed that demonstrating one's conversion by "following the law of God"—that is, observing Pentecostalism's strict moralistic requirements—allows these youth to solidify and maintain their identity. In the Honduran barrio, Wolseth found that,

> Belief in God is not enough to save one from harm; one must also continuously demonstrate this belief through one's actions in the world. God's protective path is available only to those who demonstrate their new status by their actions. If they relapse into violence, alcohol use, or drug addiction, they will be accused of "playing with God" and open themselves up to violent retribution. (2008:105)

In other words, evangelical conversion functions much like a social contract in which gang leaders say, in effect, "You keep up the strict lifestyle, we'll leave you alone." Wolseth argues that "spatial metaphors" promoted by Pentecostal pastors serve to create a distinction in the popular rhetoric of the barrio between "the streets" epitomized by the gang and "the way of God" characterized by the moralism of the Pentecostal hermanos. Young Pentecostals who maintain the moralistic lifestyle of "the way of God" help to sustain this notion that evangelical religion and the gang lifestyle are not to be "mixed."

Discerning readers will have noted by now that more than symbolism is at stake in gang leaders' maintenance of the evangelical exemption. The threats against those who would "mess with Curly" by mixing God and gang also make sense from a strategic standpoint. Gang deserters who embrace the evangelical lifestyle are not likely to join another gang or set up shop as freelancers in the drugs, weapons, and extortion trade. For this reason, gang leaders can safely assume that converts—at least those who are serious—will not be competitors for business, nor will they try to settle old scores from internal gang conflicts. Freelancers undercut the gang's income by selling drugs for their own profit and by using the gang's negative social capital—its reputation for violence—to extort business owners and bus and taxi drivers without paying the gang. By requiring gang members to take on a religious identity and lifestyle should they leave, the evangelical exemption helps ensure that gang deserters relinquish their homie identity and any opportunity for profiting from it at the gang's expense.

It is worth noting that what I have dubbed the "evangelical exemption" could also be called the "conversion exemption" or the "religious exemption" since in many cases the ex-gang members who made reference to it did not make explicit that they were referring to an *evangelical* conversion. But the vast majority of conversions in Central America, and virtually *all* of the conversions of former gang members, are evangelical in nature. Both the gangs and the larger society typically assume that a "convert" has converted to some form of evangelical-Pentecostal Christianity. Of course, many of those interviewed did refer to the evangelical nature of the exemption while others clearly assumed it when they employed the term "cristiano," which is synonymous with *evangélico*. Catholic conversions are exceedingly rare and gang youth who decide to "seek out the paths of God" almost always do so in an evangelical context.

I have no way to know for sure how many gang leaders actually respect the evangelical exemption. Although I met many converts who had managed to remain safe for years after having left the gang, I was also told of multiple cases in which a convert had been killed who had been generally regarded as having maintained his conversion and played by the rules. But more than just reprisal from one's former gang mates can end the life of an ex-gang member. Antonio attributed the death of his very active evangelical brother to a payback from his brother's former *rivals* in the MS-13. Similarly, I found plenty of evidence that not everyone who converted but then lost their religious fervor met with the violent fury of the gang. My interviews included a dozen ex-gang members who were not "practicing evangelicals" by any reasonable standard, but in ten of these cases, the "backslidden" convert belonged to a cell that had disintegrated entirely; thus, there was no one left to enforce the morgue rule or to "monitor" those professing a conversion to ensure their veracity. In another case, the ex-gang member and former convert had moved to another area of the country at a moment when his own gang had lost its leader. As a result, he was unlikely to be monitored. Finally, Antonio had also left the gang after professing an evangelical conversion but no longer considered himself an active Christian. It is at least possible, though far from certain, that Antonio's "failed conversion" had something to do with his very real reasons for fearing his former gang.

DEALING WITH ENEMIES

Gang members who leave the gang, even those professing a conversion, have more to worry about than dodging the morgue rule for deserters. Most jumped-in Central American gang members participate in violence and intimidation during their gang tenure and such participation makes them subject to the "boomerang effect" of violence from opposing gang members, vigilantes, or victims and family members of victims of past crimes. In fact, as several ex-gang members recounted being told by their *ranflero*, even those who leave with formal permission from the ranflero forfeit the gang's protection from enemies. Only *pandilleros calmados* retain the right to protection since they also carry the potential to help out as "reservists" when called upon. Ex-gang members worry about how to protect themselves from former enemies without weapons or friends-with-weapons. Converts like Oliver reported feeling protected by God. Oliver had been a ranflero in the Honduran M-18 and thus did not seek "permission" to leave the gang. His concern was rather how to keep himself safe from his former enemies:

> I couldn't sleep at night because I could feel death following close behind me. I was getting desperate and so I was carrying my guns with me everywhere. I had many enemies right here in this neighborhood. So one day I decided to go to church and I left my weapon and everything. And something happened then. I felt the need to go to church. After the service, I met three of my enemies along the way. Three enemies. I was walking with my Bible in my hands and they stopped and turned when they saw me. I said to myself, "That's it. I'm dead." But they—I don't know what

> happened to their sight. But they turned their heads down like this [lowering his head]. And we passed each other like this. And when I got home, my family was crying because those same guys had just been at my house looking for me just before. "They were just here, looking for you to kill you. One was keeping watch on each street corner," they said. They were looking for me to kill me because I used to go out every night at seven or eight to smoke up. But that night I went to church instead. And isn't God something? Because I had walked right by them and they didn't do anything to me and so that's one way that I came to realize God's purpose for me, when I started to recognize it and stay off the streets, away from my old friends, and to look for help.

Not one to take unnecessary risks, Oliver remained holed up in his home for six months during the time of his conversion. But he still attributes his safety for the next six years to divine protection. "I feel at peace now. Wherever I go, Guatemala, El Salvador, I go out with my family without any trouble. Nobody follows me, thanks to God." Raymundo, another gang member who belonged to a different cell in a nearby community, told of a similar experience on his way to an evening church service. When he passed his enemy on the way to the service, "He didn't say anything to me. He had his pistol and I had my Bible and I walked calmly by. We didn't say anything to each other."

Men like Raymundo and Oliver described the Bible as a kind of talisman protecting them from danger whenever they ventured out to attend church services. But divine protection is not the only way to make sense of such testimonies. In the symbolic world of the barrio, the Bible carries enormous weight. Barrio evangelicals, who almost always carry a Bible when walking to religious services, communicate to onlookers that they are attending to matters of eternal significance. When a young man, especially a gang member, carries a Bible, he can be assumed to have experienced or be seeking out a religious conversion. Attacking him while he is carrying a Bible would be a particularly brazen form of "messing with Curly." Just as important, the converted or "converting" gang member is no longer considered a threat since evangelical converts are generally considered "neutral" in matters of violence. Other research on evangelicals and Pentecostals in other parts of Latin America (Brusco 1995; Burdick 1993) bolsters the reports of converts being "left alone" by violent enemies. David Smilde, who researched troubled Venezuelan men who convert to evangelicalism, described *la culebra* (the snake) as an encultured form of vendetta violence that haunts macho Venezuelans who engage in violence. *La culebra* is cultural code of conduct requiring them to "settle old scores" in order to preserve their masculinity (Smilde 2011). Smilde (2007) found that "conversion to evangelicalism provides men with a way to step out of conflict-ridden situations" (2007:6). Wolseth's research coincides on this point: "Conversion lifts [barrio youth] out of everyday violence and reinscribes them in the protective social space of the church" (2008:97). Thus, when Oliver and Raymundo carried a Bible to church, their "safe passage" may have had less to do with divine intervention than with their own willingness to symbolically "forfeit" in the hyper-macho game of get-him-before-he-gets-you by openly advertising their new identity as a Bible-carrying evangelical.

DOMESTICATING LA VIDA LOCA

In addition to its benefit in providing a measure of safety from the morgue rule and from violent enemies, barrio evangelicalism offers a well-publicized method for dealing with the addictions associated with la vida loca. Not that evangelicals promise instant or immediate freedom from addiction. Although a few respondents described their own experience in this way, pastors and gang interventionists know the difficulties involved with drug and alcohol addiction. They provide support in the form of continued interaction and constant "checking-up" on new converts in order to make sure they succeed in their new commitments. It is here that evangelicals' strict Arminianism—that is, their belief that a saved individual can "fall back" out of grace—has social consequences for the converted gang member. Instead of maintaining the belief that "once saved, always saved," most barrio evangelicals believe in the ability of the individual to exercise "free will" both in the initial conversion and in the maintenance of it. It is this understanding of the precarious nature of salvation, coupled with real-world experience, which propels evangelical pastors and ministry workers to keep a close eye on converted

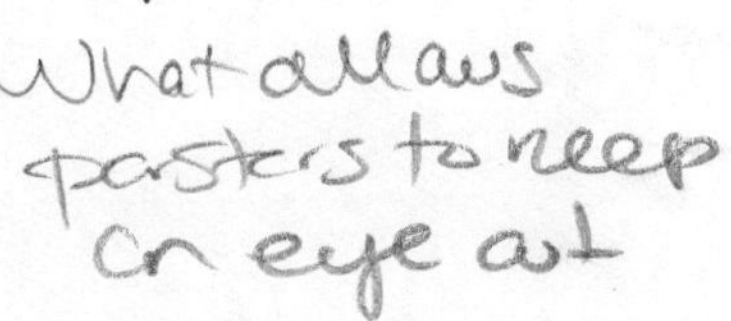

ex-gang members, encouraging them to stay on the right path by avoiding drugs and alcohol.

Still, such "encouragement," which often takes the form of social policing, is hardly enough by itself to keep new converts away from destructive addictions. A more effective means of steering converts away from la vida loca is simple time hoarding. Barrio evangelicals tend to gather with great frequency. Even more important, their largest, most important gatherings take place at night and on weekends, when the gang *mitins* (meetings) take place, the bars and discotecas are open, and drugs and alcohol are widely available. New converts are under significant social pressure from the pastor and church members to demonstrate the depth of their commitment by attending services "whenever the doors are open and the lights are on." Of course, many converted ex-gang members undoubtedly also feel the added "incentive" of vigilant homies observing to make sure the convert is not "messing with God and the gang" by using a professed conversion as cover for continued partying with a different gang. The former member who attends worship regularly, Bible in hand, tells his former gang mates that he is serious about his new religious commitment. Meanwhile, the enormous investment of time, which coincides and interferes with the peak hours of la vida loca, provide additional help in avoiding the temptations and addictions of the gang life.

But *la vida loca* includes more than just substance abuse. Abundant, casual, and sometimes violent sex was routinely cited as a key incentive drawing young males to join the gang in the first place. Sex in this context makes the youth feel like an adult—like a real man. But ex-gang members reported that these encounters sometimes resulted in unwanted pregnancies, sexually transmitted disease, and, more commonly, conflicts with other gang members competing for the same woman. Over time the negative effects began to become more evident and the experience of casual or competitive sex soured. Reining in sexuality is not easy for these youth. Thus, gang members who wished to leave the gang and "formalize" by starting a family found that their sexual "conquests" made settling down to a domestic life difficult at best. Meanwhile, evangelical congregations work hard to promote, support, and, to the degree that they are able, enforce formalized marriages as the only legitimate means of sexual expression. Thus, ex-gang members who convert are expected to end any sexual relationships (very few gang members are legally married) or, if they have a steady relationship, to make plans to marry their partner in the not-so-distant future. Not only are leadership positions within the church unavailable to individuals living in "common law" marriage, "full participation" rights can be withheld from women and men who dismiss the church's standard on sexuality.

Since I was well aware of evangelical policies regarding sexual practice, I was surprised when I found cases in which pastors were offering former gang members considerable time before contracting legal marriage with a live-in partner. One convert, in the presence of his pastor, told me that he was hoping to marry his partner soon but that she wanted a "formal" wedding with a white dress and new shoes and he lacked the money. Other converts told of similar experiences of planning to be married or of having married several months or several years after cohabiting with a partner. But barrio evangelicals do expect converts to legally marry and in the meantime to arrange any relationship with that expectation in mind. In any case, the marriage "requirement" is not just a rule but also an incentive. Congregations often help put up resources for a wedding, including providing the building and a meal. JJ's marriage in 2008 is just one example.

Taken together, marriage (or stable cohabiting en route to marriage) and weekly or nightly involvement in an evangelical congregation provide exiting gang members with an important change of routine and social networks that limits opportunities for engaging in crime and substance abuse, as well as risky sexual encounters and the conflicts that may result. Such new patterns of activity and radical restructuring of time investment resemble what criminologists John Laub and Robert Sampson (2003) refer to as a "knifing off" process. In their longitudinal study of 500 youth with delinquency charges early in life, many of the "desisters"—men who were able to desist from patterns of crime—reported that a marriage or entrance into the military played an important role in changing their lives.

Another way to make sense of barrio evangelicalism's attraction for gang members interested in leaving is by noting the structural similarities between evangelical congregations and gang cells. Although evangelical congregations are not nearly as hermitic as the gang and include members of all ages, both gang and church draw rather bright boundaries between members and nonmembers, and both place high demands on members' time and affiliation. From an institutional point of view, both gangs and evangelical churches in Central America are an example of what Lewis Coser (1974) called "greedy institutions." Jealous of their member's time and attention, greedy institutions "seek exclusive and undivided loyalty" from those who belong to them (1974:4). In return for their "omnivorous" demands of total commitment, they bestow on their members a deep sense of belonging and an efficient hierarchy of the self and its roles. As examples of greedy institutions, Coser cites the Society of Jesus (Jesuits), the Central Intelligence Agency (CIA), and "Protestant fundamentalist sects," all organizations that tend to ask members to subordinate all other roles to that of their membership in the group. Even the traditional American family in the 1970s exemplified a greedy institution for Coser, since it placed enormous demands on the housewife to be at the beck and call of each and every member of the family. Greedy institutions do not engage in outright coercion. In contrast to "total institutions" such as prisons and concentration camps (Goffman 1961), greedy institutions do not *force* their demands upon members by erecting physical barriers to the outside world. Instead, they "maximize assent to their styles of life by appearing highly desirable to the participants" (Coser 1974:6). Time hoarding, then, via multiple and lengthy evening worship services, is part of barrio evangelicals' "greedy" practice of subordinating the social lives of members to the needs and priorities of the faith community. Prohibiting social activities such as drinking or going to bars or night-clubs—frequent and much-anticipated pastimes among young barrio males—helps to erect barriers between the ex-gang member and his former life, "knifing off" the past to an extraordinary degree.

GIVING CONVERTS A "CHANCE"

In many cases the most difficult obstacle facing the homie who has left the gang is landing a steady job. Good jobs are difficult to come by in the barrio and most employers are extremely hesitant to take the risk of hiring an ex-gang member, tattoos or no tattoos (Loudis et al. 2006). Perhaps even more than in the United States, social ties are key to finding *un chance*. Gang members spend years developing relationships within the gang itself. Because these relationships exist within a highly homogenous group, with few ties to the world outside the gang, exiting gang members have few if any social networks from which to seek information or a recommendation in order to obtain paid legal work. Indeed, the typical gang member spends his teenage years ignoring, even alienating, non-gang neighbors and relatives. Furthermore, the age-specific nature of the gang means that ex-gang members have especially few social ties to the older adults who could be of the most help in finding a job or getting an interview. At precisely the moment when a youth is most in need of abundant "weak ties," he finds himself bereft of them.

In this context, joining a church provided many of the ex-gang members I interviewed with the crucial social ties they needed to obtain paid work. Why was this the case? First, frequent worship services and other church activities provide numerous activities for converted ex-gang members to inquire about job possibilities and make themselves available for permanent or temporary work. Joining an evangelical "family" wherein all adult members address each other as "brother" and "sister" means that all members are at least *expected* to take seriously the plight of their spiritual siblings. To the extent that the ex-gang member is able to convince his new family of the genuineness of his conversion, he gains a helping hand from nonrelated adults who possess hitherto unavailable contacts and vocational ties. Of course, few barrio evangelicals are well-connected professionals with an abundance of expertise, insider knowledge, and social capital at the ready. In most cases, due to their low levels of formal education and to their residing in marginal neighborhoods, barrio evangelicals face some of the same forces of social isolation and stratification that gang members face. Furthermore, as members of an organization that places high demands on their routines and their relationships while discouraging involvement in political parties (Steigenga 2001), the *hermanos* are unlikely to possess sought-after connections to professional or government jobs. Nevertheless, most congregations do have at least some members with formal jobs and a membership that is considerably more heterogeneous in age and background than the typical gang cell. The "weak ties" these members do possess become available to converted ex-gang members.

Second, and more important, pastors themselves were a crucial resource in landing a job. Several converted ex-gang members reported having found a job as a direct result of a recommendation or referral from their pastor. Danilo reported that he had been hired in a bakery only after his pastor wrote a letter of recommendation on his behalf. JJ was accepted into the USAID-funded employment program for ex-gang members called "Challenge 100" only after his pastor had vouched for the quality of his character in the two years since leaving the gang. The job, assembling computer equipment at a large computer hardware outlet, came with full legal benefits including basic medical insurance and legal bonuses—a rare find for a youth without high school diploma and with tattoos on his eyelids![4] In a few cases, pastors themselves provided work and invaluable apprenticing until a formal job could be found. At Youth Restoration, a small church-run ministry spearheaded by a Mennonite church in the gang-heavy Honduran neighborhood of Chamelecon, the pastor, a self-employed electrician, takes newly converted ex-gang members with him to construction jobs whenever these are available, employing them as apprentices in electrical circuitry and block-laying. In other cases, pastors take recent converts with them on pastoral visits or evangelistic campaigns, providing them with food and lodging while "hoarding" their time to keep them away from their old friends. When nothing else is available, some converted ex-gang members have taken to leveraging their own religious testimonies into a source of income. For instance, a few converted ex-gang members told of giving their testimony on a bus and then "passing the hat" for donations.

Finally, when jobs fail to materialize, some congregations helped converts in other ways. JJ recalled receiving material aid soon after converting, when, as a recent gang deserter, he was having great difficulty finding work:

> The people of God were very aware of what was going on. They gave me staples, food. They gave me money to buy milk for the baby and I would look for work but I couldn't find any. But that was the fruit of all those

> sixteen years in the gang, the result of the stains [tattoos] on my body, the criminal record . . . People [not belonging to the church] would look at me and decide that I was way too dangerous. I looked for work and [employers] would reject me.

Although JJ's local congregation was initially unable to provide him with a job, their ability to help him provide for his partner and their infant son allowed him to bridge the gap between the lost income from gang participation and the job that eventually materialized at the computer parts wholesaler. That job as well was provided with the help of his pastor's recommendation.

What these reports make clear is that the flipside of "greedy institutions" like the congregations of Central America's barrio evangelicals is their generosity. True, barrio evangelicals place great moral demands on their members, limiting their noncongregational social ties while seeking steep contributions in terms of time and energy. But such resources of time, energy, and social ties do not "evaporate" once they are relinquished to the congregation. They can be and often *are* redistributed among the members according to need. In this respect, Coser's concept of "greedy institutions" resembles economist Laurence Iannaccone's theory regarding why "strict churches" thrive. For Iannaccone (1994), these congregations thrive precisely *because* they set the bar for membership so high, limiting free-riding by members with low commitment. Since all or most members make large contributions of time and energy, strict churches have more abundant religious and social goods to offer all members. As many of the gang members who converted and joined an evangelical congregation found, new members (converts) who demonstrate their own willingness to surrender their time and loyalty, usually receive a flood of attention, be it in the form of "checking-up" on lifestyle commitments, help with finding a job, or bridging the gap economically until a new form of income can be found. Evangelical congregations have their own reasons, both institutional and theological, for providing such support to converted gang members specifically, as well as to gang members who show *potential* to convert. From obtaining a "pass" on the morgue rule to getting help with abandoning la vida loca and finding a steady job, it pays to become an hermano.

WHY *NOT* CONVERT? THE COST OF CONVERSION

In light of the benefits encountered by gang members converting on their way out of the gang, it's worth asking why not *all* gang members who leave the gang convert to evangelical Christianity. After all, if it "pays" to convert, why not join the hermanos? Complicating the question "Why *not* convert?" is the matter of whether or not one can "choose" to be a religious convert at all. Is conversion merely a rational choice made after taking account of your options? Assuming some gang members do in fact "decide" to convert, there are real costs associated with evangelical conversion. In fact it was the very institutional "greed" of evangelical congregations that made some ex-gang members wary of converting in the first place. For example, when I asked nonconverted ex-gang members or "nonpracticing" converts why they were not active, many responded that the expectation of regular worship attendance was too great a burden. Others worried that the evangelical hermanos would judge them based on their appearance or cast them out if they ventured into a church. A few spoke of having entered a church *seeking* a conversion but had concluded from stares and indirect comments that they were not welcome. Some of these youth sought and found other congregations more welcoming to them, but others were turned off by the experience and sought out other, nonreligious alternatives.

In addition to tying up free time—and, in part, because of it—conversion also entails a severing of ties with male friends "on the street." It is a given that a converted ex-gang member will cut off friendships with erstwhile gang members, but greedy institutions, such as evangelical congregations, often require converts to sacrifice *all* friendships that have the potential to compromise the commitment and identity of the new convert. While this practice may be helpful as a means of "knifing off" a former lifestyle, it can also give pause to some gang members who would like to be free of the gang but not stripped of their former social ties and activities. Raul, a nonconverted former Vato Loco from Honduras, reported that he hoped to some day become a Christian but that for the moment, he thought it best not to make the commitment since he was not sure he could live up to its demands. He explained:

> You've got your friends. Maybe if I'm hanging out with these friends, there will be vulgarities and other things like that. Then someone will

> come along and invite me to church and I'll go. But later I can be punished because let's say that later on I decide to go to a discoteca and get out on the floor and dance. Then I can be punished even worse because then I'm just playing around. I'm not taking things seriously as I should. But I have faith in God that some day I will be able to serve him. I'm confident that some day I'll be a true Christian to serve him.

Raul did not specify who exactly would "punish" him for "playing around" by professing a conversion while maintaining ties to the vida loca of the gang. Whether it was God or the gang, Raul's comment reveals the strict moralist standards of behavior of barrio evangelicalism and how such standards raise the stakes for converting. For Raul, and other nonconverts who liked hanging out with their friends, enjoying a beer and an occasional night at the nightclub, it seemed safer to find less severe or abrupt means to "settle down" and leave the barrio than becoming an hermano. To risk angering God or the gang with a halfhearted attempt was something he wanted to avoid, at least for the moment. Raul's comment also points to the impact of conversion on the masculinity of exiting gang members. Several converts recalled receiving ridicule from other gang members. Although many gang leaders officially "respect" evangelical religion and the conversions that they deem genuine, individual gang members can offer converts plenty of ribbing for having given up the hyper-macho lifestyle of la vida loca in exchange for the teetotaling, domesticated lifestyle of the hermanos. Simply leaving the gang is itself grounds for questioning the masculinity of deserters—leavers were accused of *chavaleando,* or "backing out like a girl." Former M-18 member Ronaldo recalled being made fun of when he first considered leaving the gang. Although the Honduran youth had not yet left the gang, he had decided not to "go out on the street" for a week in order to give himself time to think the matter over. When his fellow homies came looking for him, they derided him with the worst possible accusation:

> I hadn't left my house for a week and all the guys came over and started saying, "Pucha, You've turned gay!" they said. "You're ruined! Oh no! Now the only thing left is to become a Christian."
>
> "No way!" I told them. "How could you think that? A Christian is the last thing I'll ever be. I'd rather die first." After that I fell back into the street life again because of their criticisms.

As this episode shows, the threat of a ruined masculinity looms large in the Central American barrio. Gang members use the *maricón* (fag) epithet to intimidate and humiliate those interested in joining the warm embrace of the evangelical church. Nor was Ronaldo the only ex-gang member to mention the homosexual connotations of becoming an evangelical Christian. Calín, a former MS-13 member, recalled his own inner dialogue as he described to me his "moment of conversion" while speaking by phone with a famous Honduran radio evangelist:

> The pastor said to me, "Do you want to be a Christian?"
>
> "No!" I said. "I'm a pandillero. I live for my barrio and kill for it too."
>
> [The evangelist replied] "Son, would you like to accept Jesus Christ into your heart?"
>
> When he said this it made an impact and I felt my heart might jump out of my chest. And I said to myself, "If you do this, you'll be a fag (*maricón*), you'll be a homosexual. Don't be stupid. [Think about] the money, the women. You're going to have to quit smoking. No, no, no!"

Earlier in the interview, Calín had reported that when he joined the gang at age fourteen, he felt it was "a man's thing." Now, faced with the possibility of conversion and giving up smoking, money, and frequent sex, he worried that his reputation would be ruined. His fears were not without merit. The violence, substance abuse, and misogyny of the gang represent a kind of hyper-machismo—an exaggerated form of what Raewyn Connell has called "hegemonic masculinity" (Connell 2005). Barrio evangelicals, while hardly questioning the basic tenets of hegemonic masculinity, nevertheless seek to curb its violent, exaggerated expression in the barrio by shunning personal acts of violence, proscribing alcohol, and prioritizing the home and family. Activities such as smoking, extramarital sex, and having a beer with the guys are all off limits for the *cristiano*. By converting, the gang member sets himself up for ridicule not only from the homies still in the gang but also from male friends, family, and neighbors who do not share his religious piety. Scholars such as Elizabeth Brusco (1995), John Burdick (1993), and David Smilde (2007) have written about the "domesticating" role played by evangelical religion among working-class Latin American men. Although evangelicals symbolically continue the pattern of male headship in the home and uniformly reject homosexual expression and practice as sin, even the suggestion of a man reducing his sphere of sexual influence to the home and of placing voluntary limits on his male autonomy are enough to render his masculinity subject to serious criticism on the street.

Nevertheless, gang members considering a conversion fear more than just the wrath of the gang. Many have themselves internalized the injunction not to "mess with Curly" by mixing gang and religion. Antonio, the former Eighteenth Street member murdered in 2007, recounted his own struggle not to smoke while carrying a Bible when he first began attending worship services.

> I remember sometimes on the way to church with the Bible I would feel like I HAD to smoke drugs. I remember that I would hide my Bible under my arm or my sweater to go inside the store and buy a cigarette to smoke because I couldn't stand the anxiety.

When I asked Antonio to explain further he put it this way:

> It's like this. When I would go to church it was like something inside me said that smoking on the way to church is bad. Like God was doing something inside me, CHANGING me, you know? And so I felt ASHAMED (*sentía PENA*) for people to see me carrying a Bible while smoking. And so I would hide my Bible so that I wouldn't feel ashamed if people saw me. I wasn't that cynical, you know?

According to Antonio, it was not the gang's policing of conversion that made him wary of "mixing" religion and his former life but, rather, a combination of concern for what neighbors might think as well as his own belief that smoking on the way to church was itself a "cynical" act with the potential to undermine the "change" he felt was already taking place within. After all, not just the gang but "Curly" himself is watching.

MAKING THE CONVERSION LEAP

Clearly, the prospect of an evangelical conversion represents both "benefits" and "costs" to the gang member who has become *aburrido* or "fed up" with the gang life. On the one hand, a "genuine" conversion can bring a measure of safety for the convert. At the same time, the cost to a convert's masculine reputation, the considerable time investment, and the possibility of facing a "green light" if a conversion should fail are just as real. So how do gang members considering a "leap of faith" make the difficult decision of whether to convert or to find some other pathway out such as migrating, becoming a calmado, or waiting for a window of opportunity? Furthermore, can conversion really be boiled down to a rational act of weighing known costs against potential benefits? Some converts reported their conversion as just that—a rational conclusion based on a sanguine assessment of the limited options before them. For example, the matter seemed quite straightforward and simple to former Eighteenth Street member Tomás:

> I gave my life to Christ because I was fed up (*aburrido*) with killing, bothering people; and only God can change the way we think. When I received Christ I received spiritual and moral support as well as material support from the *hermanos*.

Others reported thinking it over for at least some specified time. Danilo, the Honduran who now works in a bakery thanks to a recommendation from his pastor, converted after his partner became very ill. Desperate to find a cure as well as to make a new start with his life, Danilo reported spending a couple of days wrestling with the decision before striking a "pact" with God. "I kept thinking and thinking about it. It wasn't easy. I didn't want to leave my friends, the gang, none of it. But I kept thinking about how much I loved her and I decided to try it. 'If God exists and has power to heal, let him heal her,' I said. 'I want to see it.'" Since the health of Danilo's partner showed rapid improvement shortly after his conversion, the young man felt obliged to follow through with his side of the "pact" by abandoning the gang and la vida loca altogether. When I interviewed him, he was very active in a small Holiness congregation in his hometown on the northern Honduran coast. Such "bargains" were mentioned as instrumental in the conversion decision of multiple gang members, although it was usually the life of the gang member himself, freedom from prison, or addiction that were bargained for rather than the health of a loved one. At the same time, other gang members like Raymundo reported that the costs for conversion remained too high. Raymundo still enjoyed his freedom, including the ability to hang out with friends and go to the *discoteca*. Since he had been out of the gang for several years and the cell he belonged to was no longer active, he felt no pressing need to convert although he expected that he might well do so at some point. In short, my interviews with young men and women across Central America led me to conclude that some level of cost-benefit analysis is usually in play when gang members seeking to exit choose the pathway of evangelical conversion. Not that such "analysis" necessarily takes the form of an organized or deliberate attempt to sort out the possible outcomes. More frequently, converted ex-gang members described it as a *process* involving key moments of intense emotion in the gang, the home, or in a church.

Occasionally converts emphasized a single momentary conversion experience. For these youth, the emotional "crisis" packed a wallop that arrested the attention of the gang member. Such was the case for Emerson. In 2006 Emerson belonged to a subsidiary of the M-18 in Guatemala City, but he had become fed up with the gang lifestyle and was increasingly worried about his prospects for staying alive. Those fears came to a head one afternoon while participating in a gang battle that led to his arrest and subsequent beating at the police station. Though he was later released when police failed to testify at his court hearing, he found himself paralyzed by the fear of falling victim to the morgue rule. Emerson had already begun looking for a conversion, occasionally attending church services in the neighborhood. He had even made several "bargains" with God in the heat of gang battles, but he had so far been unable to follow through with any of these commitments. Emerson recalled that some Pentecostal women from the neighborhood had begun "pestering" him, trying to convince him to leave the gang and join the church:

> One day . . . [the women] came to my house, man, and they started to talk to me but that day, who knows what was going on because they started to pray for me and started placing their hands on me and I felt like, as if my body was getting hotter all over inside, man, and you should have seen in that instant I started—I hadn't cried, man, in maybe six or seven years, I hadn't cried but instead I would do things to get out whatever it was inside of me, I mean I would look for something like, illegal to do, something

> bad to get out whatever I was feeling but I didn't cry, man. And at that time, believe me, I was left like this [covers his face with his hands] . . . and all of a sudden I started to cry, man. I started to cry—something that, never, y'know? I mean it had been so long since I'd done it, not even while in the gang, man, not ever, because in the gang they make you feel strong like, they make you feel like "Nobody messes with me," right? And if you feel like they hurt you, you do more damage than ever, right? . . . So imagine, I haven't cried in all that time and these were chicks (*chavas*) that were praying for me, and me all shy and me with my hands over my face and like a little kid I was like [makes sobbing noises] because I felt like that. Look man, you should have seen it and I wanted to stop because like I said, you get shy if there are chicks watching you bawl, right? Like after they've seen you like with your head up high [in the gang] and then they watch you bawling. I wanted to stop and I couldn't man. I hid my face and my Mom was there too, bawling and bawling.

Afterward, Emerson recalled that word spread about what had happened and his friends in the gang wanted to know what was up. "And then they stopped by to see me and I told them I didn't want to continue anymore, right? That I wanted to stay in the church because in the church I felt really good." Emerson's conversion story is important for several reasons. First, Emerson's account makes clear references to the experience of shame while participating in the gang. His report that in the gang, "if they hurt you, you do more damage than ever," lends weight to the role of the "shame-rage spiral" as an energizer of violence in the Central American gang. Second, his account provides a close-up view of a "key moment" in conversion and how an emotional experience was interpreted as the cornerstone of conversion that had hitherto seemed impossible. Emerson had "hoped" to convert but had not yet been able to muster the resolve necessary to follow through on that desire—or in any case, to believe in its imminence. Third, Emerson's acute awareness that others were watching and assessing his embodied expression of emotion reveals the important role of emotional display during and after a crisis conversion. In short, the accounts of Emerson and others show that when the prospect of carrying out a conversion and leaving the gang seems difficult or impossible, the experience and subsequent interpretation of emotion can became a lever for bringing about

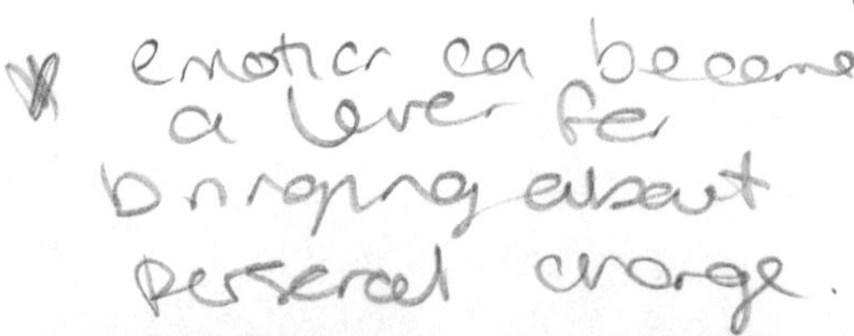

such a personal change project. Rather than ask Emerson to detail any "moment" of conversion or describe his emotions at a particular moment, I simply asked if he considered himself a Christian and allowed him to recount anything he felt important enough to relate regarding his own faith. However, like several other converts, Emerson felt it necessary to describe in detail his own means of overcoming the "rational" dilemma in which he found himself. He "wanted" to convert and leave the gang but could not find the willpower to announce to his gang that he was leaving. Thus, his "decision" came not after another round of weighing the costs and benefits of leaving but, according to his own recollection, when he found himself in the midst of an intimate, emotional ritual, surrounded by praying women. Furthermore, the role of shame in Emerson's conversion account is unmistakable. Emerson was caught in the shame-rage spiral in which young men experiencing shame and deeply damaged social bonds seek to mask shame by enacting violent outbursts of anger aimed at shaming others: "I would look for something like, illegal to do, something bad to get out whatever I was feeling but I didn't cry, man." Crying in this context was an open acknowledgement of weakness, an expression revealing vulnerability. Emerson remembered using anger, or "doing something illegal," as a means of avoiding the experience.

Several ex-gang members reported that weeping, especially in public, was strictly prohibited in the gang. As such, the prohibition illustrates what Arlie Hochschild would call the strict "feeling rules" of the gang. Hochschild notes that all societies and subcultures regulate the experience and display of emotions and these regulations are deeply gendered (Hochschild 1983). Weeping violates the gang's hyper-masculine code of pride and "respect." For Emerson, weeping marked what sociologist Erving Goffman (1963) referred to as a "bridge-burning event," and as such, it went a long way toward spoiling his identity as a macho homie. The "emotion logic" of evangelical religion, however, is markedly different from that of the gang and embraces and encourages weeping in public even for men. Thus, by weeping in the presence of other evangelicals, Emerson laid the initial groundwork for establishing his credentials as an evangelical hermano.

Emerson's account also sheds light on the way emotions can work to communicate not only to onlookers but to the individual himself. The subjective experience of emotions can be "managed" but not always tightly controlled. Thus, the experience of certain embodied states, especially those that are unfamiliar or have been repressed for some time, communicates to the individual that something "important" or monumental is taking place, a shift to which the subject cannot help but pay close attention (Hochschild 1983). Emerson reported that "I don't know what was going on" when his body became hot all over and he started to shake; he appeared to view this as proof of the authenticity of the experience since it was something he could not himself have predicted or produced. Thus, his emotional experience served as a "clue" signaling an important inner change. Later, the mere remembrance of the experience provided a biographical marker, dating the conversion with a specific time and place.

Other ex-gang members reported similar experiences even though I did not ask any interviewees for details about a "moment of conversion" or emotional details. Pancho, the Honduran MS-13 leader who expressed deep shame when recalling the experience of being abandoned by his mother, recounted the emotional content of his own conversion event. After several unhappy months in an evangelical rehab center where he had been sent by a judge, he had made up his mind to escape the following day. A visiting pastor approached him and began to deliver a "prophetic" warning regarding his future if he escaped:

> When the pastor said this to me my whole body began to shake and shake and [I started] to cry. I started crying and crying like a baby and the truth, man, is that I hadn't cried in approximately eleven years. I was a brother [English word used] and I'd always said to myself, "I'm crazy." I remember that the only day I'd let tears go, man, was the day they killed my best friend (*carnal*), but apart from that day, during that whole time I'd never cried and I began crying man, like a baby and asking forgiveness from God, right? For everything I'd done, for all that had happened, right? And for the damage I'd caused my family and then everybody was shocked, man, from watching how I cried. And I cried for approximately four hours, crying, man . . . And the pastor, man, praying for me then. And after this I said to God then, "God, you know what? I'm going to stay here after all. Help me," I told him . . .

Like Emerson, Pancho also recalled that the emotion "display rules" of the gang were even more stringent in prison than on the street. For an incarcerated gang leader like Pancho, the repression of shame had meant avoiding weeping at all costs. But when confronted by a pastor who delivered a "personalized" prophetic warning, Pancho found himself unable to continue bypassing his own shame and began weeping "like a baby." However, by "asking forgiveness" Pancho acknowledged past wrongdoings and by agreeing to stay at the center rather than escape, he took an important first step in repairing the social bonds to non-gang society that had been allowed to deteriorate for eleven years. In fact, both Pancho's and Emerson's conversion accounts display strong elements of what criminologist John Braithwaite calls "reintegrative shaming" (Braithwaite 1989). For Braithwaite, a proponent of "restorative justice," cultural ceremonies involving the public acknowledgement and subsequent discharge of unacknowledged shame provide an effective and vastly underutilized approach to dealing with crime and criminal offenders. In the modern, urban West, shame goes unacknowledged and crime is "punished" by an impersonal state more interested in dispensing punitive justice than in reintegrating offenders by obliging them to publicly acknowledge their guilt and make reparations. Such "disintegrative shaming" simply extends the shame-rage spiral by labeling offenders as hopeless criminals, consigning them to further shame and extending endless recidivism. On the other hand, since shame is a key emotional "engine" motivating ongoing violence, offenders who can be brought to acknowledge their wrongdoing in a public setting can effectively discharge shame and be reintegrated into the social fabric rather than ostracized further. Furthermore, the social, interactive nature of reintegrative shaming allows for a two-way reparation of the social bond opening up the possibility for a renewal of trust and the reincorporation of the offender (Collins 2004).

I am not arguing here that emotional conversion experiences are the same as formal restorative justice programs that bring victims and offenders together and establish a plan allowing the offender to "restore" something of value to the victim who has been violated. I am arguing instead that emotional religious conversions gain some of their impact by drawing on the same social psychological dynamics at work in programs consciously designed to promote reintegrative shaming. Most notably, public conversions like Ricardo's bear a resemblance to reintegrative shaming because by providing space for the acknowledgement of shame in a public setting, they allow offender and community to take an important first step toward restoring the social bond that was damaged by the offender's actions.[5] Indeed, in Ricardo's own account of his deeply emotional conversion experience, weeping in public drew the attention of onlookers beyond the congregation itself no doubt because of the symbolic power contained in the emotional acknowledgement of shame for past wrongdoings. Nor did the "symbolic" nature of the experience communicate solely to those watching. Ricardo remembered "feeling better" afterward—so much better that, like Emerson, Pancho, and others, he continued returning to the lively evangelical worship services, developing a "taste" for new lines of action involving other means of responding to felt shame than simply engaging in further violence. Afterward, relinquishing his weapons and disposing of his marijuana stash seemed to him like the obvious next step.

What do we learn from emotional conversion accounts like those of Emerson, Pancho, and Ricardo—or for that matter of Calín's "pounding heart" or Abner's report of "glorious" tears or Ismael's recollection of solitary sobbing? It seems clear that such emotion experiences involve more than simply feigned sincerity or conjured sentimentality. In weeping, these individuals reported finding themselves, sometimes against their immediate will, on the other side of an emotional "threshold." Crossing that threshold involved trespassing a deeply gendered feeling rule of the gang—homies don't cry. Therefore, the experience came to mark a biographical "moment zero" dating the conversion and allowing the convert a sense of security in moving forward with the project of personal reform. Emerson reported telling the gang he was finished a few days later. Ricardo turned over his weapons and destroyed his stash of pot, while Pancho abandoned his plans to escape to return to the gang. Clearly, these intentions were not completely new. Ricardo and Emerson had already been contemplating leaving the gang and all three surely knew of the "evangelical exemption" prior to their moments of emotional conversion. But neither escaping nor converting seemed fully possible prior to the emotional event. In short, their conversion involved *both* a decision to seek out evangelical religion, "hoping" for the possibility of a conversion, and a subjective, emotional experience

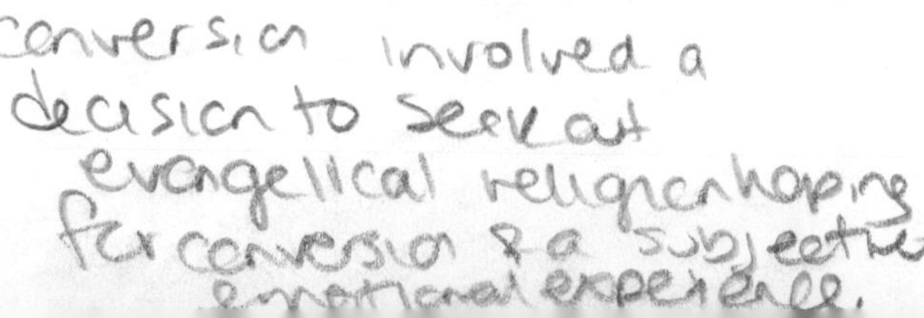

that facilitated transformation by setting in motion new approaches for dealing with shame.

EMOTION, SHAME, AND THE SOCIOLOGY OF CONVERSION

The accounts of the converted homies speak to the larger literature on the sociology of conversion. Sociologists have been analyzing religious conversions for decades, perhaps in part because they provide a means for exploring—and debating—the potential for an intensely social phenomenon, such as religion, to radically alter the habits and views of an individual. Most conversion studies debate the causal influence of social factors such as an absence of strong social networks resulting in the "structural availability" of potential converts (Rambo 1993; Snow and Machalek 1983) or emphasize the capacity of converts to freely choose conversion as individual agents (Straus 1979). Rodney Stark, a prominent sociologist of religion, argues that religious conversion represents little more than an attempt by the "convert" to align her religious views with her changing social networks (Stark and Bainbridge 1980; Stark and Finke 2000). At times, the debates over the factors leading to conversion end up resembling a tug-of-war between those who see conversion as a "caving" to social pressures and those who view it as an achievement accomplished by a rational, utility-maximizing agent. With a few recent exceptions (Frankenberg 2004; Winchester 2008), embodied experience is not a common topic in the sociological conversion studies.

In his book *Reason to Believe: Culture and Agency in Venezuelan Evangelicalism* cultural sociologist David Smilde (2007) moves this conversation in a helpful direction by asking why some Venezuelan men in the midst of personal struggles with crime and addiction were "able" to convert while others, who seemed sincerely desirous of the organization that a religious conversion might bring to their chaotic lives, were, in the end, unable to convert. He concludes, among other things, that individuals *can* "choose" to believe if they have good enough "reasons" for doing so. By "reasons," Smilde refers both to the practical outcomes of self-reform promised by evangelicalism's disciplined, teetotaling lifestyle as well as to the relatively simple theological concepts of a doctrinal system involving an empowering God and a debilitating devil. For Smilde, evangelical conversion in Venezuela provides a means for reinventing the male self-identity in such a way that the convert is lent greatly enhanced personal agency during critical moments of personal struggle. Through what he calls "imaginative rationality . . . [p]eople encounter problems, create new projects to address these problems and then evaluate the success of these projects" (2007:52). The men in his study were able to gain effective control over an array of personal struggles and setbacks in part by adopting the symbolic system of evangelical Christianity and viewing their own problems in light of this new system. This is not unique to Christianity, he notes. "People create concepts by combining and attaching existing, usually well-known images to inchoate objects of experience. They thereby gain a cognitive fix on these experiences that facilitates action with respect to them" (2007:52).

Smilde's account of the semiotic power of a symbolic system for empowering individuals to achieve personal efficacy in a moment of crisis is certainly useful. Many of the converted ex-gang members I interviewed did indeed use evangelical concepts of an empowering God or Holy Spirit and a debilitating devil to help them account for their own respective achievements and setbacks when trying to break free of the gang and its violent, addictive lifestyle. But for that matter, so did some of the nonconverts. Young men like Ovidio described themselves as caught in a struggle with the devil to overcome drug addiction and lethargy. Ovidio would like to convert but cannot seem to manage it. So far, he lamented, the devil held the upper hand. At the same time, other converted ex-gang members described their conversion not as a cognitive realization *or* a calculated decision based on an assessment of the benefits and drawbacks of conversion or gang exit. Indeed, many had long since decided that they would like to leave the gang and most *already* believed in what amounts to an evangelical Christian symbolic system. Their conversion came not when they "bought in" to a religious narrative but rather when they became emotionally overwhelmed by it, usually in the context of a religious ritual such as a sermon or a prayer service. Young men like Emerson, Pancho, and Ricardo told of converting "body-first" in a deeply emotional event, the embodied sensations and social repercussions of which caused them to both doubt their "true" identity as a homie and to place confidence in their emerging identity as hermanos. Furthermore, the power of such experiences appeared intimately connected to the transgression of well-known, gendered emotion rules in the gang and in the church. Once a gang member had violated the emotion display rule prohibiting weeping in public—regardless of whether or not he had intended to do so—the experience of emotional vulnerability (and the fact that others had witnessed it) produced a ripple effect, allowing and even obliging the convert to set aside the constant obsession with maintaining *el respeto* and the constant projection of angry dominance.

Ricardo's conversion was no accident. Worn out by the gang life, fearing that an enemy gang member would kill him, and sick of being hounded by the police, the twenty-three-year-old had been considering leaving the gang for quite some time. Furthermore, Ricardo was well aware of the potential resources that evangelical practice had to offer in terms of both providing a supportive community and offering theological concepts for gaining a "cognitive fix" on his troubles. But for Ricardo, as for at least eight of the other converts (all of them still practicing religion at the time of the interview) who told emotional stories of conversion unprompted by my questions, leaving the gang seemed somehow impossible before the emotional conversion experience. The benefits for being free of the gang were high, but so were the potential costs for converting. Thus, when Ricardo left the gang to convert, it was not, in Ricardo's estimate, merely the result of a cost-benefit analysis but rather the result of a routine-shattering, bridge-burning, deeply embodied, and highly social event during which he publicly acknowledged his shame while displaying the ultimate social indicator of "feminine" vulnerability—weeping on his knees. That the event caused a stir in the neighborhood is hardly a surprise given Ricardo's reputation as a well-known gang leader.

Of course, the emotional experience for Ricardo marked only the beginning of his transformation. There were tattoos to remove, classes to take, and relationships to mend. But as a means of discharging shame in the presence of witnesses, the conversion fit the bill par excellence. Evangelical hermanos, excited by the thrill of witnessing a spiritually "powerful" event, gathered around him to pray, undoubtedly energizing Ricardo's commitment to change by providing emotional energy from a powerful ritual in a sacred space, adding to his resolve. In short, Ricardo's conversion experience illustrates the power of emotion as a lever for human transformation. If, as theorists such as Scheff point out, shame is indeed the "master emotion" shaping interaction by establishing patterns of emotional energy, then it makes sense that symbolically acknowledging shame in a public setting forms a powerful and largely overlooked factor in religious conversion studies. Sociologists of conversion have identified changes to the convert's "universe of discourse" (Snow and Machalek 1983), "root reality" (Heirich 1977; Smilde 2007), or "usable narrative" (Smilde 2007) as the key ingredients in engendering changes in practice. But all of these perspectives place too much emphasis on changes to the convert's "way of seeing." The ex-gang members' emotion-laden conversion accounts illustrate the importance of paying attention to deeply embodied, gendered experiences of emotion that result in changes to the former homies' "way of feeling" and of expressing emotion, thereby laying the groundwork for fundamental transformations in practice or "lines of action."

CONCLUSION

We began with the question, How does conversion "work" for the homie who becomes an *hermano*? Clearly evangelical conversion provides practicing converts with some measure of safety due to the evangelical exemption and to its symbolic association with opting out of the violent code of the barrio. In addition, evangelical congregations help converts overcome debilitating addictions associated with la vida loca through social policing and time hoarding and by strongly encouraging, if not requiring, legal marriage. Finally, many gang members find help from the church when looking for work, especially from pastors who can connect them with temporary work or provide a crucial recommendation for a wary employer. Congregations are able to do this in part because of their nature as "greedy institutions" that require large investments of time and energy on the part of members but are nevertheless generous when it comes to sharing their abundance of social networks, time, and material resources with newly committed believers who show a willingness to convert and commit. Some of these findings are not new, since we know that evangelical faith offers troubled Latin American men a resource for reordering chaotic lives (Brusco 1995; Chesnut 2003; Smilde 2007). Rather, what is new and surprising is the extent to which evangelical conversion and participation in an evangelical congregation helps violent, heavily stigmatized "outsiders" (Becker 1963) like the Central American gang homies find acceptance and reintegration in communities that have come to fear and loathe them. In effect, evangelical congregations provide an entire resocialization program free of charge.

Additionally, there are nonmonetary costs associated with conversion. Gang members must surrender for good their access to a variety of rituals and pastimes that figure prominently in the maintenance of a macho identity. They can expect to receive, at the very least, a ribbing from their former gang mates and others who may question the masculinity of a new convert. Worse yet, the convert risks being violently called to account should he fail in his conversion project and be accused of "messing with Curly." Thus, the prospect of a conversion, while attractive to many, is by no means a simple "decision." Although many youth desiring to leave the gang did report weighing both the potential costs and the benefits of conversion, the key moment in a conversion sometimes came as a result of a subjective, deeply embodied emotional experience in which the gang member "tried on" the experience of acknowledging shame through weeping in public and concluded that it "felt good." In these cases, the gang member's "reasons" for believing lay in reflections on an interactive experience saturated with bodily sensations. Thus, intensive conversion experiences offer an emotional lever for effecting personal change through the forging of new lines of action motivated not by efforts to mask or bypass shame but through an acknowledgement of it, to repair the social bond and begin reforging ties to the non-gang community. If these conclusions help us to understand how and why gang members convert, at least one question remains for anyone interested in understanding the role of religion in Central America: Why do churches go to the trouble and expense of helping out gang converts in the first place?

6
Samaritans and Crusaders

I don't wait for the government to help me. I hope that the church solves [the gang problem]. Because I think the church is the one with the solution to this problem—the church as a church—because this is a spiritual problem.
—Pastor Luis Arreola, founder of "Gangs for Christ" (Guatemala City)

"The church cannot respond as a church! The problem is with society and only by responding as a society can we begin to address this issue!"
—Fr. José María Morataya (San Salvador)

After dark, the collective taxis from Honduras's northern industrial city of San Pedro Sula stop at the edge of Chamelecón. When my contact and I arrived at the entrance to this urban satellite community of 50,000 inhabitants, the taxi driver informed us that this was as far as he would take us. "You're lucky I brought you this far," he said. Chamelecón is one of several satellite neighborhoods creating a vast belt of impoverished and crime-ridden barrios encircling Honduras's northern industrial city of one million. On December 23, 2004, Chamelecón gained international notoriety overnight when armed men, ostensibly gang members, stopped a public bus and riddled it with gunfire from automatic weapons, killing twenty-eight passengers, most of them women and children. The perpetrators left a note indicating that the crime was in response to the president's all-out war on crime. When I visited the community in 2007, the barrio had become synonymous with gang violence in the minds of millions of Hondurans. After two blocks of walking the wide dirt streets—dark and eerily quiet already at 7:30 in the evening—I was glad to meet one of the planners of the event I had been invited to attend.

Five young men, two of them ex-gang members, had organized a special two-night evangelistic campaign aimed specifically at gang members. Together with the pastor of the local Mennonite congregation,[1] the young men had founded a gang exit program called "Youth Restoration." The program, which had recently celebrated its first anniversary, sought to convince gang members to leave the gang and to persuade young sympathizers to join the church instead of being jumped into the gang. Our guide, a former gang sympathizer, was visibly excited about the event and led us on his BMX bicycle to the place where the event would take place, an outdoor park with a reputation for violent encounters. The setup of a large sound system was well under way and lights had been hung from palm trees surrounding the "stage"—a former public swimming pool long-since filled with dirt. The people streaming in for the event eventually numbered 200 or 300. Some sat on chairs while others stood or milled about on the perimeter. Behind the seated audience was a row of young men and boys, the "special guests" made up of gang members and sympathizers who wore specially printed invitations, hand-delivered by the organizers in the days leading up to the event. The title of the event, as seen posted on the event's t-shirts was, "Escape with Your Life."

Heading the bill on the first evening was a Christian reggaeton group called *Soldados de Cristo* (Christ's Soldiers). After a short introduction and a pair of charismatic songs led by the pastor, who also played the synthesizer, the *Soldados* took the stage. The three young men wore ghetto-style clothing—baggy jeans, huge t-shirts, oversized baseball caps, and gold crucifix necklaces. The leader announced that his group did not normally sing in churches but rather chose to perform at secular venues and clubs, ostensibly in order to better evangelize those who frequent them. After cringing through one or two half-sung, half-shouted songs I began to feel sorry for the club patrons. But here at the campaign the specially invited gang members and sympathizers seemed thrilled. Apparently, being tone deaf is not a serious impediment to singing reggaeton. No one in the band gave the slightest indication of being able to carry a pitch. In any case, the message was thoroughly Christian as the group chanted about being transformed by Jesús and "Papa Dios." After awhile the pastor retook the stage. Pastor José, an energetic twenty-eight-year-old and father of four, preached an impromptu sermon—the invited speaker, I learned later, had been unable to find the venue. The pastor's text was Proverbs 16:6: "By mercy and truth iniquity is purged: and by the fear of the Lord men depart from evil."[2] He then launched into a blistering critique of the government's approach to dealing with gang members. "Why is [the gang] such a problem? Because the government has decided to spill blood and in doing so has made the problem even worse than before." He wondered out loud what kind of result the government might have achieved if they had instead sat down with a "man of God" to put together a different kind of approach. This point served to segue into the contrasting approach that his church was taking. "God has a different way of correcting (*corregir*) sin." He said that this evangelistic campaign was planned, "Because you're important to me, because this community is important to me and because God has a plan for you. . . . When everyone else turns their back on you, God is listening in the heavens."

Later that evening, at a gathering in his home, not far from the park, Pastor José told a small group of guests how the event had originated. An evangelical woman in the neighborhood had grown increasingly desperate for a way to convince her son to leave the gang. Eventually, she hit on the idea of planning a special evangelistic campaign targeting neighborhood gang members, but when her own pastor spurned the idea, she turned to Pastor José and the young men from Youth Restoration. Together, they began planning and raising money for the "Escape with Your Life" special event, but shortly after the planning had begun, tragedy struck. The woman's son was killed by members of the opposing MS-13 gang in a shooting only two blocks from his home. His mother had hoped that the event would provide the additional incentive that her son needed to leave the gang for good since he had already begun participating in some events at the Youth Restoration program. The woman was devastated and plans went on hold. However, a few months later, the young men approached her to ask if she was still interested in moving ahead; she agreed and even helped put up money for printing special t-shirts. Now the event was finally taking place.

My decision to attend the evangelistic campaign was motivated in part by sheer curiosity. I had interviewed the members of Youth Restoration in the days leading up to the event and they had shared with me their excitement about the campaign, which had been in the planning stages for months. They showed me the full-color invitations they had printed and had hand-delivered to their former gang mates and told me how they had participated in special work projects in order to raise money for the event. Given evangelicalism's prohibitions of hyper-macho behavior, would any of the local gang youth actually show up to an evangelistic event I wondered? And, assuming some did show up, what would be the impact of attending such a campaign? Surely there would be an old-fashioned "invitation." Would the gang youth stream forward by the dozens, making commitments to leave the gang and becoming evangelical teetotalers like the members of Youth Restoration? In fact, turnout at the two-day event met the planners' expectations. About two dozen youth attended one or both outdoor services and nearly as many participated in the daytime workshops on self-esteem and violence. Despite this, in other ways, the results of the campaign were disappointing. The youth, many of whom I was later informed were only just beginning their gang affiliation or still in chequeo, seemed curious and interested in the campaign events—especially the reggaeton concerts—but not yet ready to give up life in the gang. There were no public "decisions," much less a massive exit of gang members or sympathizers. Still, when I visited the program a year later the five youth who had organized the event reported that two of the gang youth who had participated in the event had joined the program since then. "The seeds were sown," they insisted. The campaign, they believed, had been worth the effort.

In fact evangelical "campaigns" aimed especially at gang members and other young, wayward males are not uncommon in Central America and religious ministries aiming to help gang members leave the gang are, if not plentiful, not an anomaly in the region. But what are congregations really aiming for with such ministries, the costs of which can be quite high? The goal here is to gain a better understanding of how and to what extent religious groups in northern Central America attack social problems related to youth violence and whether such programs hold out any hope for reducing such gang violence. Finally, I draw some tentative conclusions regarding the connection between two contrasting approaches to gang violence and the broader shift in the religious landscape of the region. My findings draw heavily from over thirty interviews with individuals from more than two dozen organizations working with gangs in the region. My list of contacts was developed by word of mouth and with the help of lists developed in an earlier study by researchers associated with El Salvador's Jesuit university (Cruz 2006) but I also draw from the interviews with former gang members.

AN OVERVIEW OF EVANGELICAL AND CATHOLIC GANG MINISTRIES

Evangelicals have been involved in gang ministry since at least the late 1990s, but most ministries that address gangs and gang violence directly emerged in the early 2000s. My research took me to visit nearly a dozen evangelical ministries, most of which were connected with a congregation or a denomination, while some were stand-alone "para-church" organizations with no such affiliation. Table 6.1 shows a list of the evangelical gang ministries I visited or with which I conducted at least one interview.

Staff sizes are based on my own estimate. The "approach" of the institution indicates whether a group aims to "restore" current gang members—a term explained below—or to thwart the growth of gangs or gang violence through "prevention" intended to keep youth from joining the gang in the first place. The size and structure of the evangelical ministries varied considerably. A few were well organized and highly institutionalized, but these ministries usually had a variety of institutional priorities, having added gang ministry only in recent years. More commonly, evangelical gang ministries were "mom-and-pop" organizations spearheaded by an energetic pastor and a handful of volunteers. The small size of these ministries makes sense since one of the distinguishing features of evangelical congregations is their tendency to multiply in amoeba-like fashion. Theologically speaking, there is nothing to stand in the way of an evangelical who feels a "calling" to begin a ministry from doing just that, regardless of the extent of that person's theological training or lack thereof. The same is true with evangelical gang ministries. There are no diocesan authorities whose permission must be obtained before a social or evangelical ministry can begin. Individuals

TABLE 6.1. A Sampling of Evangelical Gang Ministries in Central America

Name	*Country*	*Affiliation*	*Staff size*	*Approach*
Proyecto Jeremías	El Salvador	Evangelical	20	Restoration
Fundación San Andrés	El Salvador	Evangelical	5	Restoration
Maras para Cristo	Guatemala	Evangelical-ELIM	1	Restoration/prevention
Casa de Alcance	Guatemala	Evangelical	4	Restoration/prevention
Ministerios Jefté	Guatemala	Evangelical	1	Restoration
Casa de Restauración	Guatemala	Evangelical	5–10	Restoration
Unidos en Cristo	Honduras	Evangelical	1	Restoration
Casa Victoria	Honduras	Evangelical	5	Restoration
Iglesia de Santidad	Honduras	Evangelical-Holiness	1	Restoration
Restauracion Juveníl	Honduras	Evangelical-Mennonite	1–5	Restoration
Proyecto de Paz y Justicia (PPyJ)	Honduras	Evangelical-Mennonite	5–10	Restoration/prevention

or pastors who desire to begin such ministry are free to do so provided they are able to inspire others to contribute time or resources to support the effort. Of course, this "free market" approach to religious ministry, while encouraging the founding of new congregations and ministries, also means that a great many evangelical organizations function for only a few years and later, after the energy or inspiration of the founding leader runs out, disappear or disintegrate. At least two of the smaller evangelical ministries I interviewed, *Unidos en Cristo* (United in Christ) in Honduras and *Ministerios Jefté* (Jephthah Ministries) in Guatemala City, were in a process of reevaluating their prospects for future ministry after having seen their activity decrease significantly in recent years.

Another, the Jeremiah Project, located in San Salvador, was shifting its attention away from gang-related ministry and toward broader themes of education and capacity building among youth.

While evangelical gang ministries have sprung up in all three countries, it is not the case that most evangelical congregations or pastors engage in gang ministry. However numerous the evangelical gang ministries have become, even in neighborhoods where gangs are plentiful, most pastors desire to keep a safe distance from the gangs. They do so both out of concern for their own physical safety as well as out of concern that neighbors and outsiders could get the wrong idea about their association with the gangs. When I asked one of the members of Youth Restoration if gang ministry is common among evangelicals he reminded me of the mother of the youth who had been killed during the planning of the evangelistic campaign.

> She visited various churches, looking for people to work with and they rejected her. "Oh, it's not in [our] plans," [they would say]. That's just an excuse not to support the program out of fear. They're afraid they might get killed. Or they're only interested in saving their souls. They're not looking out for their neighbor.

Similarly, Pastor José Fernandez, who directs the project, reported hearing of mild disapproval of the project from neighbors:

> The reality is that not everyone accepts this work that the churches do. So it's happened before that people have told me that some people believe that I'm a pastor that identifies with [gang members]. That because of this work, we have some sort of a nexus [with the gangs]. That's basically the biggest risk we run. That it might hurt my testimony as a "good evangelical" [laughs].

Pastor José reported also feeling some resistance from local police after he and the members of the project had scraped together funds to hire a lawyer to represent a former gang youth who had been imprisoned, they were certain, under false accusations. Such ministry requires time, energy, and resources that most pastors would prefer to invest elsewhere. Also, sometimes fear and suspicion keep churches from exploring gang ministry. A few ex-gang members themselves reported receiving a less-than-welcoming reception from evangelical congregations they had visited when first considering leaving the gang. For example, Camilo recalled visiting a Pentecostal congregation as a young gang member living on the streets of San Pedro Sula. "I was looking for help and when I arrived the hermanos said, 'Get out of the way! (*¡Quitense!*) Here comes that thief! Here comes that gang member!' They closed their doors to me completely and I left." A decade later, Camilo again sought out the church, this time while in prison, and although he again felt rejected by some, he encountered other hermanos who responded differently. Others, like Ignacio, felt rejection and never returned. "Once I attended a church called The Philadelphia. I was discriminated against and I still have that concept with me." Ignacio, a Honduran and M-18 member at the time he visited the church, wore the "cholo" style with baggy clothes and short hair. "A lady told me that I wasn't allowed to enter [the building] and I don't know why she said that; maybe she thought I was there for something else. But ha! She told me to get out of there and I never went back."

Still, the experiences of a few ex-gang members aside, a surprising number of evangelical congregations have attempted gang ministries through formal and informal means—enough to give gang members like Ignacio the impression that an evangelical congregation could be a good place to start when rethinking your allegiance to the gang. Granted, many of the organizations consist of mom-and-pop ministries in which a pastor or layperson in effect "hangs out a shingle" advertising by word of mouth or via simple flyers their intent to work with gang members. But such local micro-organizations are numerous enough to be found in every major city and under a variety of denominational headings. Most of the organizations do not have professional staff (i.e., directors with a university degree) and thus, lacking a formal institutional structure, very few receive international funding. Instead, their strength seems to be in local connections and the ability of the staff to relate easily and in a nonthreatening way to youth who feel marginalized and on the defensive. Indeed, four of eleven evangelical gang ministries I visited were founded or directed by former gang members themselves.

GANG VIOLENCE AS A "SPIRITUAL PROBLEM"

Pastor Luis Arreola is the founder and director of *Maras para Cristo* (Gangs for Christ), a ministry affiliated with Central America's oldest mega-church, *Ministerios Elim.*[3] I first met Pastor Luis while visiting Guatemala's infamous *Pavón* prison where I was shadowing another pastor during a day-long visit with gang members and other inmates. Pastor Luis drove a white delivery truck with the name of the ministry painted in bold letters on the sides and a three-way loudspeaker mounted on top. Pastor Luis was accompanied by at least a dozen youthful volunteers wearing bright yellow ministry t-shirts bearing the phrase, "Rescue 911: Gangs for Christ." Pastor Luis seemed like the quintessential evangelical ministry coordinator. The unequivocal name of his ministry, the bright t-shirts, and the loudspeaker all spoke of old-fashioned, anything-but-subtle, evangelical ministry aimed at one goal—saving souls. When I interviewed the middle-aged pastor later in his basement office of the giant factory-turned-church-building that is the mega-church's headquarters, I expected to find a slightly fanatical, highly charismatic evangelical obsessed with saving gang members from eternal damnation. Pastor Luis does have a charisma about him and, true to my expectations, he spends a lot of his time preaching and holding evangelistic services. He has also, on many occasions, given his testimony of having been involved in street gangs, crime, and drugs as a youth in the late 1970s. Also true to my expectations, Pastor Luis defined the gang issue as first and foremost a *spiritual* problem. But as I listened to Pastor Luis speak of his ministry it became clear that the term "spiritual" for Pastor Luis, held broader connotations than mere soul-saving. On the one hand, Pastor Luis insisted that due to the risks involved in gang ministry, he tried to stick to a "spiritual agenda."

> I don't get involved in the internal problems that [gang members] have, nor with the police. My work is a spiritual work, of help, that's all. Because sometimes gang members come to me saying, "I'm fleeing because they want to kill me. Come help me get out of here and find a place to hide." "No," I tell them. I can't have anything to do with that.

And yet, "spiritual" work, for Pastor Luis, clearly involves paying attention to more than the soul. Taking clothing and food to prisoners, helping to finance burials and officiate funerals for gang members killed in gang warfare, and connecting converted gang members with work opportunities or drug rehabilitation were among the non-salvation-directed tasks in which Pastor Luis engages. In fact, he seemed frustrated that so few evangelical congregations have become involved in "social work," like gang ministry:

> I think that the church has really neglected social work (*obra social*). I'm talking about the evangelical church. The evangelical church has really neglected social work because the evangelical church has room in its budget for painting the church, buying new chairs, buying speakers, and renovating the building and so much more you know. The praise and worship team here, the praise and worship team there. But the church forgot to include its social aid (*ayuda social*). Because I think that the church is the one with the solution to this problem, at the level of the church because this is a spiritual problem, right? One that we have to solve ourselves. And God gave authority to the church from the spiritual and an economic perspective to solve it. But social aid doesn't exist in many churches. I have gone to churches and told them, 'What plans do you have for working with the streets?" And there's nothing. "What investment have you made in the streets?" Nothing there either. And so I don't look to the government for help. I look for help from the people [associated with this ministry] and they have understood and offered their cars, gasoline, their time.

On the one hand, Pastor Luis's monologue seems confusing, even contradictory. If the gang problem is in fact a "spiritual problem" why should churches bother with "social work" at all? Why not solve a spiritual problem with a "spiritual solution"? And yet for Pastor Luis, it is precisely their lack of social ministry that keeps evangelical churches from solving the problem of the gangs. Nor was Pastor Luis alone in his lament. Abner, also a former gang member who converted and later began a ministry to gang members called *Ministerios Jefté* (Jephthah Ministries), echoed Pastor Luis's language of the "spiritual problem" of gangs.[4]

> I think that the church is the first one with a solution in its hands. Why the church? Because the church has Christ and Christ is the best medicine

> for any gang member or delinquent. And so the church should be the first one on the scene, changing the situation.

Like Pastor Luis, Abner saw the gang as a problem that should be a top priority of congregations, precisely because he viewed the problem as an interior, spiritual problem within individual gang members. And yet Abner himself recognized the *social rejection* faced by gang members and the difficulty of reintegrating into a society that loathes and fears them. In fact, he went on to criticize evangelical pastors who evangelize gang members using a narrow, condemning tone and suggested that such ministers had been ignored or harassed by gang members precisely because they did not understand the "social problems" faced by gang youth. Thus, although he felt that the church should be the first "on the scene," he also seemed to intimate that more hands are needed. "What we need is an integral work. Integral. Where all organizations and institutions work together to solve this problem. Everyone. None should be left out."

One reason evangelical gang ministry leaders identify the "problem" of gangs and gang violence in ways that are at best conceptually muddled and at worst, contradictory, is that most have little if any formal training in social scientific conceptualizations of social problems like gang violence. In fifteen interviews with evangelical gang ministry staff, only three respondents possessed a university degree and none had a background in sociology or criminology. Most had only modest educational background such as a high school degree or informal theological study. Leaders of mom-and-pop gang ministries like Jephthah Ministries or pastors of small congregations tended to define the problem of gangs in terms that were familiar to them. They knew from experience that gang members tend to come from impoverished backgrounds and precarious homes, but they did not possess a working knowledge of social-structural forces that make gang membership attractive and persistent. But more than just lack of university training or exposure to the tools of social science is involved in evangelicals' labeling of gang violence as a "spiritual problem." Central American evangelicals, including those who work with gangs, tend to view social problems such as gang violence through the lens of sin, grace, and personal transformation. Like their counterparts among white evangelicals in the United States,

Central American evangelicals have an individualist, free-will theological orientation that orients their understanding of—and action with regard to—social problems. This theological outlook causes them to see social problems as reducible to a collection of individuals in need of individual transformation. Unlike the white evangelicals in Michael Emerson and Christian Smith's book *Divided by Faith* (2001), who tended to ignore or minimize the social problem of race in America, the barrio evangelicals I spoke with in Central America do not play down the social problems related to the transnational gangs. Indeed, youth violence has affected the homes and neighborhoods of almost all Central American evangelicals. But even those evangelicals who are attempting to do something about the problem have attacked it using an individualist framework that promotes the "rescue" of youth already in the gang. Most, like Pastor Luis, recognize that "social work" or "social aid" is a necessary component—gang members have real social and material needs that must be addressed if they are to successfully "escape" the gang and start over. But the problem, from the perspective of evangelicals involved in gang ministry, remains one of how to extricate individuals from the gang and help them to avoid any future involvement with drugs, alcohol, or crime.

Of course, most Central American evangelicals see evangelical conversion as a vital component of rescue and reintegration, which helps to explain why they describe the problem in spiritual terms. More important, defining the gang issue as spiritual in nature brings it into the realm of action for spiritually oriented people. Far from an attempt to wash their hands of the problem by relegating it to another realm defining the gang issue as a spiritual problem is, for pastors and barrio evangelicals like Pastor Luis, another way of holding evangelicals responsible for doing something about it. In effect, for evangelicals who undertake and promote gang ministry, understanding gang ministry within a spiritual framework is another way of making it an *evangelical problem*. As we see later, this perspective contrasts starkly with the approach voiced by those involved in Catholic gang ministries.

One result of the individualist, free-will orientation of evangelical gang ministries is that such efforts usually aim to "rescue" gang members from the gang and place them on a path to successful reintegration in their communities. Among such ministries, the most common term for this work is "restoration" (*restauración*). The term *restaurar* ("to restore") has strong spiritual connotations among evangelicals, calling to mind the conversion experience, divine healing, and being "restored" to harmony with God. I did not hear the same term used by any Catholic or nonreligious gang ministry workers. A Honduran sociologist criticized the term precisely because of its religious underpinnings. Outside the evangelical sphere, there is little agreement on what to call projects involving work with current and former gang members. Some call it "rehabilitation" in order to emphasize the enormous psychological challenges facing gang members who leave, while others object to using that term because it implies that gang members are "sick" and in need of treatment. Other non-evangelicals prefer the term "social reintegration" to underscore the fact that gang members came of age outside traditional society and need to be reintegrated into a society that fears and distrusts them. Other terms for gang intervention including "integration" and "re-insertion" also take into account the social nature of the dilemma facing exiting gang members. The director of Onward Youth, a nonreligious reentry program in Honduras, referred to the work of his own organization as that of *desarrollo de la construcción humana*, which translates into the even more unwieldy English phrase "development of human construction."

Aside from the evangelistic component of "restoration," shared by *all* evangelical gang ministries I visited, most restoration ministries also included one form or another of overt *obra social* (social work). Four of the organizations incorporate a halfway house (formal or informal) for youth who wish to be physically removed from the gang territory either because of their fear of reprisals or in an attempt to escape the temptation to abuse drugs and alcohol. At "Casa Victoria" in Honduras, ex-gang members join other men struggling with alcohol abuse in daily workshops and training. Still, many gang ministries do not have the resources or personnel to orchestrate a formal halfway home. Instead, they rely on heavy contributions of time and energy from pastors and volunteers who evangelize gang members, keep tabs on new converts leaving the gang, assist them in the job hunt, and provide occasional subsistence aid for the new convert and his or her family. In short, the notion of gang restoration combines spiritual and social aspects of gang ministry in a way similar to when Pastor Luis described the gang as a "spiritual problem." When I asked Pastor José of Youth Restoration to describe what he meant by the term, he explained it this way.

> For us restoration means precisely that: restoring worth. When we speak of youth restoration (*restauración juveníl*) our idea is that the name should produce in us as much as [the reforming gang members] the concept that you can be someone of worth again. You can once again be someone—how could we say it? It's [about] your self-concept, and others' concept toward you. We believe that the work that this title communicates has to do with returning to the person their quality of life. The quality of life in all senses beginning with the spiritual but then continuing to include giving back their emotional quality [of life] and their material quality. So in this sense we use the word restoration because we believe it's the most complete, right? It's the one that best sums up what we're trying to do for them.

Thus Pastor José's actual approach to gang ministry included a variety of social aspects. In addition to its evangelistic campaign, Youth Restoration conducts workshops on self-esteem and anger management, helps gang members in need of legal defense, and provides job training in construction and electrical work. The group even tried without success to provide employment for recovering gang members by setting up an Internet café in a small building next to the church.[5] Pastor José's broad application of the term "restoration" was probably at least partially a result of his informal ties to the Mennonite Peace and Justice Program which had developed by far the most holistic approach to gang ministry of any evangelical programs. His use of the term was also meant to imply a strong spiritual component as he insisted that the program remained "one hundred percent evangelistic."

ONWARD CHRISTIAN SOLDIER

A popular song sung at Central American evangelical youth campaigns and men's events in the late 1990s and early 2000s was *Hombres de Valor* ("Men of Courage"). Popularized by the Spanish-born musician and evangelical pastor Jesús Adrián Romero, the song challenged men to be courageous husbands and fathers who "keep their promises" and "give up [their] rights" out of "love for humanity." Evangelical gang ministries make considerable use of this long tradition of blending cultural norms of traditional masculinity with alternative values shaped by a religious tradition valuing vulnerability, nurture, and protection of the weak. Similar to the "muscular Christianity" of Billy Sunday and the YMCA movement in the United States at the turn of the last century, the evangelical pastors and lay coordinators involved in gang ministry seek to attract young men socialized toward competition and sexual predation by adopting and adapting metaphors of soldier-like "courage under fire." They recast the practices traditionally associated with masculinity in the barrio—drinking, going to the discoteca, and sleeping around—as a sign of *weakness,* and thus, the evangelical man who manages to restrain himself from these activities is praised for his success and strength in "conquering sin."

For the ex-gang member, restraining oneself from violence also plays an important role in conquering sin. For example, in his sermon delivered at the second evening of the "Escape with Your Life" campaign, Rev. Carlos Tercero, a prisoner-turned-evangelist, attempted to deconstruct the hyper-macho gang disposition by calling it a "spirit of inferiority" and "a sickness inside the soul. . . . When someone comes up to me and tells me that those gang members are bad and we should kill them, I tell them to shut up—they're children of God like us." Indeed, Rev. Carlos had a knack for reframing compassionate behaviors as courageous and masculine. "The Bible says you have to bless those that curse you," he said.

> When I see a man walking around with an AK-47, I'm not afraid. Instead, I pray to God on his behalf because a child of God doesn't need that weapon. He's just carrying it to be macho. For many years, I was macho. For many years, I carried a gun but it wasn't any good to me. It just did me harm.

Rev. Carlos also drew on the language of "spiritual warfare" to emphasize the "battlefield" nature of the challenges facing youth. Indeed, the martial metaphors appear to be especially attractive to young males who risk being called a "fag" due to their teetotaling evangelical lifestyle. Thus, the reggaeton group playing the first night of the campaign was called "Christ's Soldiers." Similarly, Gustavo, a Guatemalan ex-gang convert, remembered being encouraged by an MS-13-member-turned-evangelist with a decidedly unconventional mix of metaphors: "He told me to be firm like a soldier. Love your neighbor and your enemies. Pray that they come to Christ." Calín, who reported that he had learned in the gang to repress his feelings, since in the gang "only fags cry," reported that now things were different: "When I feel the touch of Jesus in my heart, I cry tears because I tell people that only the courageous join forces with the kingdom of heaven." Calín's statement seems like a clear attempt to rescue a sense of masculinity by attaching a risky, battlefield metaphor to the more openly expressive emotional style of the evangelical man.

Other researchers have noted the evangelical tendency to promote alternative forms of masculinity (Brusco 1995; Smilde 2007; Steigenga 2001). In his book *City of God: Christian Citizenship in Postwar Guatemala*, Kevin O'Neill (2009) explores the popularity among Guatemalan Neo-Pentecostals of spiritual warfare and "religious cartography"—creating maps that identify actual geographic terrain as belonging to God or the Devil. O'Neill concludes that spiritual warfare and the militarization of religious concepts provide a "muscular" approach to Christian faith, enhancing its appeal to men who wish to make a difference in the midst of intractable social problems. Thus, Central American evangelists who incorporate military language in order to attract young men take part in a long tradition of evangelical Christians who sought to toughen up the Christian message by presenting it as a violent clash between opposing powers. Whether or not evangelicalism promotes a true "alternative" to the traditional masculinity ideals of the barrio is a matter worthy of further analysis and debate. Although male domination of women is still alive and well in the evangelical contexts I visited, the *ideals* of abandoning la vida loca and of loving one's enemies certainly contrast with the masculine norms among barrio youth.

In addition to promoting alternative approaches to expressing masculinity in the barrio, the evangelical restoration ministries advertise the possibility of a "religious career" that is especially attractive to young men whose future holds little promise. Ricardo was ordained as a minister only two years after his conversion experience, and by the time of our interview had traveled to five countries to participate in workshops and preach in evangelistic campaigns. Camilo, a Honduran ex-member of the M-18, had traveled to Guatemala and had preached weekly during month-long evangelism services in his native country. In all, six of the thirty-eight converted ex-gang members I interviewed had worked or were currently working as pastors or evangelists even though most had not finished high school when they began preaching. Other converts coordinate or direct evangelical gang ministries, modeling the possibilities available to converted ex-gang members who "keep the faith." Nelson directs a neighborhood Bible study for men struggling with alcoholism and feels happy that he can "give back" to his neighborhood by "working hard in the Lord's work."

Impressed by the men who had helped them convert and leave the gang, some ex-gang members told of *aspiring* to be pastors or evangelists. However, they may also have been attracted to the prospect of holding a position of leadership in a church or ministry. Evangelicals promote such religious careers—at least for men—in ways that attract outsiders. Intentionally or not, the invitation to Rev. Carlos, an ex-prisoner himself, to speak at "Escape with Your Life" told the gang youth present that should they decide to convert, opportunities for leadership awaited even those unable to produce a diploma or a clean record. When he pointed toward one of the gang youth at the back of the audience and told him, "You are going to be a pastor some day," he confronted at least one of the youth—probably more since it was not clear to whom he was pointing—with the possibility of leadership and a religious career. The action also emphasized to everyone present that even barrio youth with a troubled past can aspire to evangelical leadership. Similarly, the meteoric religious careers of men like Ricardo, a grade-school dropout who has traveled to several countries and pastors his own congregation, provides attainable models to young (male) gang members desperate for the prospect of an alternative career. After all, the odds of launching a career by the traditional route of getting a university degree are minuscule for adult youth without a high school diploma. By modeling a religious career, pastors and gang ministry coordinators offer one more means of attracting youth to leave the gang and reintegrating them into their communities.

Finally, a few evangelical gang ministries have recently begun to expand their work to include "prevention"—that is, helping youth to avoid joining the gang in the first place. Pastor Luis reported that Gangs for Christ was taking a turn in this direction due in part to the fact that the gang members he had been evangelizing for years were now mostly dead or in prison. In addition to his continuing prison ministry, he had begun a church among children of imprisoned or deceased gang members. Pastor Luis is convinced that such efforts are preventive since children who grow up in the church and are "well-rooted in the word" will not, he believes, join the gang when they get older. The Mennonite Peace and Justice gang project in La López Arellano, Honduras has taken a less overtly religious approach to prevention by teaching conflict resolution in local schools and by organizing a youth group and soccer team involving children and orphans of former gang members.

EXPLORING MOTIVATIONS FOR EVANGELICAL GANG MINISTRY

Gang ministry, whether religious or not, is risky. Many gang members and ex-gang members struggle with substance abuse, fear the "morgue rule," and are under the constant threat of the "boomerang effect" of barrio violence. Bringing gang members or recent deserters into one's church or ministry presents both challenges and hazards, and nowhere were such threats more boldly—some would say naïvely—confronted than in the home of María de la Luz Hernandez. María de la Luz, whose name means "Mary of Light," lives with her husband and their six children in a one-story cinder-block home on the dusty outskirts of La Ceiba, Honduras. In 2002, accompanied by a handful of members from her own Pentecostal congregation and a few other local churches, Luz began a ministry to gang members in the northern coastal city of La Ceiba. The program, loosely known as "United in Christ," began simply as a visitation ministry aimed at evangelizing gang members on the streets and in the local prison, and at helping them to leave the gang and overcome the challenges to living a crime- and drug-free life. But when the crackdown of the Maduro administration went into effect, many local gang members found themselves on the run and forced into hiding in the nearby mountains. When a fifteen-year-old gang member approached her asking for a place to stay, Luz invited him to come and stay in her home with her family. Shortly thereafter, Luz invited Camilo, the former M-18 leader, to join her household as well. Camilo had just finished a prison term and was running for his life. The ex-gang member remembered when Luz approached him after a worship service in the prison chapel shortly before he was to be released. "She said to me, 'God has made me a mother to you.'" Since he himself had learned of his orphan status as a young teen, Camilo felt deeply moved by her pronouncement. After his release, Camilo spent several months in the Hernandez home, and soon word began to spread among those most desperate to find a way out of the gang, that safety and a modicum of stability were available at the home of "Hermana Luz" (Sister Luz). Eventually, Luz and her husband came to provide a halfway house for gang members trying to escape the gang. A total of fourteen recovering gang members have found refuge in the Hernandez home. At one point eight young men lived and ate in the Hernandez home, sharing two bedrooms and a guest bathroom while Luz, her husband and their six children (including four young daughters) shared a bathroom and two bedrooms.

When I asked Luz to explain how and why she had allowed her home to become a halfway house for recovering gang members, she answered matter-of-factly, "Well, it wasn't something that I had been planning for. All at once when I was about twenty-four, a relative of mine fell into a gang and that's when we started to live the pain of the youth and the families." Thus, on the one hand, the decision of Luz and her husband to place their household at risk by taking in gang members during the "hunt-down" was motivated by a simple, humanistic empathy.

> No one was doing anything for them and we realized that they were dying. . . . We never made an open decision like, "Let's bring home a youth!" because we didn't know how. It's just that along the way a case came up . . . where we couldn't really see another option than to bring them into our home.

Indeed, one could think of plenty of "options" besides housing not one but several gang members at a time, especially in a home with four young daughters! But Luz seemed uniquely prone to viewing gang youth as though they were members of her own family—as if they were her children. Still, Luz's motivation goes beyond maternal compassion as her actions are also guided by religious conviction. She spoke of feeling motivated by the spiritual rewards of helping converted ex-gang members find eternal salvation whatever the outcome of their immediate future.

> Early on when so many youth were getting killed, there was a moment when every week one or two of our [ex-gang member converts] would be killed after getting out of prison. I got to the point where I said, "I don't want to do this anymore because I don't want to see them get killed." But when I said that I remembered that God is interested in what happens with our soul and where our soul goes. And so I realized that they had Jesus inside of their hearts so it didn't matter if they died because that soul was not lost—although I still cried every time they died—but I realized that that youth was going up there to rest with Jesus. That was the most important thing.

Such "purely" spiritual rewards as the confidence that saving souls would lead to the eternal rest of slain gang members did not dominate Luz's description of her work. Rather, her satisfaction at the eternal salvation of these converted youth merely coincided with the motivation of seeing individual gang members "transformed" during their stay in her home. She spoke proudly and by name of former gang members who had found a stable life with a job and a marriage following their time in her home. Most stop by to visit or call her from as far away as California. Although Luz and her husband made the decision in 2006 to temporarily discontinue their hosting of gang members in their home for a time, they remain active in gang and prison ministry and did host another youth in early 2007. She stated, "I get passionate, passionate when I am with these youth—those that have left the gang or those that are still active or in prison. That's where I feel really capable." From her own account then, Luz is motivated by a "mixture" of religious, social, and personal motivations. This "mixing" of motives was quite common among the evangelical gang ministry leaders I interviewed.

In fact, "separating" religious and social motives is difficult if not impossible when listening to leaders of evangelical gang ministries. As Christian Smith and others have pointed out, religion provides a narrative about how things "ought to be" that can motivate risky or "disruptive" action when the world does not align with such values (Geertz 1973; Smith 1996). Evangelical gang ministry leaders tended to borrow frequently from biblical narratives and injunctions when explaining the motivational framework for their ministry. Luis and Nahum, two university students who work in the Salvadoran government's pro-youth program called *JóvenES*, conduct *proyectos ambulatorios* (walking projects) by walking through "red zone" neighborhoods to seek out gang members and attempt to persuade them to leave the gang. They also visit prisons, organizing games and nonviolent recreation for El Salvador's thousands of imprisoned gang members. Though this "day job" has no formal religious component, they see the work as part and parcel of a larger effort—that of helping El Salvador's gang youth find an escape from violence and drugs through Jesus. On evenings and weekends the two "check up" on gang members they know who have recently left the gang, hoping that through such visits and by bringing the young men with them to church rallies and religious rock concerts, recent gang leavers will remain motivated to retain their commitments. While traveling to a prison outside San Salvador, Luis, a Baptist, and Nahum, a Pentecostal, described to me their motivation using a variety of biblical texts and themes. Nahum began the conversation but before long Luis had turned around in his seat to face me and spoke excitedly about gang work and its relationship to biblical themes such as the story of "the good Samaritan." "The story shows that Christians must come to the aid of those in need," Luis said. He pointed out that while others walked past the man who had been robbed and left for dead, the good Samaritan came to his aid, took him to a hotel, and paid for his stay with his own money. Drawing a parallel between the victim in the story and gang members in general, he added that, "We don't know what that man had been involved in before the robbery."

As I listened to Luis's passionate monologue about the need for the church to take risks in order to get involved in gang ministry, it occurred to me that this young man possessed some of the marks of the liberationist Catholics of a preceding generation. Luis was borrowing biblical texts and religious passion in order to motivate and frame risky and unpopular work on behalf of a marginalized population in his country. In fact, the transformation that Luis believed the gospel offers young men trapped in a life of crime and the gang had the ring of liberation about which catechists, priests, and lay workers have taught for decades now. Yet there was also a clear difference. While liberation theologians prioritize a sociopolitical transformation, the transformation that Luis promotes is an individual one and religious to the core.

Biblical stories and texts surfaced in interviews with other evangelicals as well. Pastor Luis of Gangs for Christ critiqued his own tradition because he feels that many evangelicals have ignored important aspects of their own faith by not doing enough to help gang members:

> Really the mission of the church is to support those most in need. They used to say to the Lord, "You spend your time with publicans and sinners," right? The Lord said, "I have come to seek the sick of this earth, those with the greatest needs, not the healthy, because the healthy don't need anything." So we have identified with the people. There have been criticisms as well because the same [evangelicals] sometimes say, "They ought to take all of the gang members and kill them!"

In fact the language of taking gang members into account as "the least of these," that is, as impoverished youth with great needs rather than as hardened criminals deserving punishment, was more common among evangelicals than I had expected. Evangelicals like Luis and Nahum, Luz, and Pastor Luis viewed their mission largely in light of a biblical command to protect the weak, not merely to convert the damned. Although spiritual salvation was clearly a key component of all evangelical gang ministries, such spiritual concerns were often viewed in the context of a larger humanitarian concern for the well-being and future prospects of gang members.

Not all of the motivations for engaging in evangelical gang ministry were selfless. Whether or not they were willing to admit it, evangelical congregations and pastors can realize certain benefits from gang ministry successes. After all, in the evangelical worldview, a congregation in which former gang members are active and have made an obvious and public change in their lifestyle is one that demonstrates the evangelical principle that "Jesus can change anyone." Thus, when a high-profile gang member or leader converts, he is likely to be "showcased" in the congregation in which he has converted, and should he continue to maintain the evangelical lifestyle for a sufficient period of time, he will be given visible responsibilities in the church such as playing in the band or speaking at a rally. Converted gang members often travel with evangelists to give their testimonies at evangelistic campaigns or at megachurches. A congregation with one or more converted ex-gang members participating actively is one in which "the spirit" is made visible to those in the local community.

In short, it is difficult to extricate the social from religious motivations in evangelical gang ministry. Within the evangelical worldview, Christians are to act responsibly toward their "neighbor," especially those neighbors in need, but they are also to seek the salvation of everyone, including youth involved in substance abuse, drug dealing, and violence. For evangelicals, gang ministry provides an ideal context for bringing together social concern and spiritual fervor since converted ex-gang members provide "living proof" of the evangelical message that salvation is powerful and within the realm of possibility for even the worst of "sinners." The fact that such a message of transformation is always framed within an individualist framework is a natural outgrowth of the evangelical theological perspective.

THE LIMITS OF FAITH-BASED MINISTRY

The conversionist approach and religious motivation of many evangelical gang ministries can be a weakness, especially when ministry leaders possess a limited awareness of the social contextual problems underlying the problem of gang violence. Overzealous gang ministry leaders, eager to facilitate conversions, can fall into the trap of assuming that a "change of heart" is all that is needed for a gang member to start over and desist from participating in crime, violence, and drugs. Fortunately, some evangelical gang ministries seemed to be learning from their past mistakes. For example, Pastor José reported that although Youth Restoration had begun as a purely evangelistic endeavor, he had learned along with the coordinators that more than just a spiritual conversion was needed:

> When Youth Restoration was born, the idea was to inculcate in the spirit and heart of youth the need for God, the need for a change of life starting from within. Our focus, our vision is first and foremost evangelistic. Nevertheless, as the project advanced, a more formalized, more complete proposal [was developed] where we realized that people have different demands, right? So in the case of the [gang members] it wasn't just about making them feel the love of God and changing from within but also how to produce a return to their natural environment so that they could readapt, regain trust and have resources for earning a living.

Other ministers reported learning about the limits of gang ministry. Pastor Álvaro, whose name I have changed for reasons of security, is an energetic young pastor of a large congregation in a town in southern Guatemala. He reported learning an even more difficult lesson, this one regarding the connection between gang violence and law enforcement. Pastor Álvaro's congregation has ties to the enormously popular mega-church *Casa de Dios* (House of God) that is located in an upscale suburb of Guatemala City. I interviewed Pastor Álvaro in an upstairs apartment where the congregation housed a ministry for gang members and sympathizers. The ministry, called *Casa de Alcance* (Outreach Center), began when several members of the local M-18 and MS-13 gang cells converted to evangelical Christianity and started attending his congregation. Pastor Álvaro told of encountering political resistance when seeking to protect new gang converts from reprisals by opposing gangs. When I asked him to describe this resistance in more detail he insisted that I first turn off the audio recorder. Later in the interview he admitted that he and his congregation had been naïve and didn't understand anything about gangs when they began the ministry. "We soon learned that there were limits to what we could do," he said. Although the Outreach Center continues to work with some gang members, most of its work is now done in the area of prevention through after-school activities and computer-literacy workshops.

Unfortunately, wisdom gained from past mistakes is rarely shared among evangelical gang ministries. The ministry coordinators I spoke with seldom interact and usually dismissed each other's work when they were aware of it at all. Pastor Freddy, who founded and pastors a nondenominational Pentecostal church in Guatemala City, is a short, barrel-chested man with a commanding presence and a strong voice. He wears a gold watch and a half-buttoned Western shirt revealing a thick gold chain. I interviewed Pastor Freddy in the drab cement structure that houses his congregation and which, he proudly told me, used to be a bar where he had spent considerable time as a young man. The church is located on a busy street near the center of the city. Although he had never formerly belonged to a gang, Pastor Freddy tells of a past life of crime and alcohol abuse prior to his own conversion and of founding a church and ministry for gang members and street children. When I met Pastor Freddy, three young men, recovering addicts to whom he ministered, constantly shadowed him. One of the youth had been a member of a gang. Pastor Freddy began the "dry-out" ministry in his home and now rents a house several kilometers outside the city, where the young men sleep and have their evening meal. Several days after interviewing Pastor Freddy in his church, I accompanied him along with three of his young "protégés" on a pastoral visit to a large, medium-security prison called *Pavón* where two converted ex-gang members he visits weekly were serving out lengthy prison terms. In addition to the two ex-gang members, Pastor Freddy was excited about a third inmate whom he had been visiting and who had lately begun to express considerable interest in religion. Over the course of the day, I became concerned about the nature of the pastoral relationship Pastor Freddy had developed with this inmate, *El Buso* (a fictional nickname). El Buso lived in a special private wing of the prison referred to by inmates as "the North Pole." Three inmates lived in private cells in this tiny sector and enjoyed special access to water and other amenities. Pastor Freddy seemed impressed with El Buso and the respect he commanded among the other inmates. Indeed, I found myself marveling at El Buso's seemingly unlimited resources, his gold chains, name-brand clothing, and easy-going manner. Pastor Freddy had informed me that El Buso was the most powerful prisoner in the complex and the felon made no effort to hide his influence. He treated our party of five to ice cream, an elaborate meal of traditional Guatemalan *pepián* prepared by two female visitors, and sent us on our way at the day's end with multiple bags of sweet bread from the prison bakery. During the lunch, El Buso conducted business by mobile phone, giving orders regarding a construction project in his hometown. He also sent other inmates to fetch tortillas, Coca-cola, and "bread for the gringo." During a conversation about a prison-wide New Year's Eve party financed by El Buso himself, another resident of the three-person private wing disappeared behind a curtain and reemerged holding a bottle of Buchanan's Whiskey, the pride of the men's liquor collection. I had heard of special privileges for Guatemala's most powerful inmates, but now it was clear that such stories were true. By far the most troubling moment came during a short conversation between Pastor Freddy and El Buso near the end of the meal. After discussing a number of ministry matters, El Buso offered, and Pastor Freddy accepted, the use of a Ford Ranger pickup truck "for the ministry." In addition, El Buso offered the use of a suburban home "sitting empty right now" in a gated community near the south coast—an offer Pastor Freddy refused despite the urging of one of his young protégés. When it was time for our group to leave, Pastor Freddy made arrangements to pick up the truck at the home of El Buso's fiancé the next day.

Perhaps there is an explanation for Pastor Freddy's interaction with El Buso that would eliminate any concerns. Yet, from my perspective, there were plenty of reasons for Pastor Freddy to be far more cautious and self-critical in his interaction with powerful inmates. Prior to our visit to *el Pavón* Pastor Freddy had shared with me that he sometimes did small favors for El Buso such as "purchasing" special tennis shoes from a particular vendor downtown who charges him nothing once he knows their destination. Furthermore, Pastor Freddy admitted to not being certain of the extent to which El Buso really desired to convert. True, he attended chapel occasionally and liked to talk about religion with Pastor Freddy, but he was clearly not yet ready to take on the status of an evangelical convert, especially since it would entail giving up alcohol. Nor had Pastor Freddy inquired about the nature of El Buso's offenses or whether or not he intended to change the course of his life. El Buso continued managing his business from prison and it was not difficult to imagine that such dealings included an illegal element—at one point El Buso made reference to an altercation he and another inmate had had with a group of Colombian prisoners a day earlier. Another potential cause for alarm was the fact that El Buso counted one of Pastor Freddy's prized ex-gang member converts among his closest friends, even inviting him to live in "the pole." Given reports of connections between organized crime and the gangs, it was difficult not to be troubled by this friendship. The same ex-gang member, a Salvadoran, had reportedly been a relatively high-profile member of the M-18 prior to his very recent conversion. Finally, my concerns were deepened by the fact that Pastor Freddy and his protégés clearly hail from a lower socioeconomic class than El Buso's, and like the other men in the prison, they showed El Buso considerable deference. In accepting the offer of the use of El Buso's late-model pickup, Pastor Freddy and his ministry became indebted to El Buso, especially since Pastor Freddy drove a dilapidated hatchback from the early 1980s. Was El Buso using his relationship to Pastor Freddy as cover for his ongoing activities or was he genuinely interested in the evangelical message and truly desirous of helping Pastor Freddy's ministry to alcoholics and gang members? In either case, Pastor Freddy seemed terribly naïve about the conflict of interest created when a pastor accepts gifts and runs errands for a powerful felon.

Finally, taking a decidedly different approach to gangs and gang violence are a few prominent Neo-Pentecostals who have come to view gang members as "the enemy" in both a spiritual and a literal sense. In 2007, the *New York Times* cited an anonymous source within the United Nations to report that powerful officials in the Guatemalan police, who were active in evangelical churches, were spearheading a social cleansing campaign aimed at eliminating gang members and other "criminals" through extrajudicial executions (McKinley 2007). The article, which created a firestorm of controversy, elicited a vigorous denunciation by the president of Guatemala's largest evangelical association, the Evangelical Alliance. But shortly thereafter, in a televised interview for his Christian talk show, Erwin Sperisen, then director of Guatemala's National Police, defended the practice of social cleansing and openly admitted to the existence of "death squadrons" while confirming that evangelical police personnel had been active in them. In a chilling admission, Sperison, reported, "We incurred some illegalities, but we did what was just" (Hurtado, Méndez, and Valdés 2007). As this book goes to press, a trial has begun in a Swiss court where Sperisen, whose dual citizenship allowed him to flee to Switzerland shortly after resigning as chief of police in 2007, faces charges as the intellectual author of more than twelve extra-judicial killings (Galeano 2011). I mention this incident not because I believe that a large contingent of evangelicals exists for whom social cleansing of gang members represents a religious duty. My research has led me to believe that such views are quite rare, at least among barrio evangelicals. But variation in outlook surely exists in the broader evangelical community. While my focus here is on evangelical gang *ministry*, I would be remiss if I ignored Pastor Luís's lament that not all evangelicals believe in the efficacy of such ministry. In any case, the fact that Sperisen was an active member of the Neo-Pentecostal El Shaddai mega-church, where the pastor-turned-presidential-candidate Harold Caballeros has cultivated spiritual warfare and a theology of "dominion" probably helps to explain the ousted police chief's belief in social cleansing (Smith 2007).

My review of characteristics, tendencies, and motivations of evangelical gang ministries has complicated the portrait considerably. A great variety exists among evangelical organizations and congregations working at gang ministry. A few of those I visited have multiple, paid staff members and a formal institutional structure, but most consisted of merely a pastor or a highly motivated former gang member and a cadre of volunteers. Furthermore, some evangelical gang ministry coordinators seem aware of the complexity surrounding gang ministry while others appear not to have yet recognized the dangers and pitfalls associated with it, confident instead that religious conversion can change a gang member "from the inside out." Nevertheless, a number of broad tendencies characterize nearly all of the evangelical gang ministries I visited. First, evangelicals involved in gang ministry tended to speak of the gang issue in both spiritual and social terms. Pastor Luis defined the gang as first and foremost "a spiritual problem" but implied that congregations were not engaging enough in "social work." Abner felt that congregations must understand the struggles faced by gang members before engaging in gang ministry but believed firmly that only Christ could truly transform gang members since religious conversion effects change in "the heart" of the individual.

Second, evangelical gang ministries take a highly individualist approach, focusing almost entirely on extricating gang members from the gang rather than mobilizing to attack the social problems that make gang membership attractive in the first place. Evangelicals call this ministry "restoration" and those involved use a variety of tools to help gang members leave the gang and reintegrate into society. Among their favorite tools are religious conversion, the knifing off of the old social environment through time hoarding, the promotion and supervision of an alternative masculinity, and the offer of a religious career to take the place of a delinquent career.

Third, evangelicals are highly motivated by a combination of personal, ethical, and spiritual commands and incentives and they tend to articulate such motives with the help of biblical injunctions to take care of the disadvantaged and the down-and-out. These three broad tendencies—framing the gangs as a "spiritual problem" as well as a social one, addressing the gang issue through outreach to *individual* gang members, and drawing inspiration from biblical stories—all contrast sharply with the most common perspectives I encountered among those involved in Catholic gang ministries.

A SOCIAL APPROACH

Evangelicals are not the only religious people addressing gang violence. Catholic parishes and nonprofit charities have also developed ministries for addressing gangs and gang violence in Central America. While these programs and institutions vary considerably in size, budget, and mission, they also share some similarities. Table 6.2 shows a listing of eight Catholic institutions devoting at least a portion of budget and program toward the reduction of gangs and gang violence at the time of my visits in 2007 and 2008. Since there was no agreement among Catholics on what to call gang violence reduction programs, I distinguish between ministries aimed at promoting gang exit from those seeking to prevent entrance by calling the approach of the former "reinsertion" and the approach of the latter "prevention."

I did not encounter any "mom-and-pop" gang-related ministries with Catholic affiliation. Although some Catholic gang ministries, like *¡Adios Tatuajes!* (Goodbye Tattoos!) and *Rincón Juveníl* (Youth Corner), had only a small staff, these programs were always integrated within a larger administrative structure such as the local diocese or a larger

TABLE 6.2. A Sampling of Gang Ministries in Central America

Name	*Country*	*Affiliation*	*Staff size*	*Approach*
El Polígono de Don Bosco	El Salvador	Catholic-Salesian	10+	Prevention
CrisPaz	El Salvador	Catholic	8	Reinsertion
Fe y Alegría	El Salvador	Catholic-Jesuit	10+	Prevention
Adios Tatuajes	Honduras	Catholic-Maryknoll	3	Reinsertion
Unidos por la Paz	Honduras	Catholic	4	Reinsertion
Adios Tatuajes	Guatemala	Catholic-Maryknoll	3	Reinsertion
Rincón Juveníl	Guatemala	Catholic	3	Prevention
Grupo Ceiba	Guatemala	Catholic/ecumenical	10+	Prevention
FEPAZ (Foro Ecuménico por la Paz y la Reconciliación)	Guatemala	Catholic/ecumenical	1–5	Scholarship

Catholic nonprofit. In five cases, a priest was involved in the administration of the institution while in the other three institutions—FEPAZ (Forum for Peace and Reconciliation), Unidos por la Paz, and CrisPaz—the director held a college degree at the very least. As a consequence, Catholic gang ministries tended to be more institutionalized and better organized and had better access to funding at the local and the international levels. At least four of the organizations drew a considerable amount of their resources from international donor agencies. Before I began my on-site research, I had been informed that Catholic gang ministries were dedicated to gang prevention rather than intervention or "reinsertion." But this division did not always hold. While evidence exists for a Catholic preference for promoting alternatives to children who might otherwise be involved in the gangs, I found a few Catholic-affiliated ministries promoting gang exit through reinsertion as well as two that formerly promoted reinsertion but have shifted their focus to prevention. An example of the latter is Fr. José María Morataya's technical high school called "El Polígono de Don Bosco." Located in las Iberias, one of San Salvador's most dangerous neighborhoods, the Catholic-owned and -operated institution enrolls hundreds of students from the neighborhood and the surrounding communities and operates as a kind of "reform school" for young men needing vocational skills for entering the job market. Hundreds of youth study trades there while obtaining a high school diploma. Through an agreement with the Salvadoran juvenile justice system, young offenders can choose to serve out a part of their sentence at the school. Over the years, but especially in the late 1990s and early 2000s, a number of former gang members have entered and graduated from the school learning trades such as bread baking, welding, and machinery that have helped them gain a fresh start after leaving the gang. The school's innovative approach to reform has attracted national attention and international funding for the entrepreneurial cooperative program developed by Fr. Morataya. "Padre Pepe," as he is affectionately called by students and the media, has a reputation for "specializing" in reforming gang youth and maintains communication ties with active gang leaders both in prison and on the outside. It is easy to see why they trust him. Padre Pepe has a lively personality and a "tell-it-like-it-is" conversational style that is both engaging and disarming. When I interviewed him in 2007, he seemed eager to correct what he believed were widely held and inaccurate stereotypes regarding the gangs in El Salvador. He argued that the gangs are a foreign import (from Los Angeles) and that, contrary to the results I found, gang members no longer can escape the gang. When I asked him about religious responses to gang violence, he became emphatic: "The church cannot respond as a church! The problem is with society and only by responding *as a society* can we begin to address this issue!" This perspective contrasts sharply with the views expressed by Pastor Luis, Abner, and other evangelical gang ministry leaders who believed gang ministry ought to begin by promoting a change of heart among current gang members. Instead, Padre Pepe insisted that the real sources of growth and violence of the gangs lie in unemployment and migration. Only the government, pressured by civil society, can effectively address the problem. Just as important, Padre Pepe believes that the Salvadoran gangs no longer allow exit, and the school had not accepted gang members for some time now. Although he did not rule out the possibility of helping to reform gang members in the future, he would only do so if they came honestly seeking to leave and, by his own admission, such cases were quite rare if they exist at all. Turning the question around, I asked Padre Pepe how the gangs view religion. This time his response was even more intense. "That's just the problem—they're USING us! The churches are being USED by the gangs. They're PLAYING with us!" Padre Pepe insisted that the gangs are constantly evolving and learning to take advantage of anyone naïve enough to trust them. He told me of a recent meeting with an imprisoned gang member who showed him his certificate of baptism. "See how they use the churches?" he said. "He was just *playing* the pastor for the good image of being a Christian now. [Getting baptized] might help him to get out earlier."

Clearly, Padre Pepe saw religious conversion as a ruse—a way of gaming gullible religious people, especially evangelicals, by playing to their religious sensibilities. For him, gang ministries that seek conversion are merely a distraction from the hard work that must be done to provide youth with what they really need—a job. As evidence, he recounted a meeting in which religious gang ministry leaders had tried to coordinate their efforts and speak with one voice to the government and promote pro-employment reforms. To his disappointment, a Baptist minister stood up and gave an impromptu sermon on what "the Bible says," insisting that what these men really need is Jesus. The sermon was greeted with numerous "amen's." "I just hung my head," he recalled.

Friar Miguel, a Peruvian Franciscan who pastors a satellite neighborhood of Guatemala City, holds a similar perspective, although his manner is far less outspoken. In 2006 his parish was awarded a sizable grant from USAID to found a youth center for children and youth of the neighborhood of Búcaro and the surrounding area called Mezquital. The *Rincón Juvenil* (Youth Corner) is an after-school youth center with workshops for children and adolescents and was just getting off the ground when I visited in 2007. The center had been constructed on open land belonging to the parish and housed a beauty academy, a gymnasium, and a computer lab and was managed by a small paid staff as well as a larger core of adult and young adult volunteers from the community. Although a handful of gang sympathizers and former members had participated in workshops at the center, the lay organizer stated that the center's main approach to gang violence was that of prevention. Fr. Miguel does not share Padre Pepe's perspective of gang members as powerful, wily criminals. He described them rather as youth from precarious and impoverished families and lacking options for a viable future. However, he does share Padre Pepe's conviction that only by teaching gang youth a marketable trade can they be helped to leave the gang and establish a crime-free life. Furthermore, Fr. Miguel is equally pessimistic about the evangelical churches' approach to the gang phenomenon. In the surrounding Mezquital area, he noted, the "separatist" (i.e., evangelical) churches have grown as the gangs have multiplied. Furthermore, some ex-gang members who had been taken in by local evangelical churches had recently been killed. "So when you look around and see this you realize that getting gang members out isn't enough. We have Protestant youth that come here for career preparation."

The indictment of evangelical gang ministries as overzealous "spiritualists" was a common theme among those working in Catholic gang ministries, voiced especially by the priests I interviewed. Fr. Julio Coyoy, who directs a pro-youth vocational school in Guatemala's crime-ridden "El Limón" neighborhood, accused the evangelical churches of offering little more than "song therapy." Furthermore, he expanded his critique to include what he called the "fundamentalism" of charismatic Catholic youth groups. "What's missing is to make the gospel real and practical," he said. The organization he directs, "Grupo CEIBA," has also been a beneficiary of USAID funds aimed at reducing gang violence, and like many of the Catholic-related gang ministries, CEIBA aims at prevention of gang affiliation by helping local children and youth learn trades and skills useful for finding employment. Fr. Coyoy emphasized that CEIBA, though founded in the late 1980s by the Catholic parish next door, is now a fully secular organization and does not promote a religious stance of any kind, although it does host volunteer groups from a progressive Catholic parish in Quebec. He seemed eager to distance himself from mainstream Catholicism and noted that his group no longer maintained friendly ties with the current diocesan priest.

Ironically, even Catholic ministries with an overtly religious name were reticent to promote spirituality in any formal or theologically specific manner. Such was the case at *Fe y Alegría* (Faith and Happiness), a Jesuit-founded youth center promoting popular education and technical trades among children in a rough barrio of San Salvador. The center had worked with local gang members during the late 1990s and administered a special program encouraging gang exit from 2001 to 2004. By the time of my visit, however, the center had changed its approached and now sought to promote peaceful alternatives to gang life among children not yet affiliated. When I asked Santos, the youth director, about the "spiritual component" of the group's ministry he explained:

> We call it values formation. It's not catechistic or anything. It's more general than that. When we pray we want everyone to be able to participate, no matter what their religion. We also try to help them to develop a personal project.
>
> [*You mean like a life plan?*]
>
> Yes. We try to help them think about what they want to do in life and how to get there. We also try to help them cultivate the values that are necessary in the work place. We teach all of the values.

Like Fr. Miguel and Fr. Julio, Santos criticized the evangelical efforts at gang ministry due to their highly religious, conversionist approach. He saw the evangelical churches as offering little more than spirituality in the form of *terapia del culto* (worship service therapy). "They lack any real process," he argued. "All they can offer is a religious experience—you accept, you're forgiven and that's it. They don't use scientific tools such as psychological counseling, job training or therapy." Santos did not argue that evangelical conversion never "works" as a pathway out of the gang, but he believed that it provides little help for the really tough cases involving those most deeply involved:

> [F]or many gang members, becoming a Christian has worked but it's mostly just the ones who hadn't advanced very high in the system. They could get out more easily.
>
> [*So you're saying there's a point of no return?*]
>
> I'm one who believes there are those who just can't go back. Once you get so deep into it you can't change. They're crazy. A guy, after killing so

> many people, he is a psychopath—he's gone crazy. If you talk to this guy he narrates his sadistic crimes with ease (*tranquilo*).

In this respect, Santos's perspective on gang exit mirrored that of Padre Pepe. Because leaving the gang becomes increasingly difficult after years of activity or leadership, it seems advisable to them not to try to persuade long-time gang members to leave the gang since doing so may lead to naïvely believing a transformation has taken place when it has not. "Many of [the graduates] have made us look bad. One guy we helped place in a carpentry shop busted up his boss's face one day. Others have robbed from their boss or just don't like the job. They'll come back and complain that the job is no good."

One way to avoid the challenge of having to discern whether or not a former gang member is adequately prepared to succeed as a drug- and crime-free member of the community is to reduce the scope of programming. The Maryknoll community, a progressive Catholic order founded in New York State in the early twentieth century, has helped to develop tattoo-removal clinics called *¡Adios Tatuajes!* (Goodbye Tattoos!) in all three countries of northern Central America. The clinics incorporate inexpensive infrared technology capable of burning off a tattoo in three visits over the course of one month. The treatments are attractive because of their very low price but the method is time consuming and can sometimes lead to painful, ugly scarring. Figure 6.1 shows a tattoo in its second of three treatments required to fully "erase" the tattoo.

Although the clinic in Honduras closed after providing more than 30,000 treatments, tattoo removal at other Catholic-funded clinics in Guatemala and El Salvador continues to be an important service offered to gang youth and anyone else whose tattoo has become a barrier to job opportunities (Sibaja et al. 2006). Lately, though, the practice has come under scrutiny since a number of studies have suggested that gang leaders now remove their tattoos in order to more freely be able to go about their work. In other cases, tattoo removal attracts the ire of gang leaders and places ex-gang members at a greater risk for a "green light." Still, for ex-gang members who have been given their "squares," tattoo removal greatly enhances the prospects for getting a job and makes traveling in rival gang territory far less dangerous. The clinics ask no

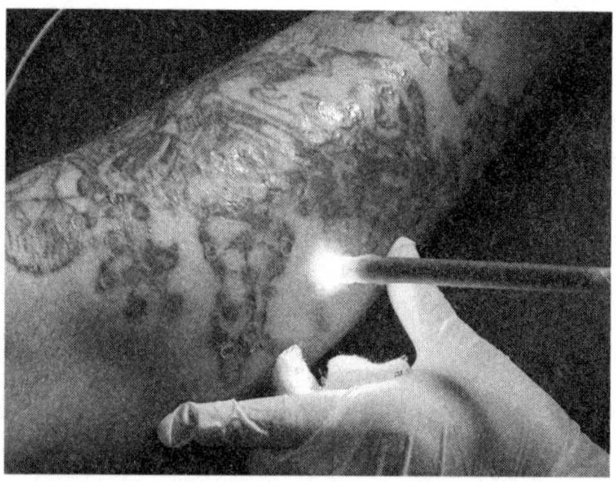

FIGURE 6.1. shows a nurse technician administering stage two in a three-stage treatment of tattoo removal at *¡Adios Tatuajes!* in Cuidad Quetzal, Guatemala City. Local anesthesia renders the initial treatment painless, but subsequent inflammation, scabbing, and scarring cause considerable discomfort during the month-long process.
Photo Credit: Robert Brenneman

questions, simply providing a low-cost service to men and women wishing to be free of their tattoos.

SEEKING JUSTICE

A few Catholic bishops and priests in Guatemala and Honduras have approached the issue of gangs as a matter of social justice, denouncing the "scapegoating" of gang members by politicians for political advantage. In Honduras, both the Archbishop of Tegucigalpa and, especially, Auxiliary Bishop Rómulo Emiliani Sánchez were outspoken opponents of the heavy-handed militarized approach of the Ricardo Maduro administration and its "zero tolerance" legislation. After the Maduro administration and its hard-line party lost the elections to a left-leaning candidate from the opposition, Msgr. Sánchez offered to act as a mediator between the gangs and the government. The bishop's proposal met with strong disapproval from hardliners who viewed the overture as akin to "negotiating with terrorists" (Replogle 2006). The bishop has also played an instrumental role in helping a local rehabilitation center called "Unidos por la Vida" (United for Life) seek funding for the building of a rehabilitation and job training center, but after some early successes, additional funds have been slow to materialize and the project was at a standstill in 2008. In Guatemala, the Catholic bishop's conference has also released statements promoting a more humane approach to dealing with gang violence. Catholic educational institutions have contributed to advocacy efforts indirectly by providing objective, social scientific research regarding the rise of gangs (Cruz 1999; Cruz and Portillo 1998) and investigating possible social causes contributing to the presence of gangs in particular communities (Cruz 2004). The Jesuit Universidad de Centroamérica de Simeón Cañas, popularly known as the UCA, has produced some of the best empirical research on the gangs to date. Both through publications of its own faculty and by organizing and overseeing research institutes in the rest of Central America, the UCA has been able to produce balanced scholarship on a topic that is all too often subject to generalization and hyperbole. Jesuits at the ERIC research institute in Yoro, Honduras have also contributed empirical research (Castro and Carranza 2005).

Thus the approach of Catholic-affiliated ministries works at the local and national level to combat the demonization of the gangs and at the community level to provide alternatives to gang affiliation to youth who might see the gang as an attractive possibility. Although they may not have put it quite as emphatically as Padre Pepe did, all of the Catholic priests and lay workers I interviewed agreed that the proper approach to gang ministry is a *social* one. Most emphasized that they tried to downplay or avoid religious topics altogether when working with youth so as not to offend or scare off youth from evangelical families. Some of the organizations, such as *Grupo CEIBA* and *Fe y Alegría*, were founded as a direct outgrowth of the liberation theology movement of the 1970s and '80s while others came from less progressive traditions such as the Salesians. Still, in all cases, the priests and lay directors are well aware of the social roots of gang violence and firmly believe that education and job training are the best means of both preventing gang affiliation among youth and luring current gang members out of the gang. Religion, they agreed, is of little use in addressing the gang phenomenon. While some doubted the efficacy of religion in relation to gangs, they did not allude to the religious motivations of their work. Whether they took religious framing as a matter of course or because they believed explicit religious discourse is offensive to cultural pluralism, coordinators of Catholic gang-related ministries, including priests, avoided religious language altogether.

COMPARING STRATEGIES

What do we learn from reviewing and comparing evangelical and Catholic strategies for addressing gangs and gang violence? First, despite the diversity of strategies and discourse that exist among Catholics as well as evangelicals addressing the gang issue, some clear differences emerge. Across the board, evangelicals were intent on extracting gang members from the gang, and religious conversion was assumed to be the best pathway for bringing about such an exit. A few ministries were now involved in prevention, but these groups always continued to promote gang exit. All evangelical groups incorporated a significant evangelical-spiritual component as part of their ministry. Catholic ministries on the other hand, avoided topics of spirituality except in a very broad sense (such as "values education") either out of deference to the evangelical youth who participated or because they deemed it irrelevant to the topic at hand. Although some Catholic ministries were involved in social reinsertion (the nonreligious equivalent to evangelical "restoration"), more than half approached gang ministry from the angle of prevention, advocacy, or scholarship. Additionally, whereas evangelicals described the gang issue as "a spiritual problem," and thus an ideal target of religious ministry, Catholics like Padre Pepe believed that churches, Catholic or evangelical, must recognize that only the government can adequately address the gang issue by providing jobs and reducing poverty.

Another way to conceive of the diverging tendencies between evangelical and Catholic-inspired approaches to the gang phenomenon is that of two very different ways of dealing with shame. If my argument is correct, that shame and the shame-rage spiral are key factors motivating youth to join the gang and to participate in criminal violence, then it may be useful to differentiate between the varying approaches to gang outreach and how these programs deal with shame. Evangelical gang ministries invariably seek to provide gang members with opportunities for acknowledging and discharging shame by setting the stage for a conversion experience that is public and that incorporates an emotional-symbolic recognition of guilt for past deeds. When such acts lead to a successful exit, as they sometimes do, both the individual and the congregation gain emotional energy. The faith of the congregation in its message and its pastor is renewed and the individual is able to lay the groundwork for a new identity as an "hermano"—a sibling belonging to a new family possessing time, energy, and a vested interest in helping the convert establish a stable lifestyle. On the other hand, the failure of a public conversion to result in visible changes in behavior and lifestyle can drain the emotional energy of a congregation. If too many conversions fail, a pastor, a congregation, or a ministry will be labeled gullible or naïve. Nor are evangelical gang ministry promoters unaware of the role of shame. When Rev. Tercero preached of an "inner sickness" that drives gang youth to carry weapons and look macho, it was surely of shame that he spoke.

Catholic ministries, which tend to favor prevention over working with individuals, approach the topic of shame indirectly. Groups like the Youth Corner or Grupo CEIBA in Guatemala City or el Polígono vocational school in San Salvador seek to provide youth from impoverished backgrounds with the skills they need in order to find employment and a steady income, both of which can protect them from the shame of not being able to provide for their own needs or those of their families. Providing safe after-school programs that help children and youth to stay in school or that provide alternative career training for those who do not, especially in marginal neighborhoods where the gangs are prevalent, may have a less "visible" impact, since they do not produce a bible-toting ex-gang member. But to the extent that these programs provide attractive, nonviolent pathways to pride and a robust self-identity for children from precarious households, they are undoubtedly impacting their communities. Even Catholics who advocate on behalf of the dignity and human rights of current or former gang members are in effect attacking the sources of shame by trying to leverage against the social stigma defining gang youth as dangerous and worthless elements of society.

WHAT GANG MINISTRIES TEACH US ABOUT CENTRAL AMERICAN RELIGION

These distinct approaches to gang ministry also speak to a larger story—one regarding the diverging trajectories of evangelicalism and Catholicism in Central America. Evangelicals in Central America have grown dramatically in number and as a percentage of the population. In the 1980s and '90s, most of the attention in the media and among academics was on Protestant growth in Guatemala. However, evangelicals in El Salvador and Honduras appear to be catching up or even surpassing (in the case of Honduras) those of Guatemala in the most recent polls of religious affiliation. Furthermore, despite modest increases in the number of religiously unaffiliated Central Americans, evangelicals continue to gain most of their adherents from the ranks of the Catholic church. In a region of the world where a few short decades ago the Vatican could claim nearly universal religious dominance, adherence to the Catholic Church is in dramatic decline. In the very near future, if not already, Roman Catholicism will no longer enjoy majority status in the Northern Triangle. Scholars have been debating the reasons for evangelical gains and Catholic declines for at least two decades, and in Central America, wars and political instability were often cited as key factors. David Stoll argued that evangelical congregations, by virtue of their apolitical theology, provided political refuge from Guatemala's raging civil war (Stoll 1991, 1993). That explanation provides some power for countries like Guatemala, which experienced dramatic evangelical growth during the height of the civil war—growth that leveled off significantly during the 1990s (Gooren 2001) as the war drew to a close. But the same explanation of political conflict does not apply for Honduras, which did not undergo an open civil war,[6] and where an explosion of evangelical growth has taken place in the last two decades. For this reason, a number of researchers have simply expanded the notion of "refuge" to include seeking shelter from economic rather than merely political catastrophes. Sheldon Annis argued on the basis of ethnographic work in a rural Guatemalan town that evangelicalism provides economic advantages for indigenous families that convert, better positioning them to succeed in a changing economy (Annis 1987). Virginia Garrard-Burnett (1998) has argued that evangelical theology provides a source of solace for Latin Americans facing crises and offers a means of adapting in ways that give converts a new sense of leverage despite difficult odds. John Burdick (1993) studied economically disadvantaged Pentecostal churches in Brazil and concluded that such congregations provided refuge from status judging while uniting members in a "cult of affliction" (Burdick 1993). Andrew Chesnut, borrowing loosely from Rodney Stark's supply-side theory of religious economies (Stark and Finke 2000), contends that in places like Brazil and Guatemala, "Pentecostal churches responding to popular consumer demand, developed products that offer healing of the afflictions of poverty and positive personal transformation for those who have been rejected and stigmatized by societies that have the steepest socioeconomic pyramids in the world" (Chesnut 2003:63).

My interviews with ex-gang members and leaders of religious gang-related ministries provide further evidence that evangelicals in the region are highly motivated religious marketers, promoting religious goods for addressing social problems. That is, while most of the evangelicals I interviewed did not ignore the social context surrounding the problem of gang membership and violence, evangelicals insisted that a spiritual rebirth is by far the most effective means of addressing the problem. In fact, evangelicals' emphasis on the possibility of individual transformation for all propels them toward identifying gang members as *ideal* targets for ministry. Although the risks and complications associated with gang ministry mean that only the most ambitious evangelical pastors and laypersons will actively engage in gang ministry, gang members continue to be viewed as "ripe" for ministry since conversion can lead to powerful new testimonies with special payoff to congregations that host them. Conversely, the Central American Catholics I interviewed—including priests who are under considerable pressure to slow or stop the attrition in their own parish—were reticent to bring religion into the picture when dealing with the gang issue. Convinced that the problems surrounding gangs are eminently social, political, and, economic in nature, they avoided religious language when addressing gang violence. Even those groups, like *Unidos por la Paz* (United for Peace) and *Fe y Alegría,* that work with ex-gang members (or used to do so) were reluctant to promote Catholic faith as providing pertinent answers or special relevance to the plight of gang members.

As we have seen, one factor contributing to continued evangelical growth is the tireless work of its clergy and lay ministers including evangelical gang interventionists who seek out converts by promoting conversion as a "refuge" from the debilitating effects of chronic shame. Recognizing that many gang members are tired of the hyper-machismo mentality and lifestyle of the gang, evangelical gang "restoration" promotes alternative masculinities, often borrowing military metaphors and language in order to reframe non-macho behaviors as risky and courageous. For example, Emerson used violent language to describe his motives in evangelistic outreach with two other converted ex-gang members in an attempt to find and convert new gang members. "If we used to fire away [at the enemy], why not fire at them again but this time with the Word," he explained. In fact, the project of reform itself can become a source of masculine identity. For young men, like Emerson, abandoning la vida loca, eschewing weapons, and taking up the lifestyle of a teetotaling, domesticated husband together became a project of "conquering sin." At the same time, evangelical religion provides men—especially those who can provide evidence of having been "beyond hope," and thus serve as an inspiration to others trying to change—with opportunities for leadership and public recognition at every level. From internationally traveled pastors and evangelists, such as Ricardo and Camilo, to home bible study leaders like Nelson or worship band members like Armando, such converts found opportunities to reconstruct an identity waiting for them upon their conversion.

At least one poll shows evidence that evangelical masculinity holds considerable appeal among Central American men. While reliable data on religious affiliation by gender are difficult to find, a recent poll conducted by the Center for Public Opinion Research at San Salvador's highly respected Jesuit university provides a surprising view of religion and gender presented in Table 6.3.

Incorporating a random sample of 1,200 respondents, leading to a 2.8 percent margin of error, the poll showed that *overall* Salvadoran men are less likely to report being religious when compared with Salvadoran women—hardly a surprise given the well-documented preference for religion among women worldwide (Miller and Stark 2002). But still, Salvadoran men are just as likely to report being Protestant as Salvadoran

TABLE 6.3. Professed Religious Affiliation Among Salvadorans by Gender

	Catholic	*Protestant*	*None*	*Other*
Women	57.3	28.9	12	1.7
Men	49.8	29.7	19.1	1.4
All	53.9	29.2	15.2	1.6

(Source: Instituto Universitario de Opinión Pública 2008.)

women are. In fact, although the difference remains within the margin of error, a higher percentage of men reported being Protestant than did women in the poll. At the same time, Salvadoran men are considerably *less* likely than are women to report being Catholic. Indeed, fewer than half the Salvadoran men in the poll identified themselves as Catholic while more than 57 percent of the women did so. Bearing in mind that virtually all Salvadoran Protestants consider themselves *evangélicos*, the higher proportion of males self-identifying as evangelical comes as a surprise. Most evangelical congregations seek to place serious lifestyle demands on the men who belong to them. Recall that among barrio evangelicals, an emphasis on personal piety (such as the tradition of observing "The Five P's") places considerable demands on the lives of new believers. While the prohibitions of The Five P's may be less frequently enforced than in the past, most evangelical congregations throughout Central America continue to forbid drinking and going to *discotecas*. Being an observant lay Roman Catholic on the other hand, involves fewer sacrifices for men in the barrio—at least in the eyes of the young men I interviewed. Of course, not all evangelical men follow the rules, and some Catholic men make significant sacrifices in other ways such as by giving time, effort, and money to their local parish. But, as both converted and nonconverted ex-gang members alike pointed out, becoming an evangelical *hermano* is considered a serious business in the Central American barrio precisely because it places so many demands on the lives of converted men. To convert while ignoring the rules is playing with fire, or "messing with Curly." Furthermore, the prohibitions to interpersonal violence, extramarital sex, and especially drinking hit men particularly hard because they threaten to limit pastimes traditionally associated with rituals of barrio masculinity. In fact, some ex-gang members remembered agonizing over the decision to convert in part because they feared being called gay or a *maricón* (fag). Viewed in light of such prohibitions, the fact that just as high a proportion of Salvadoran men as women profess Protestant Christianity is perplexing.

But when viewed in light of the findings here, the poll's results make more sense. Evangelical congregations and social-spiritual ministries promote conversion as *the answer* for men facing problems that seem out of their control. They provide alternatives for retaining a sense of masculinity by framing piety as "conquering sin" and by offering a variety of opportunities for the development of a religious career. Finally, due to its cadre of religious entrepreneurs motivated by religious narratives of transformation and compassion, evangelicalism is able to saturate the barrio with testimonies of males who have managed to pull off a successful transformation, thereby modeling the possibility for other youth seeking to enhance their own prospects for achieving stability (and perhaps some notoriety) in an environment fraught with insecurity. That such social and religious goods attract Central American men in general and not just gang members seems plausible at the very least. The results of the Salvadoran poll, especially when read in the context of the findings of my research on gang conversions, ought to cause scholars of Latin American religion to rethink the conclusion by Brusco (1995) and others that evangelical conversions among men result largely from an attempt by women to domesticate their men. After all, if Protestant men equal or surpass women in proportion, it is unlikely that these converted men are all being coaxed and cajoled into converting by their evangelical partners.

CONCLUSION

Both Catholics and evangelicals have spearheaded gang ministry in Central America, sometimes eliciting an outcry from neighbors and the media who believe them to be cozying up to hardened criminals. However, such ministries are motivated by very different theological frameworks and with differing perspectives on the nature of the problem itself. Evangelicals involved in such ministry tend to view the gang as a spiritual problem—exacerbated perhaps by poverty or disenfranchisement—while Catholics involved in gang ministries understand the problem within a framework of social justice. With few exceptions, evangelicals view conversion as the most important means of addressing the gang problem and thus create ministries that seek to "rescue" individual gang members and reestablish them within their communities through "restoration" programs. Meanwhile, although Catholic ministries have engaged in similar promotion of gang exit and communal reentry, most promote prevention of gang entrance through community centers and educational institutions designed to provide alternative means of personal and vocational development for children and youth in marginal neighborhoods. By promoting education, job training, and tattoo removal in marginal urban neighborhoods, and by advocating for social investment and against draconian security measures at the national level, Catholic leaders are "crusading" against the social sources of shame. They engage in this work in part because of the social justice component of Catholic social teaching and the theological inheritance of liberation theology. But their approach is also undoubtedly the result of the considerably higher level of education possessed by most of the priests and lay leaders involved in gang ministry whose access to higher education has given them some knowledge of the social-structural roots of gang formation and violence.

Comparing the impact of the evangelical "restoration" programs with the Catholic prevention-focused efforts is difficult, in part because the efforts of the Catholic ministries are aimed at producing a long-term effect. Part of what energizes evangelicals involved in gang ministry is the ability to point to converted ex-gang members who now thrive as members of a congregation and the local community, and they hold up these cases as verifiable, if not especially numerous, "success stories." Still, evangelicals involved in gang ministry may be more likely to underestimate the social forces connecting gang members to wider problems of crime, violence, and drugs. Some evangelical pastors such as Rev. José and Pastor Álvaro may have learned these difficult lessons, but at least one, Pastor Freddy, was alarmingly unaware or unconcerned by the risks associated with evangelizing powerful gang members and their friends. In any case, evangelical gang interventionists remained thoroughly convinced of the possibility of and the need for individual transformation among even the most deeply involved gang members, while Catholics such as Santos and Padre Pepe had come to conclude that attempting to help gang members leave the gang was unrealistic at best and, at worst, an invitation to gang members to take advantage of religious naïveté. Naïveté or not, evangelicals' sheer confidence in the power of conversion to effect change suggests that one reason evangelicals continue to grow in the region despite relatively high lifestyle expectations for members relates to their insistence on promoting conversion as a response to social problems. Evangelical pastors and gang ministry leaders promote conversion to evangelical Christianity as a means of gaining control of one's life and future. When conversion works for ex-gang members, these individuals are often "showcased" by pastors and gang ministry leaders as evidence of the power of evangelical religion and may even be fast-tracked into positions of leadership in a church or ministry. In short, both the rescuer and the rescued benefit from gang conversions since the episode serves as proof of the activity of the Holy Spirit in the faith community which is seen to have effected a "faith healing" of a social nature. That the event represents a "social healing" rather than a physical one matters little. Thus gang conversions provide further evidence of the dramatic nature of "healing" promoted by barrio evangelicals. That more and more Central Americans, including men, look to these communities for healing should hardly come as a surprise, given the wounded nature of an increasingly violent society.

Conclusion

Generally speaking, violence always arises out of impotence. It is the hope of those who have no power.
—*Hannah Arendt*

Painted on the wall at the entrance to La Lopez Arellano, a sprawling urban satellite of San Pedro Sula, Honduras is a mural depicting a popular verse cited by multiple converts and evangelical gang ministry workers in Central America: 1 Corinthians 28–29: "And the base things of the world and the despised, God has chosen, the things that are not, so that He may nullify the things that are so that no one may boast before God." The mural originally held a pair of scenes. Next to the verse was a gang mural representing important symbols of the Vatos Locos gang—a mother crying tears for her son, a DJ, a rose. The dual mural confused me at first. Although the Vatos Locos "pane" was not as pornographic or violent as the "unofficial" gang scenes portrayed in tattoos and on the walls of many Central American barrios, it nevertheless told a pictorial story of a chapter in the history of this community that many residents seemed eager to forget. So it came as little surprise that when I visited the community for a second time in 2008, community leaders had painted over the gang symbols due to complaints from residents. But the pane with the biblical verse had been preserved with special permission from the neighborhood officials. The dual mural was the first of many pieces of evidence I was to encounter supporting the hypothesis I had come to investigate—that evangelical religion provides a widely recognized refuge from the gang—a way out for weary gang members. Indeed, to many of the young men and women I interviewed, both those who had converted and those who had chosen another pathway, my interest in the evangelical pathway seemed almost sophomoric and obvious. Nearly all of the former gang members interviewed knew of the "evangelical exemption," and many brought it up without my even asking about religion. Moreover, many ex-gang members spoke of the unofficial but widely referenced follow-up to the exemption—that gangs monitor those who profess a conversion, and anyone caught violating evangelicalism's well-known prohibitions to drinking, smoking, or carrying weapons will be subject to a "green light."

Safety from a death warrant is not the only reason gang leavers seek out evangelical religion. Evangelical congregations provide many of the resources ex-gang members need most in order to start over after the gang. Since converted gang members represent the quintessential "sinner-turned-saint" testimony that gives credibility to the evangelical belief that "God can change anyone," members and especially pastors of these congregations have a vested interest in helping converted ex-gang members to succeed in finding work, to overcome addictions, and to avoid crime. Pastors use resources of time and social networks in their attempts to find work for converts and to keep tabs on their behavior. Meanwhile, expectations regarding frequent worship attendance and the prohibition of alcohol and dancing help keep converted ex-gang members out of the social circles where gang friends and activity dominate while "proving" the genuineness of deserters' motives to gang leaders and members. Indeed, viewed in light of what conversion can do for the ex-gang member, evangelical religion appears to be pragmatic—a convenient tool for getting out of an incredibly tight jam. That is in fact how several converted ex-gang members described their decision to convert. Reflecting on an increasingly bleak future in the gang, cognizant of the evangelical exemption, and well-aware of the resources offered by evangelical religion for overhauling a deeply stigmatized identity, these young men reported making a strategic decision to accept the invitation of evangelical Christianity to be "born again," trading in a homie identity for that of an evangelical *hermano*. Such strategic conversion narratives undercut the mystic view of religious conversion as the sudden and unexpected blinding light that stops an unsuspecting individual in her tracks, forcing a change of course. Rather, in these instances, evangelical conversion resembled a kind of "Twelve-Step plan," albeit one accompanied by a more particularized religious doctrine, rituals, and symbols than the one offered by Alcoholics Anonymous.

My research has revealed that more than mere strategy was at work in the conversion of some of the ex-gang members. In a few cases, former gang members told of experiencing conversion in spite of their immediate plans to remain in the gang. Other ex-gang members remembered *wanting* to convert, even hoping for a conversion, but not being able to carry through with the project for some time. After all, conversion to evangelical Christianity offers benefits but also costs to one's freedom and identity, especially for young men in the barrio, where drinking constitutes an important gendering ritual (Pine 2008). In six cases, ex-gang members, without prompting, dated their conversion to an emotional experience, usually that of weeping, that allowed them to believe that something important and not entirely under their control was afoot. That is, the experience of weeping provided a biographical marker representing to the struggling gang member that a fundamental change was in fact already under way. Just as important, crying in the presence of sympathetic and even enthusiastic onlookers allowed ex-gang members to publicly express remorse for their acts and gain a measure of trust with a subpopulation (the congregation) of the community. In that sense, emotional conversions played a role akin to what Braithwaite (1989) has called "reintegrative shaming." Evangelical churches provided a safe space where ex-gang members were allowed and encouraged to publicly express remorse for prior acts and lifestyles that violated the trust of the community. I argue that such shaming and reintegration provides an important first step in discharging chronic shame and exiting the "shame-rage" spiral that helps to fuel participation in gang violence.

CONTRIBUTIONS TO THE SOCIOLOGY OF RELIGION

Max Weber famously claimed that religious *ideas* can be the "track switchers" of history, playing the role of a catalyst in a particular time and place in history (Weber 1963). Track switchers do not lay the tracks to determine the course of the train, nor do religious ideas guide the course of history, but they can and sometimes do set the stage for a change in course that would not have occurred but for the persistence of a particular religious worldview held by a particular people. I suggest that emotional, embodied conversion experiences can and do play a similar role at the level of the individual and his or her life trajectory. Men like Emerson, Pancho, and Ricardo experienced conversion as a profoundly embodied, subjective experience that set in motion a series of events that dramatically changed the course of their lives. In effect, their bodies, having rebelled against the hyper-machista emotion display rules of the barrio, gave them permission and even led them toward the pursuit of a new set of ends. Joining a congregation subsequently provided further social supports affirming the new identity project and offering resources for framing and extending such a project. But I have argued that the effective *lever* for such attempts at personal change is not limited to religious ideas or even networks of social support but includes and sometimes begins with an embodied experience marked by weeping and trembling. The public, embodied acknowledgment of shame before a sympathetic audience such as the congregation or, in the case of Emerson, the *hermanas*, laid the groundwork for a newly energized project of identity reconstruction.

Recognizing that religious conversion experiences can play such a role does not mean that conversion, or evangelical religion for that matter, can run roughshod over the economic and social landscape, ignoring the "tracks" which restrict the life outcomes of barrio youth. Although a few of the converted ex-gang members have experienced an impressive turnaround in terms of life outcomes, in part due to the evangelical community's desire to showcase such testimonies, most have achieved only a very modest "success." Evangelical congregations do their best to provide access to a job, but even when successful, the jobs they provide usually entail manual labor with dismal pay. Since poverty and especially relative deprivation were key motivators in the decision of such youth to join the gang in the first place, further follow-up work is necessary before we can adequately judge the long-term effectiveness of this religious escape route from shame. Will the converted ex-gang member be able to avoid new rounds of chronic shame if and when it becomes clear that his long-term prospects for economic success are only marginally improved by his religious transformation project?

It is clear that evangelical congregations in Central America are firm believers in the track-switching potential of conversion. The efforts and resources poured into evangelistic campaigns in neighborhoods like Chamelecón, Honduras testify to the deep faith possessed by evangelicals like Pastor José who believe that even the most violent youth of society can "switch" tracks in the midst of a carefully choreographed service aimed at arresting both the attention and the emotions of gang youth. Though only a minority of evangelical congregations take risks and expend resources aimed at promoting gang conversions, the fact that nearly all evangelical gang ministries insist on promoting gang exit rather than engaging in prevention reveals the faith of evangelicals in the track-switching enterprise. Nor are Central American evangelicals, the vast majority of whom self-identify as charismatic or Pentecostal, the first to promote an emotional, conversionist solution to personal and even social problems. Emergent religious movements and denominations, from the trembling Quakers of sixteenth-century England to the raucous, revivalist Methodists and Baptists of late eighteenth- and early nineteenth-century America, to the electrified Pentecostals of present-day Brazil, have all promoted emotional religious services aimed at setting the stage for conversion. That a great many sociologists have studied the theology and institutions of such groups rather than the emotional and embodied aspects of their worship practice simply reflects the rationalist bias of our discipline. This book joins a swelling call among sociologists of religion to reclaim the Durkheimian attention to religion as an embodied affair, engaging the emotions through rituals of interaction (McElmurry 2009; Neitz 2004; Smith 2008; Warner 2007; Winchester 2008). Recent developments in the sociology of emotions, including Scheff's (1988, 1991, 2004) emphasis on the central role played by shame in the maintenance and deterioration of social bonds, and of Randall Collins (2004) in the chaining of rituals, provide enormous opportunities for sociologists and other scholars of religion to  better understand how religion "works" at the level of the individual and how such individual experiences are tied into ritual chains extending beyond the individual in both space and time. Doing so may require us to conceptualize a denomination or religious tradition as what Hochschild (1983) calls an "emotion institution" whose emotion logic plays a no less formative role in the lives of its members than does its theology or its structure. However, the potential payoffs are significant since doing so would allow us to forge conceptual links between religious institutions and the lived experience of the people who populate them. The study of how and to what effect religion "takes root" (or withers) in the individual and his or her daily practices can be deeply illuminated by just this attention to emotion, the body, and the rituals meant to engage them.

SO WHAT?

A larger question still looms over my study—one that haunted me during three years of research, interviews, and analysis of gang deserters and converts. Do evangelical gang conversions make any difference? That is, what, if any, is the overall impact on the gang phenomenon of exit-by-conversion? Although the question had been on my mind for some time, I felt especially confronted by it when I met Chuz [CHOOS], a twenty-eight-year-old paraplegic living in a ramshackle tin room perched precariously on a steep hill in the community of La Lopez.[1] Chuz was one of two disabled former Vatos Locos I interviewed who had lost the use of their legs in gang shootings. Both had also converted to evangelical Christianity. But whereas Ramón dressed well, had a job in his family's cell phone repair business, and spoke at length and with glowing optimism about his church and his future, Chuz answered my questions with a single word or a short phrase and without any enthusiasm. He referred repeatedly to "this thing that happened to me" as if the shooting had all but ended his life. Chuz's dismal tone was mirrored by the dilapidated conditions of his surroundings. In a nearby lean-to, Chuz's partner and two daughters sold tortillas which they made by hand, browning them the old-fashioned way on a wood-fired skillet called a *comal*. The "door" to his abode consisted of a dirty piece of fabric hung lengthwise in front of his bare foam mattress. When Chuz mentioned that he went to church, I asked him to tell me more about that experience. He said that on Saturdays and Sundays *hermanos* pick him up and take him to the "The Potter's House," a mega-church located a few kilometers down the highway. There, he had "accepted Christ" some time ago, and he enjoyed going to the services because he liked "to hear the word." Later, I wondered about the meaning and impact of Chuz's conversion and attendance at worship. If, as evangelicals insist, the gospel can save and transform anyone, why was Chuz so clearly struggling to access that optimism and move forward with his life even after a professed conversion and an ongoing participation in the amped-up worship and social networks of the *hermanos*? And why did his situation and his outlook so clearly contrast with those of optimistic Ramón?

Chuz's story is an important reminder that while religious beliefs, networks, and experiences can and do make a difference in certain situations, "switching the tracks" of a life trajectory, sometimes those "tracks" veer only a little from the current course. Human experience and social context extend far beyond religion. A great deal of the difference between the trajectories of Chuz and Ramón can be attributed to differences in networks of family support. Chuz had little support from extended family but instead was responsible for at least three dependents. Meanwhile, Ramon, slightly younger and still single, had no dependents and was able to rely on his family of origin for housing, an income, and a steady job. Indeed, his role behind the counter in his family's mobile phone sales and repair business was the perfect place for Ramón to cultivate an identity as a capable contributor despite his disability. Although they lived in the same barrio and had belonged to the same gang cell, the diverging trajectories of the two young men illustrate the inequality that exists even within low-income barrios and that follows youth into the gang as well as out of it.

Religious conversion and evangelical Christianity alone cannot put an end to the problem of violence committed by and toward gang members. Although conversion and communal experience of emotion-laden religious rituals can provide important resources for personal projects of change among worn-out gang members, conversion and evangelical religion appear to have done little to stem the flow of children and adolescents into the gang. In fact, eight of the youth I interviewed reported having grown up in evangelical homes governed by at least one devout, church-going parent or grandparent. Ricardo remembered hating the evangelical faith of his father who would taunt his gang-leader son with the Bible itself. "When my father would see me passing by on the street" Ricardo recalled, "he would recite the biblical text, 'The whip for the horse; the rod for the stubborn!'"[2] Ricardo's statement is a reminder that growing up in an evangelical household does not necessarily protect children and adolescents from the experience of shame that pre-disposes so many toward joining the gang. Strict evangelical religion can easily be turned into a source of further disintegrative, stigmatizing shame and strengthen a youth's resolve to participate in the gang.

In fact, the many "faces" of evangelical Christianity in Central America help explain the as yet unfulfilled promise of bringing prosperity and democracy through cultural shift. Two decades have now passed since David Martin argued, and not without some persuasive evidence, that Pentecostal sectarianism could provide a cultural cocoon out of which cooperative, democratic social skills could emerge. Like their spiritual ancestors the British non-conformists, the Pentecostals, Martin argued, are a "periphery religion" drawing converts from the poor and empowering them to "make their autonomy visible" via conversion (Martin 1990). Christian Smith advanced a similarly Weberian culturalist argument in the 1990s, holding that evangelicalism, not liberation theology holds the most promise for a democratized future in Latin America (Smith 1995). And yet if evangelical religion is helping to usher in democratic reform, it has taken a very long route to doing so. In spite of continuing growth among evangelicals, including a recent poll showing that 36 percent of Honduran adults now profess evangelical Christianity (CID-Gallup 2007), true democratic reform seems as elusive as ever. Indeed, the June 2009 coup staged by the Honduran military with full support of its congress, stands as evidence that the structures of democracy continue to be weak and subject to the authority of the gun barrel.[3] Meanwhile, heavily evangelical Guatemala continues to be plagued by corruption scandals reaching all the way into the president's cabinet. El Salvador, a country where nearly 30 percent of the population now professes evangelical faith, also holds the ignominious title of the most violent country in the hemisphere (Portillo 2008). In light of such social and political realities, one cannot help but ask when thousands of religious conversions to evangelicalism may add up to lowered levels of violence and a political culture of transparency.

Anthropologist Adrienne Pine is among the skeptics. In her book *Working Hard, Drinking Hard: On Violence and Survival in Honduras* (Pine 2008), Pine contends that evangelical religion advances an "achievement ideology" all-too-popular among working-class and poor

Hondurans. This ideology justifies enormous economic inequality by convincing wealthy and poor alike that economic success is the result of sober, hard work and therefore the same achievement ideology claims that the poor have themselves and their "weak nature" to blame for their impoverished circumstances. Alcohol and vice (including violence) play a role in this ideology insofar as alcoholics and violent "delinquents" are thought to represent weak-willed men in need of a cure and a program. Pine argues that evangelical Hondurans mistakenly believe that the solution to such problems as poverty, widespread addiction among men, and street violence lies not in structural reform or in a movement demanding social and economic justice but, rather, in individual projects of self-reform and self-discipline rooted in spirit-filled conversion. Borrowing Bourdieu's concept of "symbolic violence," Pine claims that evangelical religion provides Honduran elites and the government with a convenient means of subjugating an impoverished majority while protecting neoliberal economic policies that benefit only a few and undermine social spending. Although Pine's research is not based on extensive empirical research on religion, her argument is worth considering.[4] After all, it is certainly possible that the social benefits brought about by the religious conversion of a handful of gang members could come at the cost of exacerbating a larger social ill. If it is true that Central American evangelicals' individualistic theology of self-reform, which includes guarding and controlling one's body, has the effect of shutting down possibilities for reform, we should at the very least question the practice of sending international aid to gang ministry projects that include evangelical organizations.

But there are reasons to be skeptical of the practice of drawing a clear and direct line from evangelical theology to conservative ideologies and practice. For starters, researchers have found little if any evidence of conservative voting tendencies or even abstention rates among Central American evangelicals, who vote with the same frequency, for roughly the same candidates, as their non-evangelical counterparts (Steigenga 2001). As the research of Timothy Steigenga (Steigenga 2001, 2005) and Paul Freston (2001) has shown, evangelicals in Latin America tend to vote and get involved in political movements in ways that reflect local dynamics rather than a single, self-evident ideology. Nor is evangelical theology—or religious enthusiasm for that matter—historically pre-disposed toward conservative politics or against social movements. Social movement scholar Michael Young has argued at length that at least in the case of the United States, the earliest social movements were thoroughly evangelical and deeply confessional in nature. In the abolitionist and Temperance movements of the mid-nineteenth century, evangelicals found a way to fuse a notion of individual and social "sin" with their rituals of public confession and created the practice of "confessional protests" wherein the personal became political and gave birth to a movement (Young 2002). Furthermore, we need look no further than the contemporary African-American church in the United States to find evidence of an evangelical tradition that combines an emphasis on self-reform and self-discipline with progressive politics and political organizing (Harris 2001).[5]

In short, I believe that the self-reform perspective undergirding evangelical efforts at "gang rescue" has an as-yet-unrealized potential for congealing into critical consciousness and a movement for economic and social justice. Although several evangelical gang ministry coordinators were critical of their government's criminalization of gang youth and the heavy-handed tactics that came with it, their work remained at the level of social aid aimed at rescuing gang members one at a time. As we have seen, the gang phenomenon is no different than the larger political problems facing Central America. In order to arrest the gang violence in Central America, more than conversion, indeed, more than the exit of all current gang members, is needed. For as long as chronic shame is abundant in the barrios of northern Central America, the symbols, drugs, sex, and weapons of the gang will continue to hold irresistible allure for thousands of youth. Additionally, chronic shame will continue to persist and even increase as long as its sources go unchallenged. The steep pyramids that separate and stratify Central Americans on the basis of class and race remain intact, held together by tacit agreements between a handful of elites and a military with little claim to legitimacy. Nor will the temptation to engage in gang violence diminish as long as the small arms flow continues, buoyed up by an ever-more-intensive battle between drug cartels competing for territory and personnel. And only when the United States learns to deal with its insatiable demand for illegal drugs in ways other than by declaring a war on those attempting to meet that demand, will the temptation to bypass shame by making a fast buck for an afternoon's work begin to fade. Already, the extension of the U.S.-led war on drugs into Mexico has pushed the violence of the drug trade deep into Central America despite additional weapons and logistics aid to the whole region (Associated Press 2009; McKinley 2009). Providing more sophisticated weapons and helicopters to national governments will do little to stem the tide of violence.

Simply stated, the gangs of Central America are not likely to disappear any time soon. Street gangs have been present in the barrio for at least four decades and they will likely find many new joiners to replace those who exit by the church door or by the morgue. Nor are the transnational gangs likely to renounce violence since it represents such a powerful source of solidarity and income. Indeed, if there is any wisdom in the view of Hannah Arendt that violence is "the hope of those who have no power," then we should expect to see the transnational gangs continue to "advertise" violence among the marginalized youth of the Central American barrios. Instead of resorting to social cleansing or neighborhood "roundups" and incarcerations, the larger task facing local neighborhoods, national governments, and the international community is that of tackling the structures that perpetuate shaming through persistent inequality, unemployment, and failing schools while undermining the accessibility of weapons and drugs. Churches can join in the effort through social and religious programming, but by themselves they will not be able to solve the problem of gang violence with preventive *or* restorative programs. That will require a multipronged effort between civil society, government, and the international community and it must involve significant changes in educational spending, tax collection, judicial structures, law enforcement, and trade agreements. In the meantime, however, the task of providing gang members with safety, a job, and a transformed identity is a worthy goal, well suited to the social shape of barrio evangelicalism. If evangelicalism struggles to deliver on the promise of democratic reform and economic progress, society is hardly the worse for its contribution of an army of good Samaritans ready and willing to believe in the transformation of the "despised." Helping "worn-out" homies become hermanos—and fathers, husbands, and employees—is a Samaritan effort that most Central Americans can surely live with.

APPENDIX A

Methods

The transnational gangs of Central America constitute a deeply stigmatized social group disenfranchised within whole societies already relegated to the margins of the global economy. Research on social groups that are poorly understood by outsiders begs for a qualitative approach in order to gain a more complete understanding of the marginal social world, with its particular symbols, values, and contextual features. Developing or testing formal hypotheses of narrow claims regarding causes or impact must come later. My qualitative research design relied heavily on interviews with ex-gang members, and I supplemented these with interviews of local experts in the field of youth violence and short ethnographic forays. My data gathering took place during four months spent in the field over four separate trips, the first of which took place in January 2007 and the last in March/April 2008. The decision not to spend a longer period of time in the field was driven mostly by practical considerations involving stateside commitments to work and family. My familiarity with the region and my existing social networks, based on over six years of having lived and worked in Guatemala City's working-class barrios and from having traveled around northern Central America, gave me a head start, and at least partially compensated for the fact that I did not compile extensive ethnographic field notes during years of fieldwork. Although I would never have been able to conduct participant-observation on life in the gang since I am not and never could be a member of a transnational gang or for that matter an ex-gang member, I do not deny that more time in the field could have strengthened my claims and nuanced further my conclusions. I also would have preferred to enhance my data with interviews of current gang members in order to compare their reports of why they have not yet chosen (or managed) to leave the gang with the reasons reported by the leavers. Despite this desire, gaining privileged access to this particular social group involved certain risks that I ultimately decided not to accept. Although my initial decision not to interview active gang members owed more to the urging of my wife and Guatemalan in-laws, after hearing multiple ex-gang members recall the popular gang warning, "Trust no one!" (in heavily accented English), I came to accept as reasonable my trade-off of less-than-perfect methodology in exchange for lowered anxiety for me and my family. In any case, researchers of gangs in the United States have observed that interviews with current gang members are not always highly reliable. As Irving Spergel has noted, "Gang members have a tendency to feed outsiders and themselves a set of standardized answers" (1992:124). Central American gang intervention directors agreed with this assessment, warning me that most *active* gang members would have little if any motivation to speak with transparency in an interview, given their commitment to protect and enhance the image of the barrio. Whatever my experience might have been had I chosen to seek out active gang members, the ex-gang members I interviewed were more than willing to critique the gang even while defending it against facile stereotypes circulated by the media and the government.

INTERVIEWS WITH GANG EXPERTS

The first leg of my research involved hearing from those who study gangs or work with gang members. I entered the field in January 2007 after having read as many studies on Central American transnational gangs as I could find. I began interviewing gang experts including professionals, academics, and practitioners, all of whom helped me to deepen my knowledge of the process of gang exit by sharing with me their expertise based on years of experience or research. I continued to carry out these interviews with knowledgeable outsiders throughout my research such that by May 2008, I had conducted thirty-two interviews in person with individuals employed at nearly two dozen agencies including think tanks, churches, parishes, nongovernmental organizations, and government-related institutions. Since my research questions leaned heavily toward religion and the responses of religious institutions, a number of those interviewed were clergy, including five evangelical pastors (not including three ex-gang members-turned-ministers), three priests, and one Presbyterian minister. Among the secular professionals who helped me to deepen my understanding of gangs and gang exit, and who provided me with access to ex-gang members willing to be interviewed, were four psychologists, three sociologists, two social workers, and a clinical psychiatrist. I also interviewed several lawyers, an undercover police officer, and the presiding judge for Guatemala's only juvenile court. Most interviews were recorded for later analysis, but in six cases, either because the individual preferred not to be taped or because taping seemed an intrusion to the particular context, I took careful notes and later reconstructed the interview based on my memory of the conversation. About half of the interviews with experts and interventionists were later transcribed and coded for analysis.

One outsider who shared with me his opinions regarding the nature of "the gang problem" was Honduras's former president, Ricardo Maduro. At a public debate of former and aspiring Central American heads of state hosted by my university, President Maduro defended himself against reports stating that his "iron-fist" policies had led to a number of alarming human rights violations by giving tacit permission for off-duty police or vigilantes to engage in "social cleansing" (Medina and Mateu-Gelabert 2009; Ribando 2008). Since my question during the forum obliged him to elaborate further his defense, the former president approached me afterward, eager to correct what he felt sure was a misunderstanding regarding his government's response to the gangs. By an awkward coincidence, the gringo doctoral candidate was later seated next to the former president (and long-time business magnate) at a follow-up dinner, giving Mr. Maduro even more time to describe his approach as that of a "multipronged strategy" aimed at increasing efficiency and collaboration between government agencies. Not surprisingly given the setting, he was careful not to refer to the policy by the names his campaign had used to promote it and to win his election. So much for *mano dura* (iron fist) and *cero tolerancia* (zero tolerance). Nevertheless to his credit, the former president seemed to relish open, honest debate. His responses pushed me to think more critically about the challenges facing an incoming politician who inherits corrupt, inefficient police and judicial structures charged with protecting the citizenry in a violent society.

INTERVIEWS WITH FORMER GANG MEMBERS

The most prominent element of my research design involved interviewing former gang members themselves. In-depth, semistructured interviews with ex-gang members formed the cornerstone of my research. I chose this approach for several reasons. First, many of the youth interviewed shared with me their considerable knowledge of the various norms, and forms of organization maintained by gang cells, and many of these features tended to vary considerably from one context to the next. As a neophyte to the topic of gangs, and having been exposed to many sensationalist accounts of gang life in the newspapers and on television, I wanted to hear as many "insider" accounts as possible. Interviewing ex-gang members helped me to develop a sense of both the commonalities shared across gangs and *clicas* as well as the differences between them. More important, extended interviews provided firsthand retrospective accounts of joining, participating in, and eventually leaving the gang from the perspective of the ex-members themselves. In this sense, the interviews provided a window into the process by which youth shape and are shaped by gang roles and role expectations. Other examples of well-recognized studies that rely heavily on interviews to illuminate the process of role entry and role exit are Arlie Hochschild's classic study of the training of airline attendants (Hochschild 1983) and Helen Rose Ebaugh's study of religious clerics and others who left a vocation with strong role expectations (Ebaugh 1988).

I am aware, of course, that retrospective accounts delivered in an interview setting do not represent a perfect re-rendering of the past. Instead, interview subjects highlight certain events in their past while downplaying or suppressing others, often in an attempt to create a coherent personal narrative or biography. The act of telling one's story is itself an exercise in identity construction. Through the telling and retelling of stories we make sense of our lives and locate ourselves with respect to larger narratives that elevate certain symbols and ethics as virtuous and cast others as dangerous or simply a waste of time. Employing in-depth interviews exposed me to the process by which ex-gang members draw meaning from personal stories of triumph, defeat, and ongoing struggle. These personal stories illuminate the experience of gang life and of leaving the gang and starting over afterward, but they also draw attention to the ways in which individuals "make sense of" their past, creating a meaningful or "usable" past that situates an anticipated future. Other studies of persons with a difficult past, such as violent offenders, have noted this tendency to create a former life with definite lessons and meaning for the future (Laub and Sampson 2003; Presser 2004), but the practice is by no means unique to former gang members or ex-offenders. For example, quite a number of conversion studies have relied on interviews as a means of analyzing religious conversion (Beckford 1978; Staples and Mauss 1987; Streiker 1971; Stromberg 1993).

In order to provide ex-gang members with ample opportunity to "tell their stories" I incorporated an open-ended interview format that almost always began with the question, "Tell me how you came to be a member of the gang." In addition to allowing the subjects themselves to identify the elements they felt were most important to their experience before, during, and after the gang, the open-ended format, especially in the opening question, helped to reduce the nervous tension that some ex-gang members obviously felt at the beginning of the interview. After all, how could they be sure that the gringo sitting before them did not work for the FBI, which had recently established a special regional office in San Salvador for countering gang activity? If I had begun with a battery of questions regarding the personal characteristics of the participant, I could easily have alienated her or him and diminished the likelihood of establishing a context of trust for open dialogue. Over time, I learned to unobtrusively intersperse questions about age, family background, and specific gang affiliation over the course of the interview as it became clear that trust was established. Of course, in many cases such details emerged during the open-ended monologues.

The ex-gang members varied enormously in their willingness and capacity to articulate their past. A few ex-gang members preferred speaking only in vague generalities about a part of their lives that it seemed they would rather forget. In these cases my challenge was to persuade participants that their recollections held value and meaning and were worth recounting, even if they included mistakes that carried pain and regret. I did not pry but I did learn how to rephrase questions in order to "prime the pump." In addition, I was also reminded each time I traveled from one country to the other that even in the tiny republics of Northern Central America, each of which shares a border with the other two, there are significant linguistic differences from one context to the next. A Guatemalan *patojo* (male youth or teen) is a *bicho* in El Salvador and a *cipote* in Honduras. In many cases, the greater challenge was not eliciting responses or interpreting local slang but guiding subjects in such a way as to ensure that the interview touched on topics of interest to the study while also allowing themes to emerge that were not contemplated at the outset of the project. For example, in my very first interview with an ex-gang member conducted in La Lopez Arellano, Honduras I found that the former Vato Loco wanted to talk about one topic and one topic only—vegetable gardens! Since I had been presented as a *gringo menonita* and the only prior contact the ex-gang member had had with my kind was via social projects promoted through the very active Mennonite Central Committee, the young man was bound and determined to convince me to supply funding for an urban gardening project he was sure could transform his neighborhood. I politely reminded him that my role was that of a researcher, not an agriculturalist or community development worker, but in places like Honduras, where white North Americans have traditionally taken the form of tourists, missionaries, or development workers, a gringo in a popular neighborhood means one thing—access to resources.

In fact, dealing with requests for money was one of several factors involved in negotiating my own subjectivity as a gringo interviewer. I had been advised by a Honduran gatekeeper not to offer monetary compensation for interviews since doing so could a create conflict or a sudden increase in the population of "ex-gang members with a story to tell." Still, I felt a strong desire to compensate in some way for the enormous gift of time and transparency given me by the participants and so in place of cash I offered an *obsequio* (small gift) in the form of a college baseball cap. Doing so assuaged my guilty conscience only a little. After all, I was asking individuals to set aside time to talk about potentially dangerous topics associated with painful moments in their lives. On the other hand, several ex-gang members saw me as an advocate who was "getting their stories out" in order to help other youth who are thinking of joining or contemplating leaving the gang. One youth asked for a copy of his *testimonio* because he hoped to some day write a book about his experience in the gang and his life afterward. It was not an evangelical "testimony"—he is not particularly religious. Rather, the young man was convinced that barrio youth need to hear stories of life in the gang in order to be able to judge for themselves what belonging to the gang is "really like." This youth began his interview, "Good afternoon, my name is . . . and I am twenty-six years old and thanks to God[1] I have left the gangs." In these cases, my role was that of someone who could "get their story out" in order to help other youth avoid the same fate.

Given that religion represented a key topic of this study, how to present my own relationship to religion was an important concern. Where you stand on religious questions is especially critical in Central America, where many evangelicals see themselves at odds with the Catholic Church, if not in direct competition with it. In effect, revealing your religious (or nonreligious) identity is a matter of declaring "which side you are on" in the religious competition for cultural hegemony. Whenever possible, I tried not to divulge my own religious identity as a Mennonite since most Central America Mennonites consider themselves evangelicals, even if some of their religious neighbors are not sure how to classify them. Since in most interviews it was not clear from the outset whether the ex-gang member held any religious convictions, I did not want to enhance reactivity by giving the impression that I was "fishing" for a particular kind of exit story, that is, one with a "religious" moral. Nevertheless, establishing rapport with gatekeepers at evangelical churches or gang exit programs made it necessary at times to flash my religious "credentials" as an hermano. This was especially important given the traditional association in Central America of higher education—especially sociology—with Marxism and religious skepticism. One Honduran social worker expressed shock after her questions forced me to disclose my identity as a religious person *and* a sociologist—she had not known that one can be both at the same time! In any case, evangelicals do not wish to be analyzed as specimens of a particular form of cultural naïveté, and those who work in gang ministry were understandably protective of the ex-gang members in their care. Thus I found it helpful, and even necessary in some cases, to assure that I was a person of faith who could be trusted. I tried to be transparent about the nonreligious motives of my research, and, in at least one case, that transparency cost me an interview. One converted ex-gang member whom I contacted via another convert, decided after consulting with his pastor that he preferred not to undergo an interview. When he telephoned to inform me of his decision, the ex-gang member told me that had the interview been conducted in order to help other gang members "leave the gang and come to Christ" he would have been willing. But he was not willing to give the interview merely for the purpose of extending research on gang exit.

In fact, the question, "What are you planning to do with my story?" was a common question for which I was underprepared at first. Institutional Review Boards in the United States generally assume a certain familiarity with and at least mild support (however unenthusiastic) for academic research and its purposes among the population from whom researchers draw their samples. However, in the urban barrios of Central America, to say that a proposed interview will be conducted "for the purpose of social scientific research" falls pretty flat. Of more interest, especially to those unfamiliar with higher education and its goals, is the question, "Whom will the research benefit directly?" The most honest answer to such a question is that the research will benefit first the gringo researcher and his career through the production of a *tesis* (dissertation), graduation, and perhaps the publication of a book useful for gaining tenure. Fielding this question over and over pressed me to expand my future research goals toward more directly addressing questions of how and why youth join the gangs and what might be done at a meso- and macro-level in order to reduce youth violence and help Central American children of the barrio avoid the traumas faced by so many of those I interviewed. Although this book takes only minor steps in that direction, I hope to be able to move further toward that goal in future research. Finally, having to describe the goals of my project again and again helped me to see the interview itself in a different light. Interview subjects wanted to know "to whom" exactly they were talking when they spoke into the voice recorder.

As mentioned above, interview subjects always engage in some level of conscious shaping of their own accounts based on deeply held commitments to a larger narrative or repertoire of stories. So how could I be sure that the accounts presented to me correspond in some way to the actual experience of the youth who spoke? After all, I *was* interested in hearing firsthand accounts of actual, lived experiences, but there is *no* way of ensuring that interview subjects are not making it up as they go. As in all research methods, the interview format poses both advantages and drawbacks, one of the latter being that the researcher cannot verify beyond all doubts that everything reported to him actually took place. On the other hand, interviewers do possess tools for diminishing the chances that interviewees will engage in outright fabrication or gross exaggeration and strategies for spotting such instances should they occur. One means of motivating forthrightness was to work hard at establishing rapport with ex-gang members beforehand or in the early stages of the interview. My ability to speak Spanish *puro chapín*, "like a Guatemalan" helped me here. The presence of a *canche gringuote* (big, blonde gringo) who spoke with little if any perceptible gringo accent helped me to avoid a number of gringo stereotypes while providing a topic for conversation prior to the interview. Furthermore, having lived in working-class barrios for several years, I was able to engage in a certain level of joke telling and idiomatic expressions that surprised and delighted many of the respondents and put to rest at least some of their reservations stemming from the unfamiliarity of the interview situation.

In a minority of cases I was able to compare the broad outlines and major features of an ex-gang member's autobiography with the story shared with me by the pastor, priest, or gang intervention coordinator who knew them. In these cases I found no major discrepancies. In other cases I was able to corroborate stories of specific events via accounts from members of the same *clica*. However, in most instances I had no means of formally verifying accounts, especially the specific events of gang entrance, activity, or exit, or for that matter, for conversion to evangelical Christianity. Still, most accounts possessed one or more features that lent credibility to the biographies as representing actual lived experiences that had been passed through the lens of personal interpretation. First, I looked for and found evidence of internal consistency in the interviews in terms of the chronology of major events and the years that had passed since they had occurred or other major political events with which I was familiar. Second, evidence of emotional remorse, occasionally enough to slow down the interview while the participant took the time weep or to simply regain control of his emotions, made it plain to me that the individual's report of a particularly painful memory or the participation in a heinous or "shameful" crime was almost certainly not a fabrication. No self-respecting Central American man, converted or not, looks for opportunities to weep, much less in the presence of a little-known foreigner. These moments affected me greatly and left me with the indelible impression that many participants were exposing aspects of their lives that continued to be a source of deep shame. They also provided me with the first "clue" that I needed to pay closer attention to the role of shame and the emotions in the process of both entering and leaving the gang. In addition, participants who wept, or who had to work hard not to do so, helped to convince me that on the whole, interview subjects were not trying to merely strike a pose or project a carefully crafted image of themselves or the gang. Indeed, some of the converted ex-gang members told stories of ongoing struggle that would fall flat as a motivational speech in a church or at testimony time. If they were "manufacturing" accounts of gang exit or conversion, they were borrowing only loosely and from very different templates. My last strategy for ensuring significant reliability involved interviewing as many ex-gang members as I could find from the most diverse contacts I could locate, thus providing for ample opportunities of comparison and contrasts and lowering the chances that I would hear only standardized accounts. This "multisite design" also bolstered the generalizability of my claims (Glaser and Strauss 1967) regarding the nature of life in the Central American gangs and the challenges associated with leaving.

In total, sixty-three ex-gang members provided me with a usable interview (see Appendix B for complete listing). I conducted all interviews onsite and in Spanish, with two exceptions involving ex-gang members who had recently returned from the United States and preferred to speak in English. Nine ex-gang members were Salvadoran (one lived in Guatemala at the time of the interview), twenty-one were Guatemalan, and thirty-three were Honduran. Two were interviewed while serving time in a medium-security prison in Guatemala. Fifty-nine were men and four were women. A few had left the gang more than a decade earlier while a half dozen had left less than a year prior to the interview. Most, however, had been out of the gang for at least two years. The interviews were not, strictly speaking, life histories, although some ex-gang members shared at length about nearly every aspect of their lives from their earliest memories until the present. A few lasted over two hours, but most were shorter with the average ex-gang member interview lasting about thirty-eight minutes. Three participants asked not to be tape-recorded and in such instances I took extensive notes and drew up an account of the interview afterward incorporating both verbatim and paraphrased segments. All audio recordings of ex-gang member interviews were later transcribed, yielding more than 650 pages of transcripts in Spanish.

FIELDWORK

My study is not ethnography in the formal sense since my time in the field was limited and taken up largely with locating participants and conducting interviews. Nevertheless, during four months in the field, I managed to shadow pastors on pastoral visits, attend an evangelistic campaign aimed specifically at ex-gang members and sympathizers, spend time at a tattoo-removal clinic, and accompany Salvadoran gang interventionists in their *proyectos ambulatorios* (walking gang-exit projects). After such occasions, I wrote field notes in the evenings. I also took field notes on my interactions with ex-gang members and promoters during and after interviews of particular significance. In these notes I recorded aspects of the setting, any noteworthy physical features of the participants, and any important elements not available in the text of the interviews. Finally, I wrote memos during and after my time in the field and this practice helped me to better see my thinking as it took shape and to monitor my own emotions for clues to future questions I wanted to address during the more formal stage of analysis.

ANALYSIS AND PRESENTATION

Andrew Abbott has argued that, "Science is a conversation between rigor and imagination. What one proposes, the other evaluates. Every evaluation leads to further proposals and so it goes, on and on" (Abbott 2004:3). In other words, science is a dialogue between creativity and process. Good social science is that which allows time for developing and pursuing creative hunches while following careful procedures for analyzing them and discarding or elaborating on them accordingly. I incorporated a number of tools for enhancing rigor at the analysis stage of my data while allowing for unexpected themes or patterns to emerge, giving rise to new insights, further analysis, "and so on." One tool for enhancing the conversation between rigor and creativity involved coding all transcripts of interviews with ex-gang members using the qualitative data analysis software MAXqda. Each participant was coded on several dimensions such as religion, gang affiliation, and family background. Transcripts were coded paragraph by paragraph and, in some cases, line by line for broad themes such as religion, family, and violence as well as more specific subthemes such as "conversion" and "domestic violence," allowing for easy comparison across many texts and quick testing of assumptions. Memo-ing continued during the coding process and all analysis was conducted in Spanish. Only those excerpts selected for quotation were translated to English. I am responsible for all translations although I was able to rely on my wife's native ear for more difficult or culturally complex words or phrases. I took some minor liberties when quoting from transcripts, for example, by dropping vocalized pauses except when they appear to carry meaning. I also dropped repetitive words or phrases such as *¿Me entiendes?* (Do you know what I mean?).

Most chapters begin with an extended quotation in order to contextualize the material to follow and to minimize what some qualitative researchers have described as "fracturing the data"—that is, chopping up long interviews involving deeply personal and highly contextual stories into micro-bytes useful only for making a point here or there (Charmaz 2000). Since to some extent the incorporation of short quotations cannot be avoided and allows for illustrating the variety of perspectives and tendencies in the data, beginning with a longer narrative selection from a particular individual allowed me to humanize the data by setting it within the context of a single life trajectory. Excepting Juan José, who granted permission to use his name, the names of all ex-gang members have been changed to protect the identity of the interviewees while the names of all clerics and ministry coordinators (except for Pastor Álvaro) are not fictitious.

CODING CONVERTS

One methodological issue that I fretted about even before I reached the field was the matter of coding "converts." What constitutes a "convert" and how would I know if I had found one? Definitions of "conversion," when they are discussed at all, vary considerably in the sociological literature. Among the more well-known definitions is the one offered by Snow and Machalek (1983) positing that a conversion involves a radical change in a person's "universe of discourse". The authors suggest using "rhetorical indicators" such as "the suspension of analogical reasoning" and "biographical reconstruction" to identify converts since it is assumed that the *discourse* of a convert will set him or her apart from nonconverts. There are a number of problems with such a definition, not least of which is the fact that all biography involves "reconstruction" to one degree or another. Thus, determining who is a convert becomes a matter of degree and depends largely on one's familiarity with the "actual" events or trajectory of the subject's prior life. In any case, as other research makes clear, the Snow and Machalek definition equates religious conversion with religious conservatism since many religious conservatives are taught to speak in ways that reflect the "rhetorical indicators" of conversion even if they grew up in the faith (Staples and Mauss 1987). A very different approach to defining conversion is to simply follow the lead of the Supreme Court in its ruling on pornography—that is, to define a convert by concluding that "you know one when you see one." This approach is not so far out as it may sound. In Central America evangelical converts, especially young men, tend to dress, speak, and, yes, even comb their hair differently than their non-evangelical peers in the barrio. And in the theologically conservative context of barrio evangelicalism, an hermano generally carries his Bible with him, in a figurative if not a literal sense. Not only is it customary to carry a Bible to *culto* (worship), evangelical converts are taught to memorize scripture and recite it, and a surprising number of converted ex-gang members did just that. Of course, not all evangelicals are "converts" in any substantive sense. Many actually grew up in the church. But since evangelical piety and the gang lifestyle are so diametrically opposed, among those formerly belonging to the gang a practicing evangelical is, by definition, a convert, or at the very least, a re-convert. Still, in methodological terms, identifying converts through behavioral patterns such as speech, dress, and manner is not necessarily less problematic than using a conceptual definition such as the "radical shift" in a person's "universe of discourse." After all, many of the ex-gang members I interviewed still possessed tattoos, and more than a few, religious or otherwise, were still attempting to "unlearn" the *homie* manner. Nor had all converts adopted the evangelical demeanor as thoroughly as had Ricardo, now a reverend. Furthermore, as I suspected when beginning the project, some ex-gang members had in fact "attempted" an evangelical conversion but failed to pull it off completely or had in any case abandoned the project. Were these youth "converts" in any practical sense?

Given these difficulties I chose to take a route somewhere between the conceptual definition emphasizing "rhetorical indicators" and the substantive one underscoring radical, "visible" change from the homie lifestyle. On the one hand, I asked participants if they had any religious preferences, following up a "yes" with further questions about affiliation, beliefs, and practices. In many cases I simply asked, "Do you consider yourself a Christian?" and followed up an affirmative answer with *¿Por qué?* and a negative answer with *¿Por qué no?*

In any case, recognizing the need to go beyond discourse, albeit within the limitations of a methodology based on interviews, I sought information about current practices including church attendance and pastimes. Since barrio evangelicals strictly prohibit drinking alcohol, any mention of current alcohol use meant that an individual was probably not a "practicing" evangelical convert. Worship attendance is also extremely important to barrio evangelicals and when a participant professed a conversion but did not report current or recent activity in a congregation, I tried to probe for a better sense of the individual's current religious status. In short, I used a combination of three criteria in coding converts: profession of a religious commitment or a conversion experience, activity in a local congregation, and adoption of the evangelical lifestyle. I coded as "practicing" converts all ex-gang members who exhibited at least two of these three criteria and as nonpracticing, those who reported a conversion but did not attend worship *and* were making no attempt at carrying through with evangelical lifestyle prescriptions. Except for one Mormon convert, none of the youth professed a conversion to anything other than evangelical religion. Whenever possible, I checked individual self-reports regarding religiosity against the assessment of an informant such as a gang ministry coordinator or another ex-gang member himself. I recognize that my coding of converts and conversions reflects a certain degree of imprecision, but, I feel that a certain humility of approach is warranted, if nothing else, by the ongoing *lucha* (struggle) among the converts themselves to maintain their own conversions.

APPENDIX B

Selected Characteristics of Interviewed Ex-Gang Members

Name	*Former Gang*	*Country of Origin*	*Gender*	*Religion at Time of Interview*
Lucas	M-18	El Salvador	male	No professed religion
Elmer	M-18	El Salvador	male	Evangelical
Lico	M-18	El Salvador	male	Evangelical
Otoniel	M-18	El Salvador	male	Evangelical
Eric	MS-13	El Salvador	male	Evangelical
Lalo	MS-13	El Salvador	male	Evangelical
Andrés	MS-13	El Salvador	male	Catholic
Enrique	MS-13	El Salvador	male	Catholic
Tomás	M-18	El Salvador	male	Evangelical
Lacho	Break	Guatemala	male	Evangelical
Ester	Las Calacas	Guatemala	female	No professed religion
Abner	Los Charcos	Guatemala	male	Evangelical
Umberto	Los Condes	Guatemala	male	No professed religion
Olivia	M-18	Guatemala	female	No professed religion
Emerson	M-18	Guatemala	male	Evangelical
Gustavo	M-18	Guatemala	male	Evangelical
Isaac	M-18	Guatemala	male	Evangelical
Pablo	M-18	Guatemala	male	Evangelical
Roberto	M-18	Guatemala	male	Evangelical
Antonio	M-18	Guatemala	male	Lapsed Evangelical
Iván	MS-13	Guatemala	male	Evangelical
Saúl	MS-13	Guatemala	male	Evangelical
Miguel	MS-13	Guatemala	male	Lapsed Evangelical
Lester	MS-13	Guatemala	male	Mormon
Uriel	Not Divulged	Guatemala	male	Evangelical
Ismael	other	Guatemala	male	Evangelical

(Continued)

Name	*Former Gang*	*Country of Origin*	*Gender*	*Religion at Time of Interview*
Abel	Ramsta-Sureños	Guatemala	male	No professed religion
Neftalí	White Fence	Guatemala	male	Evangelical
Nestor	White Fence	Guatemala	male	Evangelical
*Juan José	White Fence	Guatemala	male	Evangelical
Oscar	M-18	Honduras	male	No professed religion
Beto	M-18	Honduras	male	Evangelical
Calín	M-18	Honduras	male	Evangelical
Camilo	M-18	Honduras	male	Evangelical
Ernesto	M-18	Honduras	male	Evangelical
Oliver	M-18	Honduras	male	Evangelical
Ronaldo	M-18	Honduras	male	Evangelical
Ignacio	M-18	Honduras	male	Catholic
Rina	MS-13	Honduras	female	Lapsed Evangelical
Danilo	MS-13	Honduras	male	Evangelical
Meme	MS-13	Honduras	male	Evangelical
Osvaldo	MS-13	Honduras	male	Evangelical
Pancho	MS-13	Honduras	male	Evangelical
Ramón	MS-13	Honduras	male	Evangelical
Leonardo	Sur 16	Honduras	male	Evangelical
Leti	Torres 13	Honduras	female	Evangelical
Raúl	Vatos Locos	Honduras	male	No professed religion
Armando	Vatos Locos	Honduras	male	Evangelical
Nelson	Vatos Locos	Honduras	male	Evangelical
Raymundo	Vatos Locos	Honduras	male	Evangelical
Ricardo	Vatos Locos	Honduras	male	Evangelical
Rolando	Vatos Locos	Honduras	male	Evangelical
Vito	Vatos Locos	Honduras	male	Evangelical
Edgar	Vatos Locos	Honduras	male	Lapsed Evangelical
Gaspar	Vatos Locos	Honduras	male	Lapsed Evangelical
Pedro	Vatos Locos	Honduras	male	Lapsed Evangelical
Ricky	Vatos Locos	Honduras	male	Lapsed Evangelical
Sergio	Vatos Locos	Honduras	male	Lapsed Evangelical
Wilmer	Vatos Locos	Honduras	male	Lapsed Evangelical
Emanuel	Wonder 13	Honduras	male	No professed religion

Name	*Former Gang*	*Country of Origin*	*Gender*	*Religion at Time of Interview*
Ovidio	Wonder 13	Honduras	male	No professed religion
Leonel	Wonder 13	Honduras	male	Lapsed Evangelical
Melchor	Wonder 13	Honduras	male	Lapsed Evangelical

*Indicates actual name.

APPENDIX C

A Primer of Gang Vocabulary

Term	Translation/origin	Meaning
jomi	Homie/homeboy	gang member
carnal	perhaps related to *primo carnal* or "first cousin"	blood brother or close friend in the gang; sometimes used interchangeably with *jomi*
clica	clique	local cell of a transnational gang composed of 15–75 members
maje		dude (can be masculine or feminine)
ranfla		the local cell or *clica*; sometimes refers to gang activity
ranflero		A local or regional leader of one or several gang cells; also called *el mashín* (machine)
letras	letters	referring to the *Mara Salvatrucha*, represented by the letters "MS"
números	numbers	referring to the Eighteenth Street gang, represented by the digits "1–8"
vivo	alive	"on the ball"; smart, driven, ready for anything
Crazy	crazy	name or title given to the most daring local gang member; usually this title is reserved for ranfleros and sometimes distinguished from others as in "Crazy Little" or "Crazy II"
clecha	from the Calo word for school or grade	Rules, code, or vision; sometimes associated with tattoos, as a kind of military badge of honor that must be earned

(Continued)

Term	*Translation/origin*	*Meaning*
la nueva clecha	the new code	The new environment brought about with the breaking of the "Pacto Sur" or Southern peace treaty that had formerly held for all MS-13 and M-18 interaction in nondisputed public territory
placas	license plates	tattoos; sometimes used as a verb, as in "*Me plaqueé.*"
jaina	perwhaps related to gyne-	female gang member or sympathizer; sometimes used to refer to young women in general
paisa	from "paisano" or countryman	Youth who does not belong to a gang
peseta (Honduras)	(Spanish currency)	gang deserter or traitor; most serious when tattoos are crossed out
cuadros	squares	permission to leave the gang and settle down without repercussions
cohete	rocket/firecracker	pistol or gun
sortear	to gamble	to shake down or rob
chavalear	from *chava* or girl	to back down or back out "like a girl"
livar	live	to drink, have a good time and "live it up"
rifar	to gamble	to risk, gamble or hazard one's safety for the gang
tirar barrio	to "throw" the neighborhood (symbol)	to make the sign of the gang using special hand signals; a sign of camaraderie when done among fellow members but a first-class offense when done "outside" the gang's own territory or in disputed territory
chequeo	checking	time of checking out during which sympathizers are observed for their worthiness of membership

Term	*Translation/origin*	*Meaning*
luz verde	green light	a "go-ahead" sometimes issued as a release from the gang; often issued as a death warrant, granting permission for a kill
luz rojo	red light	a "stop" sometimes meant to stop gang members from killing, but most often issued as a death warrant to "stop" a deserter or traitor

Notes

Introduction

1. *Aquí solo hay una manera de salirse, y es con tu tacuche de madera.*

2. I use JJ's name here with his full permission and endorsement. In all other cases I have changed the names of interviewed former gang members in order to protect their identities.

3. *¿Para qué enamorarme de la vida si estoy casado con la muerte?*

4. Central American gang members refer to one another with the English term "homie," which they write in Spanish as *jomi*.

5. While gangs also exist in Nicaragua and Costa Rica, they are mostly local, are not well organized, and do not engage in lethal violence on anything close to the scale of their counterparts in the transnational gangs of the north.

6. See the Appendix for a more complete description of my methods and the logic behind them.

Chapter 1

1. As of 2010, only Honduras did not yet have an urban majority, with 49 percent of its population living in cities.

2. Many Central American gang studies erroneously report members of this gang as belonging to the "Waifers."

3. John Hagedorn mentions the use of the term "franchise" by an expert on South African gangs, and Aguilar, Carranza, and IUDOP also mention the metaphor in their 2008 report. But I am not aware of any extensive application of the term.

4. Although police estimates are often inflated at first, local and national police authorities often have political reasons for citing lower numbers after several years in leadership.

5. A popular phrase among many Guatemalan *ladinos* (people of mixed European and Mayan descent) used to describe an unexpected angry outburst is, *¡Me sacó el indio!* ("It brought out the Indian in me!")

6. According to a study by the Facultad de Ciencias Sociales in Costa Rica, in 2006, there were 536, 236 registered handguns in the Northern Triangle and an estimated 1.5 million unregistered firearms.

7. Female gang members are usually given a choice between undergoing a beating or having sex with all male members of the clica.

8. It is possible that the more recent rise in the murder rate was due to the withdrawal of Maduro's reforms following the exit of his party from power in 2006, but I have yet to encounter a strong and careful argument in favor or against this conclusion.

Chapter 2

1. Anglican missionaries had begun religious work much earlier on the north coast and Bay Islands of Honduras, but these English-speaking missionary efforts died out by the mid-twentieth century.

2. It is probably the case that many of the Protestants who described themselves as "charismatic" in the Pew study belonged to Neo-Pentecostal congregations which are generally "nondenominational" and do not include the term "Pentecostal" in their title.

3. Sociologist Steve Offutt reports that in El Salvador, the pastor of the Iglesia Bautista, Amigos de Israel (a conservative, pro-Israel mega-church with friendly ties to conservative Baptists in the United States) prayed a blessing at the inauguration of conservative President Tony Saca. But when the leftist FMLN candidate Mauricio Funes won the presidential election in 2009, the pastor of the Elim denomination prayed a blessing at his inauguration. Differences in social class among the membership of these two churches probably explain much about the political proclivities of the leadership in each.

4. Pentecostals do not accept the strict dispensationalism of conservative evangelicals since it relegates the practice of the gifts of the spirit to an earlier dispensation, thus precluding its practice in the church today. At the same time, the theology of the rapture is very common among Pentecostals and this fact may help to explain some of the reticence among Pentecostal leaders to invest time and resources in social causes aimed at promoting this worldly peace or social justice.

5. Long-time evangelical-Presbyterian-cum-Mennonite pastor Rafael Escobar first told me about "the Five P's," although others including my wife confirmed the widespread knowledge of the alliteration among evangelicals.

6. While there is a vague resemblance between evangelical or Pentecostal denominations and commercial franchises, the Neo-Pentecostals have unashamedly adopted branding strategies that mirror the franchise system of the corporate world. Local congregations market CDs, DVDs, and literature produced by the mother church (and its celebrity pastor) in exchange for the rights to adopt the name and logo of the mother church.

Chapter 3

1. This is a minced oath for expressing shock or emotion. It is derived from the far more vulgar term *puta* or "bitch."

2. Gang members refer to their closest friends in the gang as *carnales*. Although the term is probably at least related to *primo carnal* or "first cousin," my rendering of it as "blood brother" is a loose translation intended to convey the sense of "companion *in the flesh*."

3. Here Pancho uses the English word "brother" in a Spanish accent and with the Spanish plural (-es) ending.

4. Of course, this is a danger that haunts survey data gatherers and polling firms as well although it is less common to hear about these shortcomings from quantitative social scientists who analyze such data.

5. Some of the best, most widely cited sociological studies of the twentieth century, most notably the many classic works by Erving Goffman (1959, 1961, 1963), simply employed the astute comparison of everyday behavior with concepts from another context such as theater or gambling. Such comparisons made possible abundant insights into human behavior hitherto ignored or misunderstood.

6. Some criminological theories use the language of Goffman and "face-work" to describe the same phenomenon. These theorists emphasize violent interaction as a struggle to maintain one's own "face" by humiliating or physically eliminating one's enemy. See, for example, Papachristos. 2009.

7. In Central America the word *desquitar* is sometimes used interchangeably with *vengarse* which means "to get revenge" even though the literal meaning of the verb refers to "sloughing off" a weight or "getting out from under" a burden. Thus, it would be only a mild stretch to translate the phrase JJ uses here as, "I wanted to discharge all of that humiliation." Interestingly, a common usage for this word *desquitarse* is when small children hurt themselves by bumping a table, desk, or other blunt inanimate object to which a parent typically responds by encouraging the child to strike the offending object with the phrase, *¡Desquitáte hijo!*

8. I suspect that the actual percentage of interviewees who participated in homicide was actually larger than this. In any case, even if no others did so, the proportion here is equivalent to the findings of a 2001 survey of Salvadoran gang members conducted by Santacruz and Concha-Eastman.

9. I am unclear regarding the origin of this word. Although the term appears to have biological roots—resembling a mix of the Spanish and English pronunciations of "gyne"—the Spanish-speaking youth I interviewed were unaware of the relationship. If there is a physiological etymology, it is an Anglicism that was "lost in translation" so to speak.

10. Although Nicaragua also has a high rate of emigration, a large portion of Nicaraguan emigrants live in Costa Rica and are thus able to return to visit family members whereas millions of Central American emigrants to the United States face enormous legal and financial barriers for doing so.

11. Although men still outnumber women among Central American emigrants, this is only due to an enormous increase in male emigrants that has kept ahead of the increasing migration among women.

12. See also Philippe Bourgois. 1996.

13. The term *simpatizante* is used in many different ways by gang members and experts alike. Here I use the term in the same way that many, though not all, of the ex-gang members interviewed used it—to denote youth and children who shared both an affinity and a low-level commitment to the gang but were never officially "jumped-in" and were therefore free to pursue other pathways when their interest in the gang waned.

Chapter 4

1. Although Antonio and his partner were not legally married, they had been cohabiting for three years at the time and he referred to her as his wife.

2. Antonio used a minced oath here—a softened, far more palatable version of the term *puta* (bitch). Elsewhere, he was less guarded with his language.

3. The car wash, I was told, was also employing only one person six months after the television series. Since then, the USAID-funded project has wisely turned toward placing ex-gang members as employees in already-functioning businesses.

4. One former leader contended that the letters S.U.R. stand for *Razas Unidas Sureñas*, or "United Southern Races," forming a backward acronym of the word *sur*. Obviously, the notion that "we're all Latinos after all" makes more sense in the U.S. context where other reference groups such as blacks and non-Hispanic whites compete or interact with Latinos.

5. A major exception to this rule was the group of ex-gang members who had simultaneously exited two neighboring cliques in a satellite community of San Pedro Sula, Honduras. Between those two cliques, while about a dozen youth had been killed and several others lived in the United States, the majority of former members, about twenty-five in all, still lived in the neighborhood.

6. A gang-related death does not imply that a gang member has been killed. It simply means that authorities suspect gang involvement in the killing.

7. I have no way of knowing for sure the motive behind Antonio's death. However, given the totality of Antonio's interview and a follow-up interview with his widow, who witnessed the crime, a good deal of evidence exists to suggest that the killing was meant to complete "unfinished business" related to earlier attempts on his life.

8. Interestingly, I have never heard anyone use the term *"marero calmado"* to refer to the same phenomenon. The fact that *"marero,"* the newer term for gang member, is never paired with "settling down" seems to indicate that "settling down" is associated with the older street-corner gangs (*pandillas*) but is less common among the transnational gangs (*maras*).

9. I do not mean to suggest that female gang members are treated with special gloves. In fact, Olivia herself recalled her horror when witnessing the brutal "execution" of a pregnant gang mate by gang leaders, ostensibly for the crime of "treason." Clearly, at least *some* of the exponential growth in femicide in Guatemala can be attributed to the murder of female gang members and sympathizers.

10. Sometimes, especially in El Salvador, work or a job is known popularly as *chamba*. Working hard is called *chambeando*.

11. Although the racial pyramid has more variety in Mesoamerica than in the typically two-tiered North American heritage, brown skin and indigenous-mestizo facial features put most barrio youth at an enormous disadvantage when seeking employment whether or not they have ties to the gang.

12. Tomás resides in a medium-security prison that allows inmates a remarkable amount of independence—like visiting day when family, including wives and partners, is allowed private visitation throughout the large prison farm, including within cells.

Chapter 5

1. This is a direct translation to English of Ricardo's recollection of this oft-repeated verse, not a reproduction of the text, 2 Cor. 5:17, in an actual Bible translation.

2. I am not aware of the exact origin of this nickname, although it seems likely that it may have something to do with some traditional religious images I have seen of a white-haired celestial statesman with a voluminous, curly beard. One other ex-gang member, a Guatemalan, also used the term for God and reported that the term is used commonly by the gang.

3. I have chosen to translate "no se juega" as "don't mess with" rather than the more literal "don't play with." The phrase could also be rendered as "don't *mess around* with God."

4. In fact, the director of *Challenge 100*, himself an evangelical, confided to me that a pastoral recommendation was the key element in deciding whom to accept for the nearly fifty youth involved in the work program. Such "faith-based" practice in international aid would, no doubt, raise eyebrows were it to become publicized in the United States.

5. It is not uncommon for neighbors to feel strong resentment, even hatred toward the gang members in their community and many are themselves victims both directly and indirectly. I spoke with several residents of Ricardo's neighborhoods who described the years of intense gang activity as a terrible blight to the community because it caused both financial hardship and physical insecurity to *all* residents.

Chapter 6

1. The Honduran Mennonite Church, one of the largest "historic" Protestant denominations in the country, is made up of Honduran nationals belonging to congregations founded by North American missionaries arriving in the 1950s. It does not include conservative "ethnic" Mennonites such as those living in "colonies" in Belize or Mexico.

2. I use the King James Version here and elsewhere because it approximates the archaic and gender-exclusive language of the Spanish *Reina Valera* version from which Pastor José read.

3. Although the central congregation is a mega-church, the Elim church and its network of satellite churches have strong roots in the working class and resemble

traditional Pentecostal churches more than they do the neo-Pentecostal congregations of the wealthier neighborhoods.

4. The Biblical character of Jephthah—an outlaw-turned-judge of Israel who later sacrificed his daughter to fulfill a vow—is a curious figure to choose as a namesake for a church ministry. Abner reported with pride that the ministry was named thus because "Jephthah was a gang member."

5. Not surprisingly given its location in Chamelecón, the café never had enough paying customers to be viable.

6. Although the Honduran military did exercise considerable control over the population, no open guerrilla resistance took shape in that country and forced extrajudicial killings were in the hundreds compared to the thousands in El Salvador and in the tens of thousands in neighboring Guatemala.

Conclusion

1. I do not include Chuz among the sixty-three ex-gang members listed in Appendix C because the brevity of his responses to my questions led me ultimately to disqualify the interview.

2. Indeed, it is difficult to imagine a more blatantly counterproductive attempt to shame a child into submission than to appropriate Proverbs 26:3: "A whip for the horse, a halter for the donkey, and a rod for the backs of fools!" (New International Version).

3. Ousted President Manuel Zelaya was anything but a paragon of democratic leadership, but the manner of his arrest and deportation make clear the profound lack of faith among elites and the ostensibly supportive majority in due process or legal impeachment.

4. The author did conduct considerable research on everyday life in Honduras where, not surprisingly, she bumped up against the topic of religion quite often. But her claims about evangelical religion are built on very little direct observation of religious activity. Essentially, she builds her claims on the basis of her attendance at a revival campaign, from the transcript of a sermon by a religious televangelist, and in everyday conversations with Hondurans.

5. The Foucauldian view that bodily self-discipline represents acquiescence to the state does not always find evidence in the historical record. From the Nation of Islam to Tibetan Buddhism, religions that emphasize strong self-reform and a tight discipline of the body have generated powerful social movements that critique state control.

Appendix A

1. In Central America the phrase *gracias a Dios* does not necessarily imply religious devotion on the part of the speaker.

References

Abbott, Andrew. 2004. *Methods of Discovery: Heuristics for the Social Sciences.* New York: W.W. Norton.

Aguilar, Jeanette. 2007a. *Diagnostico de El Salvador.* San Salvador: Instituto Universitario de Opinión Pública y ITAM.

Aguilar, Jeannette, Marlon Carranza and IUDOP. 2008. *Las Maras y Pandillas como Actores Ilegales de la Región.* San Salvador: IUDOP.

Aguilar, Jeanette and Lissette Miranda. 2006. "Entre la Articulacion y la Competencia: Las Respuestas de la Sociedad Civil Organizada a las Pandillas en El Salvador." Pp. 37–144 in *Maras y Pandillas en Centroamérica: Las Respuestas de la Sociedad Civil,* vol. 4, edited by J.M. Cruz. San Salvador: UCA Editores.

Aguilar, Rita Maria. 2007b. "Ven Debilidad del Estado." *Siglo XXI,* June 28.

Anderson, Allan. 2004. *An Introduction to Pentecostalism.* Cambridge, UK: Cambridge University Press.

Anderson, Benedict. 1991. *Imagined Communities.* New York: Verso.

Anderson, Elijah. 1999. *Code of the Street: Decency, Violence and the Moral Life of the Inner-City.* New York: W.W. Norton.

Annis, Sheldon. 1987. *God and Production in a Guatemalan Town.* Austin: University of Texas.

Arana, A. 2005. "How the Street Gangs Took Central America." *Foreign Affairs* 84:98–+.

Associated Press. 2009. "U.S. Targets Three Mexican Drug Cartels." Heard on *MSNBC.* Washington, DC.

Baker, Mark. 1995. "Evangelical Churches in a Tegucigalpa Barrio, Do They Fit the Escapist and Legalistic Stereotype?: An Ethnographic Investigation." Working Paper Series, Duke-University of North Carolina Program in Latin American Studies.

Bardales, Ernesto. 2007. *Proyecto de Seguridad Ciudadana para los Municipios de la Region del Valle del Sula.* San Pedro Sula: Oficina de Paz y Convivencia.

Barnes, Nielan. 2007. *Executive Summary: Transnational Youth Gangs in Central America, Mexico, and the United States.* Mexico City: Center for Inter-American Studies and Programs.

Barrios, Luis. 2007. "Gangs and Spirituality of Liberation." Pp. 225–248 in *Gangs in the Global City,* edited by J.M. Hagedorn. Chicago: University of Illinois.

Becker, Howard. 1963. *Outsiders: Studies in the Sociology of Deviance*. New York: Free Press.

Beckford, James A. 1978. "Accounting for Conversion." *British Journal of Sociology* 29:14.

Blumer, Herbert. 1967. *Symbolic Interactionism: Perspective and Method*. Berkeley: University of California Press.

Boueke, Andreas. 2007a. "Exportando Violencia." *El Periodico*, February 11.

———. 2007b. "Hay que Respetar al Barrio. Las Maras y su Mística." *El Periodico*, February 25.

Bourgois, Philippe. 1996. *In Search of Respect: Selling Crack in the Barrio*. London: Cambridge University Press.

Braithwaite, John. 1989. *Crime, Shame and Reintegration*. New York: Cambridge University Press.

Brenneman, Robert. 2010. "Peaceful Pentecostals: Pietistic Interpersonal Pacifism in the Central American Barrio." Paper presented at annual meeting for the Society for the Scientific Study of Religion, Baltimore, MD.

Brotherton, David C. 2007. "Toward the Gang as a Social Movement." Pp. 251–272 in *Gangs in the Global City: Alternatives to Traditional Criminology*, edited by J.M. Hagedorn. Chicago: University of Illinois Press.

Bruneau, Thomas C. 2005. "The Maras and National Security in Central America." *Strategic Insights*, 4(5): (12 pages). Retrieved January 6, 2006 (http://www.nps.edu/Academics/centers/ccc/publications/OnlineJournal/2005/May/bruneauMay05.html).

Brusco, Elizabeth. 1995. *The Reformation of Machismo: Ascetisism and Masculinity Among Colombian Evangelicals*. Austin: University of Texas Press.

Burdick, John. 1993. *Looking for God in Brazil: The Progressive Catholic Church in Urban Brazil's Religious Arena*. Berkeley: University of California Press.

Casa Alianza. 2009. *Análisis de las Ejecuciones Arbitrarias y-o Muertes Violentas de Niños/as y Jóvenes en Honduras*. Tegucigalpa, Honduras: Casa Alianza Honduras.

Castro, Misael and Marlon Carranza. 2005. *Maras y Pandillas en Honduras*. Tegucigalpa, Honduras: Editorial Guaymuras.

Charmaz, Kathy. 2000. "Grounded Theory: Objectivist and Constructivist Methods." Pp. 509–536 in *Handbook of Qualitative Research*, edited by N. Denzin and Y.S. Lincoln. Thousand Oaks, CA: Sage.

Chesnut, R. Andrew. 2003. *Competitive Spirits: Latin America's New Religious Economy*. New York: Oxford University Press.

CID-Gallup. 2007. *Catolicismo Cede Terreno en Honduras*. San Jose, Costa Rica: Consultoría Interdisciplinaria en Desarrollo S.A.

Cojtí, Cuxil D. 1999. "Heterofobia y Racismo Guatemalteco: Perfíl y Estado Actual." Pp. 193–216 in *¿Racismo en Guatemala? Abriendo el Debate sobre un Tema Tabú*, edited by C. Bianchi, C. Hale and G. Palma Murga. Guatemala: AVANCSO.

Collins, Randall. 2004. *Interaction Ritual Chains*. Princeton, NJ: Princeton University Press.

Connell, R.W. 2005. *Masculinities*. Berkeley: University of California Press.

Cooley, Charles Horton. 1902. *Human Nature and the Social Order.* New York: Scribner's.

Coser, Lewis A. 1974. *Greedy Institutions: Patterns of Undivided Commitment.* New York: Free Press.

Cox, Harvey. 2006. "Spirits of Globalisation: Pentecostalism and Experiential Spiritualities in a Global Era." Pp. 11–22 in *Spirits of Globalisation: The Growth of Pentecostalism and Experiential Spiritualities in a Global Age,* edited by S.J. Stalsett. London: SCM Press.

Cruz, Jose Miguel. 1999. "Maras o Pandillas Juveniles: Los Mitos sobre su Formación e Integración." Pp. 101–125 in *Sociología General. Realidad Nacional de Fin de Siglo y Principio de Milenio,* edited by O. Martínez Peñate. San Salvador: Editorial Nuevo Enfoque.

———. 2004. "Pandillas y Capital Social en Centroamérica." Pp. 277–326 in *Maras y Pandillas en Centroamérica: Pandillas y Capital Social,* vol. II, edited by ERIC, IDESO, IDIES, and IUDOP. San Salvador: UCA Editores.

———, ed. 2006. *Maras y Pandillas en Centroamérica: Las Respuestas de la Sociedad Civil Organizada,* vol. IV. San Salvador: UCA Editores.

Cruz, Jose Miguel, Marlon Carranza and Maria Santacruz Giralt. 2004. "El Salvador: Espacios Publicos, Confianza Interpersonal." Pp. 81–114 in *Maras y Pandillas en Centroamerica: Pandillas y Capital Social,* vol. II, edited by J.M. Cruz. San Salvador: UCA Editores.

Cruz, Jose Miguel and Nelson Portillo. 1998. *Solidaridad y Violencia en las Pandillas del Gran San Salvador. Más Allá de la Vida Loca.* San Salvador: UCA Editores.

Decker, Scott H. and Barrik Van Winkle. 1996. "Slinging Dope: The Role of Gangs and Gang Members in Drug Sales. *Justice Quarterly* 11:21.

Dimaggio, Paul. 1998. "The Relevance of Organization Theory to the Study of Religion." Pp. 7–23 in *Sacred Companies: Organizational Aspects of Religion and Religious Aspects of Organizations,* edited by N.J. Demerath, P.D. Hall, T. Schmitt and R.H. Williams. New York: Oxford University Press.

Durkheim, Emile. 1982 [1895]. *The Rules of the Sociological Method.* New York: Macmillan.

———. 1995 [1903]. *The Elementary Forms of Religious Life.* Translated by K.E. Fields. New York: Free Press.

Ebaugh, Helen Rose. 1988. *Becoming an EX: The Process of Role Exit.* Chicago: University of Chicago Press.

Ehrenreich, Barbara and Arlie Hochschild. 2003. "Introduction." Pp. 1–14 in *Global Woman: Nannies, Maids and Sex Workers in the New Economy,* edited by B. Ehrenreich and A. Hochschild. New York: Metropolitan Books.

Emerson, Michael and Christian Smith. 2001. *Divided by Faith: Evangelical Religion and the Problem of Race in America.* New York: Oxford University Press.

Foro Ecuménico por la Paz y la Reconciliación. 2006. *El Fenómeno de las Maras Desde La Perspectiva Socio-Religiosa: Un Desafío a Las Iglesias, la Sociedad y el Estado.* Guatemala City, Guatemala: Author.

Fernández, Jorge and Víctor Ronquillo. 2006. *De las Maras a los Zetas.* México, D.F.: Grijalbo.

FLACSO. 2007. *Armas Pequeñas y Livianas: Una Amenaza a la Seguridad Hemisférica.* San Jose, Costa Rica: Facultad Latinoamericana de Ciencias Sociales.

Fleshman, Michael. 2001. "Small Arms in Africa: Counting the Cost of Gun Violence." *Africa Recovery* 15.

Frankenberg, Ruth. 2004. *Living Spirit, Living Practice: Poetics, Politics, Epistemology.* Durham, NC: Duke University Press.

Freston, Paul. 2001. *Evangelicals and Politics in Africa, Asia and Latin America.* Cambridge, UK: Cambridge University Press.

Galeano, Gladys. 2011. "Suiza Investiga a Sperisen en Paquete de Seis Casos." *El Periódico*, May 25.

Garrard-Burnett, Virginia. 1998. *Protestantism in Guatemala: Living in the New Jerusalem.* Austin: University of Texas.

———. 2000. "Introduction." Pp. xiii–xxv in *On Earth as It Is in Heaven: Religion in Modern Latin America*, edited by V. Garrard-Burnett. Wilmington, DE: Scholarly Resources.

Geertz, Clifford. 1973. "Religion as a Cultural System." Pp. 87–125 in *The Interpretation of Cultures*, edited by C. Geertz. New York: Basic Books.

Gilligan, J. 1996. *Violence: Reflections on a National Epidemic.* New York: Vintage.

Giralt, Maria Santacruz and Jose Miguel Cruz. 2001. "Las Maras en El Salvador." Pp. 15–107 in *Maras y Pandillas en Centroamérica*, vol. I, edited by ERIC, IDESO, IDIES, and IUDOP. Managua: UCA Editores.

Glaser, Barney and Anselm Strauss. 1967. *Discovery of Grounded Theory: Strategies for Qualitative Research.* Chicago: Aldine.

Goffman, Erving. 1959. *The Presentation of Self in Everyday Life.* Garden City, NY: Doubleday.

———. 1961. *Asylums: Essays on the Social Situation of Mental Patients and Other Inmates.* New York: Penguin.

———. 1963. *Stigma: Notes on the Management of Spoiled Identity.* Englewood Cliffs, NJ: Prentice Hall.

Gomez, Ileana and Manuel Vásquez. 2001. "Youth, Gangs and Religion Among Salvadorans in El Salvador and Washington, DC." Pp. 165–187 in *Christianity, Social Change, and Globalization in the Americas*, edited by P.J. Williams, M.A. Vasquez and A.L. Peterson. New Brunswick, NJ: Princeton University Press.

González, Rosmery. 2011. "Capturan a Sospechoso de Elaborar Bomba Incendaria." *El Periódico*, January 12.

Gooren, Henri. 2001. "Reconsidering Protestant Growth in Guatemala." Pp. 169–204 in *Holy Saints and Fiery Preachers: The Anthropology of Protestantism in Mexico and Central America*, edited by J. Dow and A. Sandstrom. Westport, CT: Praeger.

Hagedorn, John M. 2009. *A World of Gangs: Armed Young Men and Gangsta Culture.* Minneapolis: University of Minnesota Press.

Harris, Fredrick. 2001. *Something Within: Religion in African-American Political Activism.* New York: Oxford University Press.

Hayden, Tom. 2004. *Street Wars, Gangs, and the Future of Violence*. New York: New Press.

Heirich, Max. 1977. "Change of Heart: A Test of Some Widely Held Theories About Religious Conversion." *American Journal of Sociology* 83:28.

Hochschild, Arlie. 1983. *The Managed Heart: Commercialization of Human Feeling*. Berkeley: University of California Press.

Holland, Clifton. 2001. "An Historical Profile of Religion in Honduras." *PROLADES-RITA Database*. Retrieved April 6, 2010 (http://www.prolades.com/cra/regions/cam/hon/honduras.html).

———. 2002. "An Historical Profile of Religion in Guatemala." *PROLADES-RITA Database*. Retrieved April 6, 2010 (http://www.prolades.com/cra/regions/cam/gte/guate.html).

———. 2008. An Historical Profile of Religion in El Salvador. *Religion in the Americas Database*. Retrieved April 6, 2010 (http://www.prolades.com/cra/regions/cam/els/salvador.html).

———. 2009. "Census Documents & Religious Public Opinion Polls on Religious Affiliation in Central America: 1950–2008." *Religion in the Americas Database*. Retrieved April 6, 2010 (http://www.prolades.com/cra/regions/cam/campolls.htm).

Honneth, Axel. 1995. *The Struggle for Recognition: The Moral Grammar of Social Conflicts*. Cambridge, MA: MIT Press.

Hurtado, Paola, Claudia Méndez and Mirja Valdés. 2007. "El Ultimo Adios." *El Periódico*. April 15.

Iannaccone, Laurence R. 1994. "Why Strict Churches Are Strong." *American Journal of Sociology* 99:1180–1211.

Instituto Ciudadano de Estudios sobre la Inseguridad. 2010. "Estadísticas sobre Inseguridad Pública." Retrieved June 6, 2011 (http://www.icesi.org.mx/documentos/estadisticas/estadisticasOfi/denuncias_homicidio_doloso_1997_2010.pdf).

Instituto Universitario de Opinión Pública. 2008. *Encuesta de Preferencias Políticas para Las Elecciones Legislativas, Municipales y Presidenciales 2009*. San Salvador: Instituto Universitario de Opinión Pública Universidad Centroamérica.

Jankowski, Martin Sanchez. 1992. *Islands in the Street: Gangs and American Urban Society*. Berkeley: University of California Press.

Katz, Jack. 1988. *Seductions of Crime*. New York: Basic Books.

Klandermans, Bert and Dirk Oegema. 1987. "Potentials, Networks, Motivations, and Barriers: Steps Towards Participation in Social Movements." *American Sociological Review* 52:519–531.

Klein, Malcolm. 1995. *The American Street Gang*. New York: Oxford University Press.

Klein, Malcolm and Cheryl Maxson. 2006. *Street Gang Patterns and Policies*. New York: Oxford University Press.

Klinesmith, Jennifer, Tim Kasser and Francis T. McAndrew. 2006. "Guns, Testosterone, and Aggression: An Experimental Test of a Mediational Hypothesis." *Psychological Science* 21:568–581.

Kraul, Chris, Robert J. Lopez and Rich Connell. 2005. "Gang Uses Deportation to Its Advantage to Flourish in U.S." *Los Angeles Times*, p.1.

Lacey, Marc. 2008. "Abuse Trails Central American Girls into Gangs." *The New York Times*, April 11.

Latinobarómetro. 2010. *Informe 2010*. Santiago, Chile: Corporación Latinobarómetro.

Laub, John H. and Robert J. Sampson. 2003. *Shared beginnings, Divergent Lives: Delinquent Boys to Age 70*. Cambridge, MA: Harvard University Press.

Leggett, Theodore. 2007. *Crimen y Desarrollo en Centroamérica: Atrapados en una Encrucijada*. New York: Naciones Unidas Oficina Contra la Droga y el Delito.

Lopez, Edgar. 2005. "Mareros Cobran por 'Planilla.'" *Siglo XXI* (Ciudad de Guatemala) 2.

López, Pedro. 2004. "Nicaragua. La Visión Comunitaria sobre las Pandillas en el Reparto Schick." Pp. 227–276 in *Maras y Pandillas en Centroamérica: Pandillas y Capital Social*, vol. II, edited by J.M. Cruz. San Salvador: UCA Editores.

Loudis, Richard, Christina del Castillo, Anu Rajaraman and Marco Castillo. 2006. "Annex 2: Guatemala Profile." *Central America and Mexico Gang Assessment*, edited by USAID. Washington, DC: United States Agency for International Development.

Manwaring, Max G. 2005. *Street Gangs: The New Urban Insurgency*. Washington, DC: Department of Defense, Strategic Studies Institute.

Martin, David. 1990. *Tongues of Fire: The Explosion of Protestantism in Latin America*. Cambridge, UK: Blackwell.

Martin-Baró, I. 1996. *Acción e Ideología: Psicología Social desde Centroamérica*. San Salvador: UCA Editores.

Martinez Ventura, Jaime. 2010. *Maras en El Salvador y su relación con el Crimen Organizado Transnacional*. San Salvador: Programa de Cooperación de Seguridad Regional.

Matza, David. 1964. *Delinquency and Drift*. New York: Wiley.

McElmurry, Kevin. 2009. *Alone Together: The Production of Religious Culture in a Church for the Unchurched*. Doctoral Dissertation, Department of Sociology, University of Missouri, Colombia, MO.

McKinley, James C. Jr. 2007. "In Guatemala, Officers' Killings Echo Dirty War." *The New York Times*, March 5.

———. 2009. "U.S. Is a Vast Arms Bazaar for Mexican Cartels." *The New York Times*, February 6.

Medina, Juanjo and Pedro Mateu-Gelabert. 2009. *Maras y Pandillas, Comunidad y Policía en Centro América: Hallazgos de un Estudio Integras*. Guatemala City: Demoscopía.

Miller, Alan S. and Rodney Stark. 2002. "Gender and Religiousness: Can Socialization Explanations Be Saved?" *American Journal of Sociology* 107:1399–1423.

Miller, Marilyn Grace. 2004. *Rise and Fall of the Cosmic Race*. Austin: University of Texas Press.

Moore, Joan W. 1991. *Going Down to the Barrio: Homeboys and Homegirls in Change*. Philadelphia: Temple University Press.

Moser, Caroline and Ailsa Winton. 2002. *Violence in the Central American Region: Towards an Integrated Framework for Violence Reduction*. London: Overseas Development Institute.

Munaiz, Claudio. 2005. "Los Hijos de Maqueira." *Revista Semanal: Prensa Libre*. November 13.

Neitz, Mary Jo. 2004. "Gender and Culture: Challenges to the Sociology of Religion." *Sociology of Religion* 65:391–402.

Notimex. 2009. "Anuncian en Guatemala Operativos contra Pandillas." *SDP Noticias*. March 24.

Observador Centroamericano sobre Violencia. 2009. "Indicadores de Violencia." Retrieved November 6, 2009 (http://ocavi.com/).

O'Neill, Kevin. 2009. *City of God: Christian Citizenship in Postwar Guatemala*. Berkeley: University of California Press.

Pager, Devah. 2009. *Marked: Race, Crime, and Finding Work in an Era of Mass Incarceration*. Chicago: University of Chicago Press.

Papachristos, Andrew V. 2009. "Murder by Structure: Dominance Relations and the Social Structure of Gang Homicide." *American Journal of Sociology* 115:74–128.

Passel, Jeffrey. 2004. *Unauthorized Migrants: Numbers and Characteristics*. Washington, DC: Pew Hispanic Center.

Payne, Douglas. 1999. *El Salvador: Reemergence of "Social Cleansing" Death Squads*. Washington, DC: INS Resource Information Center.

Pelaez, Severo. 1998 [1970]. *La Patria del Criollo*. Ciudad de Mexico: Universidad Autónoma de México.

Pew Research Center for the People and the Press. 2002. *What the World Thinks in 2002*. Washington, DC: Author.

———. 2006. *Spirit and Power: A 10-Country Survey of Pentecostals*. Washington, DC: Pew Forum on Religion and Public Life.

Pine, Adrienne. 2008. *Working Hard, Drinking Hard: On Violence and Survival in Honduras*. Berkeley: University of California Press.

Programa de las Naciones Unidas para el Desarrollo. 2009. *Abrir Espacios a la Seguridad y el Desarrollo Humano: Informe Sobre Desarrollo Humano para Centroamérica*. New York: United Nations Development Programme.

Portillo, Edith. 2008. "Gestion de Saca Acumula 16 Mil Homicidios." *El Faro*, December 29.

Presser, Lois. 2004. "Violent Offenders, Moral Selves: Constructing Identities and Accounts in the Research Interview." *Social Problems* 51:20.

Preston, Julia. 2010. "Losing Asylum, Then His Life." *The New York Times*, p. 2.

Quirk, Matthew. 2008. "How to Grow a Gang." *The Atlantic*, May, 301(4): 24–25.

Rambo, Lewis R. 1993. *Understanding Religious Conversion*. New Haven: Yale University Press.

Ranum, Elin Cecilie. 2007. *Pandillas Juveniles Transnacionales en Centroamérica, Mexico y Estados Unidos: Diagnóstico Nacional Guatemala*. San Salvador: IUDOP.

Replogle, Jill. 2006. "Honduran Catholic Bishop Prepared to Mediate Talks." *Catholic Online*. Retrieved June 6, 2008 (http://www.catholic.org/international/international_story.php?id=18975).

Retzinger, Suzanne and Thomas Scheff. 1991. *Violence and Emotions*. Lexington, MA: Lexington.

Ribando, Clare. 2005. *Gangs in Central America* (Congressional Research Service Report Order Code RS22141). Washington, DC: U.S. Congress.

———. 2008. *Gangs in Central America* (Congressional Research Service Report Order Code RL34112). Washington, DC: U.S. Congress.

Rubio, Mauricio. 2007. *De la Pandilla a la Mara: Pobreza, Educación, Mujeres y Violencia Juvenil.* Bogotá: Universidad Externado de Colombia.

Santacruz, Giralt María L. and Alberto Concha-Eastman. 2001. *Barrio Adentro: La Solidaridad Violenta de las Pandillas.* San Salvador: IUDOP.

Sassen, Saskia. 2003. "Global Cities and Survival Circuits." Pp. 254–274 in *Global Woman: Nannies, Maids and Sex Workers in the New Economy*, edited by B. Ehrenreich and A. Hochschild. New York: Metropolitan Books.

Scheff, Thomas. 1988. "Shame and Conformity: The Deference-Emotion System." *American Sociological Review* 53:395–406.

———. 1991. *Microsociology: Discourse, Emotion, and Social Structure.* Chicago: University of Chicago Press.

———. 1997. *Emotions, the Social Bond, and Human Reality.* London: Cambridge University Press.

———. 2004. "Violent Males: A Theory of Their Emotional/Relational World." Pp. 117–140 in *Theory and Research on Human Emotions*, edited J. Turner. New York: Elsevier Press.

Secretariado Ejecutivo del Sistema Nacional de Seguridad Pública (ICESI). 2010. "Homicidios Dolosos." Retrieved June 6, 2010 (http://www.icesi.org.mx/documentos/estadisticas/estadisticasOfi/denuncias_homicidio_doloso_1997_2010.pdf).

Sibaja, Harold, Enrique Roig, Anu Rajaraman, Hilda Caldera and Ernesto Bardales. 2006. "Annex 2: Honduras Profile." *Central America and Mexico Gang Assessment*, edited by USAID. Washington, DC: United States Agency for International Development.

Simmel, Georg. 1955. *Conflict and the Web of Group Affiliations.* Translated by K.A.W. and R. Bendix. New York: Free Press.

Smilde, David. 2005. "A Qualitative Comparative Analysis of Conversion to Venezuelan Evangelicalism: How Networks Matter." *American Journal of Sociology* 111.

———. 2007. *Reason to Believe: Cultural Agency in Venezuelan Evangelicalism.* Berkeley: University of California Press.

———. 2011. "Alternativas a la Violencia: Lecciones de los Evangélicos." In *Lectura Sociologicas de la Realidad Venezolana*, vol. VI. Caracas, Venezuela: Universidad Católica Andrés Bello.

Smith, Christian. 1995. "The Spirit of Democracy." Pp. 1–25 in *Religion and Democracy in Latin America*, edited by W. Swatos. Piscataway, NJ: Transaction.

———. 1996. *Disruptive Religion: The Force of Faith in Critical Movement Activism.* New York: Routledge.

———. 2008. "Future Directions in the Sociology of Religion." *Social Forces* 86: 1561–1590.

Smith, Dennis. 1991. "Coming of Age: A Reflection on Pentecostals, Politics and Popular Religion in Guatemala." *Pneuma* 13(2):131–139.

———. 2007. "Communication, Politics, and Religious Fundamentalisms in Latin America." Paper presented at annual meeting for the Latin American Studies Association. Montreal, Quebec.

Smith, Dennis and Mario Higueros. 2005. *Nuevas Corrientes Teologicos en Centroamerica y el Anabautismo Biblico.* Ciudad de Guatemala: Ediciones Semilla.

Smutt, Marcela and Lissette Miranda. 1998. *El Fenómeno de las Pandillas en El Salvador.* San Jose, Costa Rica: UNICEF-FLACSO.

Snow, David A. and Richard Machalek. 1983. "The Convert as Social Type." *Sociological Theory* 1:36.

Spergel, Irving. A. 1992. "Youth Gangs: An Essay Review." *Social Service Review* 66:121–140.

Spinelli, Stella. 2006. "Juvenile Gangs: Guatemala, El Salvador and Honduras: Crime in a State of Emergency in Central America." *Peace Reporter.* Retrieved November 8, 2008 (http://it.peacereporter.net/articolo/6819/).

Staples, Clifford L. and Armand L. Mauss. 1987. "Conversion or Commitment? A Reassessment of the Snow and Machalek Approach to the Study of Conversion." *Journal for the Scientific Study of Religion* 26:14.

Stark, Rodney and William S. Bainbridge. 1980. "Networks of Faith: Interpersonal Bonds and Recruitment to Cults and Sects." *American Journal of Sociology* 85:1376–1395.

Stark, Rodney and Roger Finke. 2000. *Acts of Faith: Explaining the Human Side of Religion.* Berkeley: University of California Press.

Steigenga, Timothy. 2001. *The Politics of the Spirit: The Political Implications of Pentecostalized Religion in Costa Rica and Guatemala.* Lanham, MD: Rowan and Littlefield.

———. 2005. "Democracia y el Crecimiento del Protestantismo Evangélico en Guatemala: Entendiendo la Complejidad Política de la Religión Pentecostalizada." *América Latina Hoy* 41:99–119.

Stoll, David. 1991. *Is Latin America Turning Protestant: The Politics of Evangelical Growth.* Berkeley: University of California Press.

———. 1993. *Between Two Armies in the Ixil Towns of Guatemala.* New York: Columbia University Press.

Straus, Roger A. 1979. "Religious Conversion as a Personal and Collective Accomplishment." *Sociological Analysis* 40:158–165.

Streiker, Lowell D. 1971. *The Jesus Trip: Advent of the Jesus Freaks.* Nashville, TN: Abingdon.

Stromberg, Peter G. 1993. *Language and Self-Transformation: A Study of the Christian Conversion Narrative.* New York: Cambridge University Press.

Sullivan, John P. 2002. "Drug Cartels, Street Gangs, and Warlords." *Small Wars and Insurgencies* 13:40.

Taracena, Arturo, Gellert, G., E. Castillo, T. Paiz and Walter K. 2002. *Etnicidad, Estado, y Nación en Guatemala, 1808–1944.* Guatemala: ASIES.

Thale, Geoff and Elsa Falkenburger. 2006. *Youth Gangs in Central America: Issues in Human Rights, Effective Policing and Prevention.* Washington, DC: Washington Office on Latin America.

Thompson, Ginger. 2004. "Shuttling Between Nations, Latino Gangs Confound the Law." *The New York Times*, September 26.

Thrasher, Frederic. 1927. *The Gang: A Study of 1313 Gangs in Chicago*. Chicago: University of Chicago Press.

Torres-Rivas, Edelberto. 2010. "La Lógica Empresarial al Servicio del Crimen." *El Periódico*, January 31.

Turner, Bryan. 1997. "The Body in Western Society: Social Theory and Its Perspectives." Pp. 15–41 in *Religion and the Body*, edited by S. Coakley. New York: Cambridge University Press.

Turner, Jonathan and Jan E. Stets. 2005. *The Sociology of Emotions*. New York: Cambridge University Press.

United Nations Development Programme. 2009a. "International Human Development Indicators." Accessed December 6, 2010. (http://hdr.undp.org/en/data/build/).

———. 2009b. *Overcoming Barriers: Human Mobility and Development*. New York: Palgrave Macmillan.

Venkatesh, Sudhir Alladi. 2000. *American Project: The Rise and Fall of a Modern Ghetto*. Cambridge, MA: Harvard University Press.

Vigil, James Diego. 1988. *Barrio Gangs*. Austin: University of Texas.

———. 2002. *A Rainbow of Gangs*. Austin: University of Texas.

Warner, Stephen. 2007. "Presidential Plenary." Paper presented at annual meeting of the Society for the Scientific Study of Religion, Tampa, FL.

Weber, Max. 1963. *The Sociology of Religion*. Boston: Beacon Press.

Williams, Philip J. 1997. "The Sound of Tambourines: The Politics of Pentecostal Growth in El Salvador." Pp. 179–200 in *Power, Politics and Pentecostals in Latin America*, edited by E.L. Cleary and H.W. Stewart-Gambino. Boulder, CO: Westview Press.

Winchester, Daniel. 2008. "Embodying the Faith: Religious Practice and the Making of a Muslim Moral Habitus." *Social Forces* 86:1753–1780.

Winton, Ailsa. 2005. "Youth, Gangs and Violence: Analysing the Social and Spatial Mobility of Young People in Guatemala City." *Children's Geographies* 3:167–184.

Wolseth, Jon. 2008. "Safety and Sanctuary: Pentecostalism and Youth Gang Violence in Honduras." *Latin American Perspectives* 35(4):96–111.

Young, Michael P. 2002. "Confessional Protest: The Religious Birth of U.S. National Social Movements." *American Sociological Review* 67:660–688.

Zilberg, Elana. "Fools Banished from the Kingdom: Remapping Geographies of Gang Violence Between the Americas." *American Quarterly*. 56:759–779.

Index